W9-BUA-282

Strategic Reading

Guiding Students to Lifelong Literacy, 6–12

Jeffrey D. Wilhelm
The University of Maine
and the Brewer Schools Professional Development Network Site

Tanya N. Baker
Brewer High School

Julie Dube
Old Town High School

JENKS L.R.C.
GORDON COLLEGE
255 GRAPEVINE RD.
WENHAM, MA 01984-1895

DISCARDED
JENKS LRC
GORDON COLLEGE

Boynton/Cook Publishers
HEINEMANN
Portsmouth, NH

Boynton/Cook Publishers, Inc.
A subsidiary of Reed Elsevier Inc.
361 Hanover Street
Portsmouth, NH 03801–3912
www.boyntoncook.com

Offices and agents throughout the world

Copyright © 2001 by Jeffrey D. Wilhelm, Tanya N. Baker, and Julie Dube. All rights reserved. No part of this book may be reproduced in any form or by any electronic or mechanical means, including information storage and retrieval systems, without permission in writing from the publisher, except by a reviewer, who may quote brief passages in a review. Reproducible forms may be photocopied for classroom use only.

Figure 3.1 first appeared in the article "Models for Teacher Education: Where Reading Recovery Teacher Training Fits" by Paula Moore. *Network News* (Fall 1997), 1–4.

"Traveler" from *Something Permanent*, copyright © 1994 by Cynthia Rylant, reprinted by permission of Harcourt, Inc.

"Direct Reading and Thinking Activity" adapted from *CRISS, Content Reading in Secondary Schools: Reading Across the Curriculum* by Santa et. al. Copyright © 1985 by Kendall/Hunt Publishing Company, Dubuque, IA. Reprinted with permission.

Library of Congress Cataloging-in-Publication Data

Wilhelm, Jeffrey D., 1959–
    Strategic reading : guiding students to lifelong literacy, 6–12 / Jeffrey D. Wilhelm, Tanya N. Baker, Julie Dube.
        p. cm.
    Includes bibliographical references and index.
    ISBN 0-86709-561-X (alk. paper)
    1. Reading (Middle school). 2. Reading (Secondary). I. Baker, Tanya N. II. Dube, Julie. III. Title.

    LB1632.W53 2001
    428.4'071—dc21   2001016199

Editor: Lisa Luedeke
Cover photo: Putman Ercoline
Cover design: Catherine Hawkes/Cat and Mouse Design
Manufacturing: Louise Richardson

Printed in the United States of America on acid-free paper

05   04   03   02   01   RRD   1   2   3   4   5

This book is dedicated to

George Hillocks, Jr.
for his work, his friendship, and especially for his teaching,
and for all of his students,
who have also taught us so much
through their teaching,

especially
Bruce Novak and Michael W. Smith

Pity us, who are caught in the endless quarrel between order and adventure.

—Apollonaire

Teachers are those who use
themselves as bridges,
Over which they invite their
students to cross;
Then having facilitated their
crossing, joyfully collapse,
Encouraging them to create
bridges of their own.

—Nikos Kazantzakis

Contents

Acknowledgments

First and foremost, all three of us acknowledge our great debt and gratitude to the work of George Hillocks, Michael Smith, and Bruce Novak, whose ideas permeate these pages. This book is really the story of how their ideas, along with those of the Russian psychologist Lev Vygotsky, completely transformed and energized our own teaching.

George Hillocks is a highly respected researcher in the area of literacy, the longtime director of the highly successful MAT in English program at the University of Chicago, and the teacher and mentor of Michael Smith and Bruce Novak. George's teaching methods and his research are the central inspiration for the work we describe in this book. And in personal ways he has been our mentor and friend. His close reading of a draft of this book was hugely helpful.

Michael Smith was a longtime high school English teacher and is currently a professor at Rutgers University. He taught Jeff at the University of Wisconsin and has remained his mentor ever since. We joke that a teaching genealogy makes George Jeff's grand-teacher. Michael has also worked closely with Julie and Tanya through the Maine Writing Project, where he introduced many of George's ideas about teaching to us, which we have applied to our own teaching of both writing and reading. The powerful changes these ideas wrought in our teaching is what we will describe in these pages. Michael's own work, particularly in his book *Authorizing Readers* (Rabinowitz and Smith 1998), has also been a powerful influence on our thinking and teaching. Michael read an early draft of this manuscript and gave us very valuable advice about how to reconceive and shape the book.

Bruce Novak is a doctoral student at the University of Chicago who has taught in a variety of settings. Bruce has had a lot to teach us about the importance of teaching through relationship. He, too, has been a mentor to us and his close reading of a draft was insight-laden.

This book is about the power of a particular kind of teaching, a kind of relational teaching embodied in the work of George, Michael, and Bruce. Such is the power of their teaching that it has helped us to evolve as thinkers, inquirers, teachers, and people. We cannot possibly acknowledge all their contributions to us. They perch on our shoulders whispering constantly in our ears.

We also draw here on the work of many other students of George. These people all went through his MAT programs and have become leaders in English Education at all levels: our thanks to Peter Smagorinsky, Larry Johannassen, Elizabeth Kahn, Tom McCann, and many others. Their teaching ideas also infuse these pages, and we think George will appreciate the "full-circledness" of this and the tribute to his teaching it clearly implies.

Paula Moore, director of the Reading Recovery Center at the University of Maine, is a colleague who lives up to that name. She has helped us think hard about teaching over the past several years. She read early drafts of the chapters on Vygotsky and was of great assistance.

We also had a wonderful editor, Lisa Luedeke, who patiently shepherded us through this project as we rethought and reshaped it several times.

Theresa McMannus, administrative assistant at the University of Maine, has been a source of constant good cheer and assistance to the Maine Writing Project site, and to many writing and teaching projects, including this one.

Gail Garthwait, in the words of Jeff's daughter Fiona, is "the world's greatest library person!" Gail chased down several books and lots of background material for us, often on a moment's notice.

Eric Waltenbaugh helped with the bibliography and other chores to help finish the book.

Now for individual acknowledgments:

Jeff: It's never redundant to thank colleagues and friends. Those listed here deserve the highest compliment I can give: they are good friends and "teachers" in the truest sense. Continual thanks certainly go out to the folks in the Maine Writing Project where this project was conceived, and to friends and teaching colleagues like Brian Ambrosius, Bill Anthony, Deb Appleman, Jim Artesani, Rosemary Bamford, Erv Barnes, Bill Bedford, Jim Blaser, Ed Brazee, Mike Ford, Paul Friedemann, Stuart Greene, Leon Holley, Jr., Bruce Hunter, Jan Kristo, Craig Martin, Bruce Nelson, Wayne Otto, Brenda Power, Bill Strohm, Brian White, and Denny Wolfe. And of course thanks to my loving family, particularly my dad, Jack Wilhelm; my wife, Peggy Jo; and my constantly delightful daughters, Fiona Luray and Jasmine Marie. A big dose of appreciation also goes to Tanya and Julie for engaging in this project with me.

Tanya: I want to thank all those teachers who have "taught me from where I am right now, but protected me and reached me into a better future." Special thanks in this regard go to my dad, Guy Baker; my mom, Marcia Lincoln; my husband, Jamie Heans; and my teacher, Jeff Wilhelm.

Julie: I would like to thank the many students in my previous classes who were so willing to participate in my teacher research for this book. You were all the best "guinea pigs" that a teacher could hope for! Also, a very special thank you goes to Martha Pojasek for her help and continued support of this project. The reading buddies chapter would not exist without Martha.

And finally, an extra special thank you to my son, Cameron; my husband, Mike; my mother and father, Shari and Kip Albert; and my other family members for your encouragement and endless support throughout this project. Where would I be without great people like you in my life?

Introduction: How Way Leads on to Way

Practice, practice! Put your hope in that!

—M. S. Merwin

Bottom Lines

My friend and mentor Michael Smith loves little party games, particularly storytelling games that make you think. He's always coming up with them. One of his games is called "Bottom Lines." You can apply the concept of bottom lines to just about anything, but because we're educators, we often apply it to teaching. Play along with me here. What are the bottom lines for your teaching? What do you *absolutely* have to get done to feel you've been successful with a group of students? If it helps, you might even think about a particular class, a particular group of students, or even an individual student.

I like playing this game, and I'm continually doing what I call "gut checks" to see if my teaching lines up with my bottom-line goals. I'm also constantly revising the list, like it's a David Letterman "Top 10" list of some kind. Sometimes I'll revise it for a particular group with whom I'm working, but I pretty much apply it generally across all my classes. Interestingly, the list doesn't change much whether I am teaching English to high school sophomores, teaching reading to seventh graders in a professional development site, or whether I am working with preservice teachers in a methods class or with practicing teachers in a graduate workshop.

I constantly play versions of this game with all my students, but particularly with my preservice teaching students. I want to get this inside their heads: Teaching is a vital and purposeful pursuit. We need to be working toward something and we need to know what that something is. Then we can consider how we can best get there.

My bottom lines developed over time through relationships I've formed with valued mentors like George Hillocks, Michael Smith, and Bruce Novak. These mentors have continually lent me their expertise and their ways of thinking and teaching so I could adapt and use these techniques on my own. I want to be that kind of mentor to my students, assisting them in forming "bottom lines" and in developing methods for meeting these goals.

My preservice students play the bottom-line game the first day of our methods class. We revisit and revise our lists throughout the year, check to see how our unit plans and teaching line up with the list, and ask how we might need to revise our lists based on our evolving understandings and relationships with kids.

To set a bottom line, you need to know what it is you are trying to do. It's a lot easier to arrive at your destination if you know where you are trying to go. I believe we should publish our goals and argue for their importance. Like the poet John Milton, I don't think truth was ever bested by a bad argument. So let your students and colleagues in on your goals. Be prepared to argue for your goals and listen to critiques.

Teaching, to me, is exactly this: sharing the secret purposes and processes of more expert practice, and negotiating meaning with others. It's up to the teacher to share what she knows about solving problems and creating meaning, and to then apply these as we create meaning together with students and colleagues.

Here are a few of my own bottom lines:

1. *Love your students.* You can't teach them if you don't know them and care about them. In my experience, they won't learn from you if you don't truly care about them—and faking it doesn't work. If you don't care about them, everybody will miss out on the joy and power of learning together. People learn through the sharing that occurs in relationships. All teaching and therefore all learning is relational, as we'll explore further in this book.
2. *Love your students as learners.* Love them for who they are right now, in their current state of becoming. Kids want and deserve to be taught for who they are and might become right now, not just for who we think they need to be later in life.
3. *Teach them for who they are right now, but protect and "reach" them into a better future.* This is the only way you can teach a person. You must consider their current interests, abilities, and problems. At the same time, the purpose of teaching is to reach them, and us too, toward the future and toward more aware, moral, affective, and powerful ways of being and acting in the world.
4. *Teach them* how *to do things.* The fun and power of learning is not in the *what* but in the *why* and the *how*—understanding importance and the mastering of ways of doing things.
5. *Make sure they have enough practice.* For example, students need lots of practice to really read and understand a particular genre, to construct an argument, to do any new and more complex task. In our constant push for coverage, we may fail to provide the time to truly support and develop seminal ways of thinking and reading.
6. *Make all learning, reading, and knowing visible and available, and make all reasoning accountable.* This is equally true for me as the teacher as for the students. I want the ways in which we know things and arrive at conclusions to be visible, and I want a high standard for accountability. We need to be able to justify and explain how we have learned and know what it is we know.
7. *Work and learn together . . . and be flexible!* Learning occurs best when teachers and students are creating meaning together. This kind of

learning is dynamic and unpredictable, so we must be prepared to
go where the energy of the class takes us. I truly believe that we can
teach all of the most important things about learning and reading
through any one engaging topic or question.

8. *Always be frying bigger fish.* Always have a higher purpose. Make it
one that can be shared and multiplied and that can grow. In this
book, we'll be making the case that our overarching purpose is
working toward better reading and meaning making. But it goes
beyond that. We teach literacy to enhance more democratic thinking and living. We ask every day how that day's lesson serves the
overall goal of our particular unit and of our teaching in general.
How is what we are doing with our students guiding them toward
the very biggest goals we are trying to achieve with them?

These bottom lines lead to the way students respond and learn
from me—and I from them.

Just as students will take what we teach and use it in independent
and unforeseen ways, so does our work with students take unplanned
turns—as Robert Frost maintained, "way leads on to way."

Way Leads on to Way

Julie, Tanya, and I began to discuss writing this book several years ago
when we were all working together as fellows in the Maine Writing
Project.

Interestingly, all of our own bottom lines segue nicely with the
ideas of Lev Vygotsky and George Hillocks, the two main inspirations
for the work we will report on in this book. Their work, which will be
explored in detail, gives us powerful ways of working toward our goals
for students as thinkers, readers, and citizens.

Our original intent was to pointedly explore the transformative
power of Vygotskian theory for the teaching of reading and writing in
our middle and high school classrooms. Vygotsky's ideas, after all, have
had a tremendous effect on early literacy and elementary language
arts teaching, but this has not filtered up to the teaching of literacy at
middle or secondary levels of education.

Vygotsky's ideas have led to a reconsideration of teaching as the
active assistance given to students as they engage in meaningful tasks.
We also wanted to integrate the ideas and strategies of George Hillocks,
whose work provides the best examples we know for providing Vygotskian assistance to readers and writers.

Consequently, for the past several years we have set off on a hike
up a set of trails blazed by Lev Vygotsky and George Hillocks that has
taken us, as we have translated and applied their work in various ways,
to previously unexplored territory.

A Trail Map of the Book

We begin our book with descriptions of the trails laid out for us by the work of Vygotksy and Hillocks. The following chapters describe the practical classroom applications that their theories and examples have helped us to develop and implement.

The book is entitled *Strategic Reading: Guiding Students to Lifelong Literacy, 6–12* because the book is about assisting students to develop the purposes and strategies they need to approach and make meaning with text. As students progress through school, they read many texts that are unfamiliar to them in terms of vocabulary, content, genre, and text structure, and these texts often require new processes and strategies of reading. We contend that the best way to teach students these new and necessary strategies is by carefully guiding them through actual readings in a context where they have a personal and social need to understand and then act on their growing understanding. We provide many concrete techniques for doing this kind of "guided reading" and we argue that this kind of teaching assists students to internalize approaches and strategies that will support their literacy and their living beyond the walls of school.

Accordingly, in Chapter 1 we explore theories of teaching and learning. We begin by maintaining that all teaching is highly theoretical and that the best teaching recognizes and makes "wide-awake" use of its theoretical orientation. We introduce a scenario ranking activity that will help you explore various contending theories of instruction. We then review Vygotsky's contributions to this debate and argue for the power of adopting his view of teaching and learning when guiding students to read.

In Chapter 2 we review theories of reading, and we show how these theories parallel the most prominent theories of teaching and learning. We describe how the transactional theory of reading is consistent with Vygotskian sociocultural views of learning and explore the usefulness of this theory for teachers attempting to support student growth as readers. We then argue that particular kinds of texts (like argument, satire, definition, ironic monologues, etc.) make particular demands on readers, and that to support student "transactions" with such texts, we must help students develop new sets of strategies that reading these texts require. We provide a procedure called the "inquiry square" that helps us understand the demands of particular texts so that we can then consider how to teach students how to develop the strategies for meeting these particular text demands. *Some teachers may prefer to skim the theory of Chapters 1 and 2 and return to it after reading the more practically oriented chapters that follow. We do believe the theory to be essential to understanding the work we propose and being able to adapt it successfully in your own classroom.*

In Chapter 3 we build the bridge from theory to the practical realm of teaching. We use the work of George Hillocks, Michael Smith, and

Peter Rabinowitz as we argue for a particular theoretical view of reading called "authorial reading" that we see as consistent with Vygotskian learning theory and the transactional theory of reader response. We describe how "authorial reading" puts a missing political and ethical edge on currently popular theories of reader response. Drawing on our argument from Chapter 2, we explore how teaching students to read texts "authorially" requires that they be taught to recognize what the text expects of them and how to fulfill these expectations.

We further argue that the theories we propose lead to the conclusion that reading is best conceived as "inquiry" and best taught in a context of inquiry. We explore how inquiry and project-based learning environments can provide powerful assistance to readers, and how these environments can motivate and support "authorial" reading. We also explain why we believe such contexts promote democracy.

We move here into practical applications as we demonstrate DRTAs (directed reading and thinking activities) and think-aloud/protocol techniques that can guide students to understand and use strategies required for more powerful "authorial" readings. The rest of the book explores various other techniques that actively guide and assist student reading in project-based environments.

Chapter 4 explores "Frontloading," the teaching that we can do before kids read that can motivate and equip them for success as they read challenging content and use new strategies. We'll explore how textual content that is too new, too distant, or too unrelated to students' current situations, can stymie their interest and comprehension. Then we'll explore how good frontloading can develop both their interest and new strategies necessary for reading with particular kinds of content, text types, or reading processes.

Chapter 5 demonstrates various questioning schemes that allow the teacher to actively assist readers to new levels of reading competence, and we explore how intelligent and humane teaching situated in inquiry situations can help students to internalize these powerful questioning strategies.

Chapter 6 demonstrates the various ways in which the technique of Symbolic Story Representation can be used to assist readers to develop their strategic repertoire for evoking text, reflecting on it, and conversing authorially with the intelligence that constructed a text.

Chapter 7 explores the notion of Assignment Sequencing and how teachers can think about creating instructional sequences that build conceptual, procedural, and textual knowledge text by text and activity by activity.

Chapter 8 describes a social project that was undertaken by students that assisted them to read authorially, and to care about and work with others as they learned to relate and interact with preschool authors.

We conclude with an epilogue that considers how our teaching has been transformed by the guidance of Lev Vygotsky and George Hillocks and how the work we have done together might inspire a re-envisioning and re-vision of how we teach and work in the English classroom.

In our conclusion, we discuss the ways in which our work has begun transforming the relationships and activities inside our classroom communities . . . and the ways in which we are now working, however experimentally, toward larger democratic purposes and communities that lie beyond the classroom door.

Back to the Bottom Line

Certainly one of our central concerns as teachers is helping our students to develop as readers. Reading is perhaps *the* foundational educational competence, and the electronic age has made this even more rather than less true. Our big bottom line for the teaching of reading is that we must always be working to support students in understanding more about how texts work and in developing strategies for reading different kinds of texts. Everything we describe in this book is centered around ways to assist students to become more motivated and competent readers with the more challenging textual demands they encounter in middle and high school.

We believe that it is essential that students learn *how* to read particular kinds of texts and that this is more complicated than most people think. In our classrooms, we particularly privilege reading texts like fables, satires, and arguments that imply and even work for social change.

Even as we teach something as important as reading, though, we are also "frying bigger fish" as we consider the ways we want our students to use literacy in terms of the way they will live their lives. Our ultimate bottom line is that we want our students to grow toward becoming more respectful, open, and caring people with the desire and skills for democratic living and citizenship.

We'll describe throughout the book how we've found ourselves rethinking our ideas about literacy and about the purpose of our classroom work and schooling itself, in terms of what we're calling "democratic community." We found that as we adapted Hillocks' ideas for our teaching of reading that our work became profoundly moral and community-centered. By transforming our notions of teaching, and by helping us build a repertoire of ways to enact our new vision, Vygotsky (in general ways) and George Hillocks (in highly specific ways) have led us to a social transformation of our classrooms. We've found that when perceptions of teaching, learning, knowing, and thinking change, ideas about transforming school and society can be changed and enacted too. We think and hope that our transformed teaching of literacy might lead our students to help transform their lives and the communities in which they live and work.

Undertaking such projects has helped us expand our conceptions of literacy. First, we've been compelled by Applebee's (1996) hope that we will "reconstrue our curriculum to focus on knowledge-in-action rather than knowledge-out-of-context." As we've worked together, we've begun to see literacy as more than just the ability to conceptually represent the world. More important, we see it as the ability to meaningfully interpret and act within the world in order to relate more thoroughly to oneself and to others.

What Do We Want for Our Students?

This leads us to consider what we want to achieve from the study of literature—indeed of any and all of the world's texts, from newspaper articles to music videos to home pages. We want our students to:

- Develop a wide repertoire of meaning-making strategies that they can deploy independently with a wide range of genres
- Question and apply critical standards to what they read
- Use texts as a way of knowing and respecting themselves, the world, and the multiple perspectives of others
- Come to know new things that will inform how they grow, behave, and take action in the world, which will help them become more humane, responsible, and democratic citizens.

We've also come to define literacy as "the ability to use the most powerful cultural tools available for making, communicating, and enacting these kinds of meanings." George Hillocks is an expert at making cultural tools and literacy conventions available to students. This has led us to encourage multiple ways of "reading" and "composing," not only through traditional notions of text but also through art, drama, video, hypermedia, and a variety of multimedia approaches. Although we concentrate in this book on reading in the more conventional sense, you'll see how we link this to literacy in a wider semiotic and social sense. This move has helped us democratize our classrooms, by bringing in various ways of knowing and exploring ideas, and by including the various interests and strengths of our diverse students in our curricular decisions. We've found that this has helped our students read and write more rather than less, to be more motivated, and to do higher-quality work that is more immediately connected to the issues of the world they inhabit. Such work has helped equip them with the tools for independent and democratic learning journeys of their own.

We hope you will enjoy taking this teaching journey with us, and that it will propel you into new and exciting journeys of your own. That's the point and odyssey, after all, of teaching and learning: to constantly outgrow our current selves, to travel toward ways of thinking and being that were previously undreamed.

1

A Theory of Teaching

One year, I had a particularly creative and zealous student teacher named Nate. We'd met early in the school year about his spring internship placement, and I had encouraged him to think about how to teach British Literature around the use of themes and issues—instead of through the typical chronological treatment.

When we met later, right before the spring semester, I was astonished at the amount of thinking my young charge had been doing. In fact, in response to my first question—*What are you planning on doing?*—he had mapped out about seventeen years worth of units. My first impulse was to blurt out, "And *just when* do you think you will have time to do all of this stuff?" But in a rare display of self-control, I held myself in check. After all, it had taken me a long time to learn that we often do more by doing less.

Two of the more interesting ideas were a unit proposal for the World War II era, with *Lord of the Flies* as the centerpiece, and another on the 1960s that would center on the rise of popular culture. I decided to concentrate on these.

As a follow-up to the question *What are you doing?* I asked Nate, "*Why are you doing this and how are you going to do this?*" I intended to get after his belief set or theory toward teaching and learning. I wanted to hear why Nate thought that these units were worth doing, what he thought the students would learn, how he would teach them in the context of the unit, and why he thought these things were worth knowing.

Instead of the rich and philosophical answer I was anticipating, Nate answered, "First off, because it fits the curriculum!"

I sputtered a bit, and then I pushed Nate to explain. He said, "You know, the anthology is organized chronologically and I'm supposed to cover the twentieth century, so I did what you encouraged me to do and thought about how to cover some really important issues of the century through themes."

Interestingly, it's estimated that more than 95 percent of elementary school teachers use the basal reader as "the curriculum," and that it organizes instructional activity through their year with students (McCallum 1988). Reviews of English teaching at the secondary level (Hillocks 1986; Applebee 1993) indicate that this is probably true there as well. Nate, with my encouragement, was trying to create a more meaningful point of contact for his prospective students, but he was still bounded by traditional notions of curricula and was not yet articulating what he believed about learning, effective instruction, or reading. Pushed a bit by me, he explained that he thought that the ideas of "persecution and survival" that pervade World War II texts, and the popular culture connections of the 1960s unit, would be "motivating" to students and would "grab their attention."

I kept doggedly on, asking Nate *what* kids would know when they were done with the unit, and what they would know *how to do* that they didn't already know. He fielded the first part of the question about conceptual learning quite nicely, but was stumped by the procedural question of what would students learn how to do that they didn't already know how to do. "What do you mean?" he asked.

I said, "With available information doubling every couple of years, what good is it to teach information? You are going after some big conceptual understandings in these units. That's good. But kids particularly need to know *how* to do things so they can deal with information and use it to think—so they'll possess generative kinds of knowledge that they can use in new situations."

We talked for a while about how to teach kids to learn and enact new reading strategies in the course of the unit. This turned the conversation to Nate's own planned teaching procedures. I asked, "How are you going to teach this stuff?" and "What evidence do you have that it will work?" and "How do you plan on gathering evidence that it's working with these kids?"

Nate seemed a little overwhelmed. "Am I going to be teaching or conducting a research study?"

"Both," I said with a laugh. "And I am here to help you do it!"

This is what I was trying to communicate to Nate: "OK, you know British literature. You have a wide knowledge of books and of literary history. You are engaged with ideas and can think. You are an expert reader and writer. But do you know *how* to teach these things to your students? Do you know *how* to lend students your expertise as a reader, writer, and thinker, and *how* to assist them to take on the strategies of other experts?"

Once Nate began proposing methods of teaching the particular texts in his units, and of teaching the strategies and approaches necessary to making meaning with these texts and understanding them, I asked, *"What reasons or evidence do you have that these methods will be successful with your kids? Why do you think this is a good way to do it?"*

What I was trying to do was to get Nate to articulate a theory of learning and then to think about how to apply it in the context of teaching reading. I was also implicitly pressing him to consider elements of my own theory of teaching.

Teacher Professionalism and Pedagogical Content Knowledge

In a conversation over breakfast this past year, Dr. James Comer, the renowned child psychologist and founder of the Comer initiative to revitalize inner-city schools, spoke with me about teacher professionalism. Dr. Comer's argument was that teaching, though certainly an art, is and should also be based on science. Otherwise, a dangerous antiprofessional attitude that any practice can be justified in particular situations and that anyone can teach begins to prevail. Dr. Comer was most adamant that teaching can and should be based on science, and that the relevant sciences are child development (an understanding of how children grow and develop so that we know how to implement developmentally appropriate education) and cognitive science (so we understand how people learn most effectively).

If teaching is a profession, then we need to know how to do things that your average person does not know. If we do not, then we do not have specialized professional knowledge, and in fact we are not a profession. A profession defines itself and its boundaries, controls entry into its ranks, sets and enforces its own standards, and maintains and creates its own methods and knowledge. It is problematic that in the United States much of what teachers should control is controlled by outsiders who are not educators—administrators, school boards, legislators—people who do not know what we know, who do not know our kids, and who may not share our concerns.

As professionals, we need to know, articulate, and justify our theory of learning. We also need to know what we are trying to achieve, the best methods for meeting these goals, and how we will know if we've done it. If we don't, then these professional functions will be taken over by legislators and test-making companies.

This book explores how we can use theory to relate to students (and help them relate to each other), to share our expertise, and to invite them into the club of expert readers to which we belong. Because texts are highly conventionalized (written according to rules made up by humans and therefore not natural or spontaneously occurring) students need our help to understand these conventions so they can become members in this club. They need to be taught the rules so they can play the game.

Tharp and Gallimore (1988), in their award-winning book *Rousing Minds to Life,* describe a problem that resonates with Julie, Tanya, and me:

> In American schools, now and since the 19th century, teachers generally act as if students are supposed to learn on their own. Teachers are not taught to teach, and most often they do not teach. The problem does not lie in individual incompetence or the incompetence of institutions. . . . All participants in the educational enterprise have suffered from the same lack of knowledge. . . . All participants in the educational enterprise have shared an inadequate vision of schooling. (3–4)

They go on to argue that educators, particularly teachers of reading and writing, assign and evaluate but do not actually teach. They maintain that teaching must be reconceived as ***guiding*** *students to more competent learning performances,* and that we must provide our guidance in meaningful contexts of use—not through traditional classroom lectures or worksheets that provide decontextualized information that has importance only in the classroom.

We'll explore ways of actually doing this kind of situated and active instruction with adolescent readers. To do so, we believe it is essential for teachers to form a conscious understanding of their teaching purposes and processes, and just as important for students to develop an understanding of *what they are doing, why they are doing it, and how they are or could be doing it.* Maxine Green calls this "wide awake" teaching and learning (1978).

What does it mean to be a "wide awake" teacher? It means we are constantly "wide awake" to our theories, articulating and testing them against our practices and student learning. We must constantly examine our instruction, asking: Is it working? How do we know? Are we happy with our orientation and what it is telling students about what to value and how to value reading and learning? Is it leading toward our big purposes and bottom lines for students or is it just a good lesson for that particular day? And if not, how can we change things? One of the most liberating possibilities of wide awake teaching is that the inevitable mistakes need not be big ones. We can adapt what we are doing and work for higher purposes from one day to the next.

> If what we do one day does not work, or doesn't truly fit our beliefs and principles, then we can change our actions. But we can only make positive changes if we are aware of our higher purposes and theories.

What Is Effective Teaching and Learning?

The following scenarios were written to highlight different perspectives on teaching and learning. Completing this activity can help you better recognize and articulate your own theories and beliefs about teaching.[1]

The scenarios are meant to be a little bit complicated, just like any teaching and learning situation, and you might find yourself agreeing and disagreeing with different aspects of the same scene. The goal is to rank the following scenes from the one in which the most effective teaching is taking/has taken place (1) to the scene in which the least effective teaching is taking/has taken place (6). Consider, as you do so, whether learning can usefully be separated from the teaching that engenders that learning.

---

[1]The original idea and scenarios were written by Michael Smith, and used here with his permission. I have deleted his last two scenes and added two of my own for the purposes of this chapter.

When I use this ranking activity with my preservice teaching students, I ask them to complete it individually, and then to work in small groups to persuade others of their ranking. Groups try, and sometimes fail, to come to a consensus. If you have the chance, you might enjoy doing this ranking with someone else and discussing it. If not, the point remains the same: to think about the principles that inform your ranking, how happy you are with these principles, and what these principles do and should mean for your own teaching.

Activity: Effective Teaching and Learning Scenarios

_____ 1. Frank has been taking golf lessons for six months. His pro is famous for basing his instruction on four key principles. Frank knows these principles by heart. In fact, he's so good at explaining them to others that his playing companions feel that they are getting the benefit of professional advice without having to pay for it. However, Frank isn't always able to put these principles into practice. Sometimes everything clicks for a hole or two but rarely for more than that. Frank scored in the low 90s when he began his lessons, and he typically scores in the low 90s now.

_____ 2. Maria has completed her dissertation and has just accepted a job in the Department of History in a major research university. As she packs up her apartment, she finds herself thinking about the course that started her on her way, an introductory course on nineteenth-century European history. Although she doesn't remember much about the specific content (in fact, she chose an entirely different area for her own specialty on the role of immigrants in the labor movement), and she has rejected the type of historiography her professor did, she does remember the passion that Professor Neal displayed in her teaching, and the profound conviction she expressed that "doing history" matters. That was the first time Maria thought that studying history could make a difference, and that being a historian was a worthwhile pursuit.

_____ 3. Peter recently moved with his two small children to a house in the city on a street far busier than the one they lived on in the suburbs. Peter explained to his kids, ages two and three, that they must never walk in the street because cars are dangerous. One day he was raking leaves while the kids were playing. He turned his back for a minute or two and looked back, horrified to see his kids jumping in the leaves he had raked into the street. He ran to the kids and slapped their hands, the first time he had ever physically disciplined them. The children were shocked and burst into tears. Neither child ever went in the street again.

_____ 4. Tom has a piano competition coming up soon. His teacher has gone through Tom's piece with him several times, note by note, explaining every detail. His teacher has also recorded the piece the way it should be played. Tom listens to it all the time; he even falls asleep with his Walkman on. Tom practices hours every day until he plays the piece exactly the way his teacher did. At the competition Tom plays the piece just as he had hoped, and he wins first place. His parents have never been so proud.

_____ 5. As Jude looks back on high school, she realizes that her favorite class was sophomore English. It was different than any other class she had ever taken—maybe it was this uniqueness that made it powerful and special for her. In this class there were no formal assignments. Her teacher, Mr. James, began the year by soliciting topics from the class that were of interest to them and that were also of social significance. He then brought a wide variety of materials in on these topics—ranging from articles and videos to classic pieces of literature. He also encouraged them to find their own information. Students spent almost all of their time reading and thinking about these issues, usually on their own. Each week, discussions and debates would be held in small groups. At the end of each quarter, groups formed and created "knowledge documents." They were free to choose their topics and their projects. During the year, Jude had participated in creating a museum display, a video documentary, a hypermedia document, and an informational website. Each quarter ended with a "Family and Friends Night" where these projects were shared. Though Jude couldn't remember Mr. James ever actually instructing her in any way, she had never read so much or been so motivated to learn. And though she couldn't really name what she'd learned, she knew it had to do with asking questions, working alone, and working with others.

_____ 6. Arlene has taken a summer job with her uncle and his partner, who are electricians. It is hard, frustrating, challenging, but fun and she feels like she is learning a lot. The first day, her uncle told her, "I know how electricity works and you don't. My job is to help you understand electricity the way physicists and electricians understand it." To this end, they began playing with batteries, conducting wire, and light bulbs to make different kinds of circuits. Her uncle then asked her to articulate rules of electrical circuits. Then he confronted her in real situations with her mistakes and what problems her misunderstanding could cause. Whenever he felt that Arlene knew enough to do a particular kind of electrical work, he would let her do it on her own. Otherwise he let her observe him, or he guided her as she did her own work. After a while, Arlene started to feel that she was really coming to understand electricity—so much so that when the electricity went out in only one room of their home, Arlene could explain to her parents exactly what the problem must be and how it could be fixed. Still, this kind of learning took a long time, and it was hard work. She was kind of relieved when the summer ended.

Evaluating the Scenarios

These scenarios are complex, and there will be disagreement among people regarding which scenes exhibit the best teaching and its relationship to learning. Our own preservice teaching students have a lot of fun debating whether the change in Peter's children's behavior really constitutes learning. Is imposing your rules on others really teaching? What if the kids' behavior changes, but not their understanding? Then again, what about Frank: his cognitive understanding has changed, but not his performance. Can that be called learning?

The issue of engagement always comes up too. Maria was totally engaged in history by her professor, but remembers no substantive procedures or concepts. Her teacher's passion and enthusiasm infected her. Certainly this is necessary to learning, but is it sufficient? Arlene really learned about electricity, but was kind of "burnt out" on it and had lost some of her motivation by the end. Must we consider current and continued engagement, an unending impulse to learn more, as part of teaching and learning effectiveness?

Is the teacher's role to prescribe behavior and transmit information (Peter, Frank, and Tom), or to provide a nurturing environment (Jude) and learning opportunities, or to actively guide, shape and assist learning by challenging misconceptions and providing greater expertise as it is needed (Arlene)? And what about the role of community?

Does this matter at all, and if it does, should it be along the lines of Jude's participation in classroom communities, or Arlene's coming to participate in a more-expert and external community of physicists and electricians? And does this participation consist of demonstrating expertise to the community (Tom), or actually participating in the construction of knowledge in the same ways that experts construct, test, and represent what they know (Arlene)?

Among the most stimulating questions that arise from these scenarios are those about the relationship of teaching and learning. Can there be teaching if there is not some kind of definable learning? What is the relationship of teaching and learning? When and how is teaching most powerfully enacted? And who or what is most responsible for learning: the environment? the teacher? the learner? or some larger notion of participating together in a community? And what do our answers to these questions mean for how we should organize education and teacher-student relationships?

Rogoff, Matusov, and White (1996) argue that "coherent patterns of instructional practices are based on instructional models, and instructional models are based on theoretical perspectives on learning" (389). Recent research (Hillocks 1999; Nystrand et al. 1997) indicates that teachers usually hold implicit theories about teaching and learning that inform their planning and day-to-day decision making. Yet these theories are typically underarticulated, unrecognized, underspecified, and quite often inconsistent if not schizophrenic in their application. It is our contention that clearly stating and coming to understand one's theory (or theories) about teaching and learning can help us to develop a coherent instructional model and then to scrutinize, converse about, and adapt our teaching in ways that hold powerful benefits for teachers and students.

Introducing Lev Vygotsky and George Hillocks

There is a powerful trend of using the theories of Vygotsky, an early twentieth-century Russian psychologist, to inform teaching at the early childhood and elementary school level. These initiatives, however, have not yet filtered up nor been widely adapted at the middle and high school levels. For example, Vygotsky's ideas about actively assisting and instructing students to do complex cognitive tasks and for guiding them through the "zone of proximal development"—the level at which they can do things with help that they cannot do alone—are apparent in highly successful programs for elementary students such as Reading Recovery. They also appear, with impressive results, in instructional strategies like guided reading, literature-rich classrooms, and the like. However, we rarely see these approaches used with older students. We want to remedy this situation.[2] The ideas of George Hillocks have helped us to do so, and to move from teacher-centered instruction to learning-centered instruction with middle and high school students or at upper levels.

The kind of teaching that most typifies American middle and high school classrooms is that the teacher tells and the student listens, then the student tells (or regurgitates information on a written test) and the teacher evaluates. The knowledge is declarative, decontextualized, and inert (think of a classroom dominated by lecture). Knowledge is not personally constructed nor applied. More progressive teaching is seen when teachers model strategies and knowledge making in the context of task completion, and then students attempt to do the task the way the teacher did it (think of Tom from Scenario 5). Vygotsky's notion of instruction would have teachers doing complex tasks in meaningful contexts with students helping as much as they can (think of Arlene in Scenario 6). Through repetitions of the task, students take on more and more of the responsibility, with the teacher helping as needed and

---

[2]There are many parallels between successful elementary school practices in literacy and potential innovations at the upper levels. For instance, older students can benefit from reading varied texts by exploring young adult literature (YAL) or using YAL as a bridge to more canonical works. Taken a step further, the highly successful "graded book programs" for beginning readers can be extended for older students through George Hillocks' ideas about text and assignment sequencing with increasingly complex reading procedures, themes, and genres (see Chapter 8). George's idea is that procedural knowledge must be constructed in one activity or the reading of one text that can be brought forward to the next task, and further developed and refined before being brought forward to the next task, and so on.

The Vygotskian notion of the classroom as a "community of learners" can easily be adapted with the creation of collaborative groups as well as inquiry and design communities in the upper-level classroom (see Wilhelm and Friedemann 1998). The idea that reading and learning are active, meaning-constructive activities can be foregrounded by the use of transactional and authorial reader response theories in middle and high school classrooms; the argument that learning must be continually assessed by teachers to match instruction to learners and groups can build on the use of teacher research methods and Hillocks' notions of frame experiments with older students (Hillocks 1995, 1999).

FIGURE 1.1
LEARNING-CENTERED TEACHING

1		2		3		4
I DO YOU WATCH		I DO YOU HELP		YOU DO I HELP		YOU DO I WATCH

naming the new strategies employed by the student. Eventually students do the task on their own. The learning here is directed by a teacher who models appropriate strategies for meeting particular purposes, guides students in their use of the strategies, and provides a meaningful and relevant context for using the strategies. Support, in the form of explicit teaching, occurs over time until students master the new strategies, and know how and when to use them.

In the learning-centered teaching process, the teacher first models a new strategy in the context of its use and students watch. As this is done, the teacher will talk through what the strategy is, when the strategy should be used, and how to go about using it. The next step on the continuum is for the teacher to engage in the task with the students helping out. The third step is for students to take over the task of using the strategy with the teacher helping and intervening as needed. Finally, the student independently uses the strategy and the teacher watches. If particular students are more advanced, they may skip ahead to a later point on the continuum. If, on the other hand, students experience difficulty using a strategy in a particular situation, the teacher may have to move back a step by providing help, or taking over the task and asking students to help.

There is clearly a need for this kind of active and sustained support for improving reading through the middle and high school years. The time is right for these Vygotskian notions of guiding reading to be widely adopted in our schools.[3] The learning-centered teaching process that we are arguing for requires *explicit teaching*, a method we outline in the figure below.

---

[3]This is another point where George Hillocks' work is so helpful. We've found that George's thinking and teaching bridges traditional concerns with acculturating students to the "language of power" (Delpit 1988), and understanding and learning from texts with new and highly progressive concerns about foregrounding the culture and meaning making of readers, about student and group-centered learning, and about active teaching.

FIGURE 1.2
STEPS IN EXPLICIT TEACHING

Explicit teaching should not be confused with drills and worksheets. Explicit teaching can be humane and holistic and can create interests and knowledge where none existed. Such instruction, when embedded in larger projects, can be highly purposeful and immediately applicable. Taylor et al. (1995) identify these steps for explicit instruction that assist student performance and that move from a teacher's direct instruction and modeling to student independence and internalization of the new strategy:

1. Teacher explanation of *what* the strategy includes (e.g., how to ask and answer an inferencing question. See Chapter 5.)
2. Teacher explanation of *why* this strategy is important (because textual meaning is often subtextual or implied. Readers will miss the point of many texts if they do not infer implied meanings.)
3. Teacher modeling of *how* to perform the strategy in a context currently meaningful to the classroom project (See Chapter 5 for full explanations of how and when to ask inference questions.)
4. Teacher explanation and modeling of *when* to use the strategy in other situations
5. Guided practice, in which the teacher and students work through several examples of the strategy together using authentic text, and then a gradual release of responsibility to the student
6. Independent use, in which the students continue to use the strategy on their own.

(See our practice chapters for examples of how we go through these steps to introduce students to new strategies, e.g., internalizing new kinds of questions in Chapter 5, or understanding main ideas in Chapter 7.)

What Is Learned Must Be Taught

An important argument in educational practice today centers on the debate of whether learning can proceed naturally and without much intervention (see Scenario 5 of the ranking activity) or whether what is learned must be taught. While we agree that creating a nurturing environment in which kids will naturally grow and learn is attractive, both Hillocks and Vygotsky would maintain that teachers who believe or enact only this vision are letting themselves off the hook. Both argue that *anything that is learned must be actively taught.*[4]

Many of our own students think that they have taught themselves some performance, such as skateboarding or cooking. Sometimes they even maintain that they taught themselves how to read. Vygotsky would argue that self-teaching is a form of high-level teaching, which depends in turn on having internalized the cognitive tools and metacognitive language to teach oneself. And an external teacher must have originally lent us the consciousness and strategies to do this. (Vygotsky himself uses the example of how teaching children to tie their shoes can become internalized and serve as the basis of learning macramé on their own.) But at some point, the basic skills were taught by another consciousness.

We make thousands of teaching decisions a day and all the decisions we make are theoretical, based on what we value, on what we think we are doing or should be doing, and on what we think will work toward those purposes. We want our decisions to work to support learning for all of our kids, even though some didn't do the reading, some did it and have no clue, some are five chapters ahead, and all are at widely different skill levels. What can we do so that our teaching is effective for all of our students in ways that work and make sense to us and to the kids? How can we teach so they can understand the purpose and use of what we do together in class, so they can all develop new abilities built on the skills they already possess, and so they can understand a higher purpose, pattern, and sense to classroom work?

George Hillocks, following the work of Shulman (1986, 1987) and Grossman (1990), maintains that teachers should and can possess specialized knowledge of students, of particular content and tasks, and of how to represent and teach this knowledge. George argues that "teaching is a transitive verb" and that it "takes both a direct and an indirect

---

[4]It's important to note that Vygotsky was not particularly concerned with drawing educational implications from his theories. Also, there are various arguments about the ways in which current theorists are interpreting Vygotsky for educational purposes. As one example, some approaches choose to focus more on the culture of the student, and others, such as ours, focus more on acculturating students—on providing them with access to cultural knowledge about texts and reading.

object" (1995). In other words, when we teach, we teach something to somebody. We need to know both our subject and student. We need to know how to teach in general, *and* in particular situations with the particular skills called for in that situation or with that text.

Shulman (1987) argues that there is a knowledge base for teaching and that it includes the following:

- Knowledge of students
- Knowledge of the subject to be taught
- General knowledge of teaching processes, management, and organization that "transcend the subject matter"
- "Pedagogical content knowledge," which includes: curricular knowledge of "materials and programs"; knowledge of how to teach particular kinds of content; knowledge of educational contexts and situations; and knowledge of educational ends, purposes, and values.

We'd include as "pedagogical content knowledge" what we as teachers know about our theoretical orientations toward learning, toward reading, toward literature, and the like. When we know these things, then theory allows practices to stem in a wide-awake way from an articulate and unified set of principles. These principles can then lead us to scrutinize our teaching and to up the ante on it, pushing us forward to more powerful teaching.

The Essential Vygotsky: A Theoretical Perspective

Vygotskian theory is the theoretical perspective that informs all of what we are trying to do in this book. You'll see that the Vygotskian perspective lines up best with Scenario 6 from the ranking activity. Our instructional model, based on Vygotsky, is consistent with Barbara Rogoff's, Matusov, and White's (1996) model of community-centered learning, or what she calls "transformation of participation," meaning that the participation of the novice in a particular pursuit is transformed into expert performance through the expertise lent the learner by the teacher (see Figure 1.2). Rogoff's theory is a general one about learning.

Our model is also similar to George Hillocks' model of environmental teaching, a model that he applies more specifically to the teaching of English, particularly writing. We've used these models to specifically inform our teaching of reading, and we've adapted them to focus on how the study of texts, literary and otherwise, can be a communal and democratic activity that leads to democratic thinking, conversation, and actions. In introducing Vygotsky, we'll provide a very brief summary of some important ideas that have helped us theorize and think about our own teaching of reading.

One of my favorite summaries of Vygotskian thinking appears in Jerome Bruner's (1986) *Actual Minds, Possible Worlds,* one of my all-time favorite books. In the final chapter, Bruner contrasts Vygotsky with both Freud and Piaget. Piaget, who still exercises a huge influence on American schooling, and Vygotsky, who is just beginning to influence early elementary instruction, do have many theoretical similarities. For instance, Vygotsky himself credited Piaget for serving as a springboard to his theory about inner speech and how it is used to regulate thinking and behavior. Both thinkers believed that there are two lines of development—the biological/natural and the social/cultural—and that these two lines interact continuously during the development of thinking, which cannot be understood in isolation from either line. Piaget emphasized the natural to a greater degree, and Vygotsky stressed the sociocultural. Both agreed that development results from experiences in the environment and reflection on these experiences. Both argued that development is influenced by social situation and interaction.

Both thinkers documented major qualitative transformations in children's thinking. Piaget argued that all children move through four stages depending on their age and readiness. Vygotsky argued that children's thinking is transformed at that point when the abilities to communicate in language are mastered, and with the development of awareness and self-direction of thinking, which is not tied to a particular age but to appropriate instructional support (Glassman 1994). The differences in their views are often accentuated, though. For me, this is because Vygotsky's particular views can be so exciting when applied to teaching.

Bruner points out that Freud looked into the past to explain development. The past history of the individual was almost a prison from which he needed to be freed. Piaget looked to the present and the child's current state of development, which allowed her to fulfill a natural readiness and biological capacity for particular kinds of thinking. Vygotsky, in contrast, looked to the future, and believed that "growth is reaching towards the future" (Bruner 1986, 141).

According to Bruner, for Vygotsky it is "the availability of the prosthetic devices of culture" that brings growth (141). These devices

Vygotsky did not believe that the mind grows naturally or without assistance.

include the social support systems of culture, and the culture's toolkit of procedures for making meaning.

Art and literature themselves are examples of cultural prosthetic devices that may use language. The *conventions* that govern the construction of art and literature and the interpretive processes for understanding and making meaning of these are also prosthetic devices. We all know, for instance, that fables convey cultural knowledge that we can use to think with. And the very conventions of these tales, e.g., that animals will represent human traits, help us to understand the tales and how to use what the tales are trying to teach us.

For Vygotsky, language is the tool of tools. Learning how to use language, and other conventional "signs," symbol systems, or ways of making meaning requires teaching—active assistance from a more expert person (a teacher) who will lend her consciousness, knowledge, and methods of thinking to the less expert person (a learner).

Zones of Development   Perhaps his most influential ideas are those related to zones of development. What a child can do alone and unassisted is a task that lies in what Vygotsky calls the zone of actual development (ZAD). When a teacher assigns a task, and the students are able to do it, the task is within the ZAD. They have already been taught and have mastered the skills involved in that task. I remember many times in my own teaching career when I made such an assignment and exulted at my teaching prowess when the most excellent projects were submitted. Vygotsky wouldn't have been so sanguine. He would say that the kids could already do what I asked them to do, and I had taught them nothing.

> When you assign a task and the students successfully complete it without help, they could already do it. They have been taught nothing.

The place where instruction and learning *can* take place is the zone of proximal development (ZPD). Learning occurs in this cognitive region, which lies just beyond what the child can do alone. Anything that the child can learn with the assistance and support of a teacher, peers, and the instructional environment is said to lie within the ZPD. *A child's new capacities can only be developed in the ZPD through collaboration in actual, concrete, situated activities with an adult or more capable peer.* With enough assisted practice, the child internalizes the strategies and language for completing this task, which then becomes part of the child's psychology and personal problem-solving repertoire. When this is achieved, the strategy then enters the student's zone of actual development, because she is now able to successfully complete the task alone and without help and to apply this knowledge to new situations she may encounter.

Of course, there are assignments and tasks that lie beyond the ZPD, and even with expert assistance the student is incapable of completing the task. I have unwittingly given many assignments and assigned many books during my career that were beyond the ZPD of most of my students. Such assignments, no matter what the curriculum might proclaim, are acts of hopelessness that lead to frustration. In fact, such texts are designated by Analytical and Informal Reading Inventories (ARIs or IRIs) to be at the student's *frustrational* reading level. If you've taught books that are at many of your students' frustrational level, then you know that teaching them lies in the teacher's frustrational level as well!

For instance, on one occasion I was studying over 40 boys who were assigned to read Shakespeare's *Twelfth Night*, and not a single one of them was actually reading the play. Each student, including quite successful ones, told me that the language was too hard ("It's in a foreign language!" "Yeah," I replied, "Late Middle English"), that the text of the play was too hard to read ("I don't get how to read the stuff in parentheses!" In fact, scripts have twelve conventions not required in the reading of any other kind of text. See Esslin 1987), that they didn't understand the purpose of reading the play, how it might connect to their lives, or how it might be useful ("Teachers do it to convince most of us we shouldn't go to college. That's the only reason for reading Shakespeare I can think of"). I would argue that reading *Twelfth Night* was beyond their ZPD in terms of vocabulary, content, text type, and reading processes required. It was an exercise in frustration for teacher and students, and what students reported learning was that Shakespeare was too hard for them, that they were not readers, and that there were ways to be successful in school without reading the assigned texts (e.g., by reading Cliff Notes, taking notes in class, watching the movie version, etc.). I'm sure that a reading of the play could have been put into their ZPD, but much sensitive frontloading (see Chapter 4) would have to have been done first. A better scenario might have been to set a purpose and read a text that was in the students' ZPD, or at their instructional level.

Texts at the *independent* level are those the student can read alone (and are therefore in the ZAD). Texts at the *instructional* level are those that students can read with help, and through which students will learn new content and new procedures of reading (because the demands of reading that book lie in the ZPD—they can be learned with the appropriate assistance). These are the kinds of texts students need to be reading. They must be carefully chosen and matched to students, and they must be accompanied with instructional assistance for developing strategies of reading. It is important to remember that the difficulty of a particular text depends on many factors, as seen in the Shakespeare example: the student's purpose for reading, motivation, background knowledge, how distant the content and ideas are from kids' experience, the vocabulary, the inference load (the amount and kind of inferences required for understanding), student familiarity with the genre, the genre expectations and the strategies that are required to comprehend it, understanding of the author's purpose, and so forth. Teaching can lead development when students are able to be successful with support. Teaching of tasks that cannot be successfully completed with assistance lie outside the ZPD.

Vygotsky viewed teaching as *leading* development instead of responding to it, if teaching is in the ZPD.

Students develop new cognitive abilities when a teacher leads them through task-oriented interactions. Depending on various factors, a teacher will lend various levels of assistance over various iterations of task completion. The goal is to allow the students to do as much as they can on their own, and then to intervene and provide assistance when it is needed so that the task can be successfully completed. Vygotsky stressed that students need to engage in challenging tasks that they can successfully complete with appropriate help. Happily, Vygotsky points out that teaching in such a way develops the teacher, just as attentive parenting matures the parent.

A metaphor that has been used to describe this kind of teaching is "scaffolding." The student is seen as constructing an edifice that represents her cognitive abilities. The construction starts from the ground up, on the foundation of what is already known and can be done. The new is built on top of the known.

Learning always proceeds from the known to the new. Good teaching will recognize and build on this connection.

The teacher has to provide this scaffold to support the construction, which is proceeding from the ground into the atmosphere of the previously unknown. The scaffold is the environment the teacher creates, the instructional support, and the processes and language that are lent to the student in the context of approaching a task and developing the abilities to meet it.

Scaffolding must begin from what is near to the student's experience and build to what is further from their experience. (Michael Smith calls this moving from "near to home" to "far from home"; you have to start from home when you journey somewhere new.) Likewise, at the beginning of a new task, the scaffolding should be concrete, external, and visible. Vygotskian theory shows that learning proceeds from the concrete to the abstract. This is why math skills are learned from manipulatives, and fractions from pies and graphs. Eventually these concrete and external models can be internalized and used for abstract thought. One of the problems with reading is that the processes are internal, hidden, and abstract. In later chapters we'll explore several techniques (DRTAs, protocols, drama and visualization strategies, symbolic story representation) for making hidden processes external, visible, and available to students so that they can be scaffolded to use and master new strategies of reading.

According to Berk and Winsler (1995), scaffolding is an interaction style that fosters cognitive growth and success in performing specific tasks. It is characterized by joint problem solving of an interesting, meaningful, collaboratively approached problem. Another quality of scaffolding is "intersubjectivity," which they define as the process whereby two participants who begin a task with different understanding arrive at a shared understanding. In other words, a student adjusts her perspective, strategy use, and understanding to gain a more mature approach to a problem, one that is exhibited by the teacher. They stress that scaffolding also includes concern, warmth, and responsiveness. Praise and feedback are important elements, as are talking through phases of the task. Scaffolding also keeps the student in the ZPD, and promotes "self-regulation." In other words, the student takes as much responsibility as possible, and eventually takes on the language and strategies to regulate independent behavior in such a way to complete the task on her own.

> Students have a need to develop and exhibit competence. Teachers must assist them to develop competence as they engage in challenging tasks in which they can be successful.

The ultimate goal, of course, is to bring the previously unmastered processes of completing a task into the students' ZAD so that they can do the task without help. Reaching this point requires lots of support and practice and is a significant learning accomplishment.

Vygotskian theorists stress that children need to engage in tasks with which they can be successful with the assistance provided. They also stress that the child needs to have strengths identified and built upon (in contrast with the deficit model of teaching, in which a student's weaknesses are identified and remediated), and requires individual attention from the teacher.

Context and situation are also essential and integral to all learning. So students need to be engaged in real everyday activities that have purpose and meaning. To quote Brown, Collins, and DuGuid (1989):

A meaningful learning context is crucial. Learning is purposeful and situated.

> Recent investigations of learning challenge the separating of what is learned from how it is learned and used. The activity in which knowledge is developed and deployed, it is now argued, is not separable from or ancillary to learning and cognition. Nor is it neutral. Rather, it is an integral part of what is learned. Situations might be said to co-produce knowledge through activity. Learning and cognition are fundamentally situated. (32)

It is important that the teacher gradually releases responsibility to the student until the task can be completed independently.

Think about coaching, which many Vygotskians use as a metaphor for teaching. A basketball coach may work her team on skills and drills, but always for the purpose of applying it in a game situation. Coaches set up practices that rehearse their teams through various game scenarios. Practice games and scrimmages always precede an actual contest. In scrimmages, the play is stopped and instruction is provided in the context in which a mistake or possibility occurred. No basketball coach would roll out the balls and let the players do whatever they wanted each day. Likewise, no coach would have her players practice at length without balls, backboards, or the chance to shoot. The coach is a teacher who instructs within purposeful situations that are directed toward clear goals. And the coach's job is to make sure her team has enough practice to be successful at playing an actual basketball game.

When students have had enough support and practice with a particular task to do it independently, they are said to have internalized the knowledge, and they have reached a new zone of actual development. The ante of instruction can then be raised and a task in a new zone of proximal development approached. In basketball, a coach teaches her players the simple one-on-one defense first. This requires each player to guard one specific player from the opposing team. Not until her players have mastered this defense, would the coach teach the more complicated "switching defense," which requires her players

Learners can only begin to learn within their individual zones of proximal development, current interests, and present state of being. *But* humane teaching can develop new interests, new ways of doing things, and new states of being.

to switch the players they are guarding under certain game circumstances—e.g., when a defensive player is screened off by an offensive player. But once the players master the one-on-one defense, the opportunity to successfully teach switching or double teaming has arrived. By continually keeping tasks in the ZPD—or slightly beyond the students' current level of independent functioning—you keep students engaged, and new capacities are continually "roused to life."

Vygotsky wrote, "What the child can do in cooperation today he can do alone tomorrow" (1934). He also noted that "instruction is good only when it proceeds ahead of development. It then awakens and rouses to life those functions which are in a state of maturing, which lie in the zone of proximal development. It is in this way that instruction plays an extremely important role in development" (1956).

Berk and Winsler (1995) further warn that "when teachers continually offer children or permit them to choose problems that they are able to handle without assistance or provide experiences that are too distant from children's independent mastery, then they fail to orient instruction so it enhances development" (104). AMEN!

In this way, we would critique natural-language-learning classrooms, like that in Scenario 4, in which children are placed in nurturing environments where it is assumed they will naturally grow and bloom. Though we know that many workshop classrooms do provide expert assistance through minilessons, and through a variety of peer interactions and projects that can provide peer and environmental assistance, we believe that such classrooms often fail to push students to learn how to engage strategically with new text structures, conventions of meaning making, and new ideas. (We are all speaking from personal experience, and are critiquing our own practice in workshop settings.) The teacher in such situations often fails to lend her full consciousness to students or to set appropriate challenges, simply encouraging and allowing students to pursue their own paths. We do not want our students to naturally unfold into what they were supposedly "predestined" to be, or imagined to be predestined to be. We want them to develop the capacity and awareness to choose who they will be and what they will do.

Another point that has become very obvious to us is that our students clearly possess not only cognitive zones of proximal development, but also social, emotional, and moral zones of development.

There are cognitive, social, moral, and emotional ZPDs.

We'll demonstrate later how Hillocks-inspired instruction assists students not only to read and learn more competently, but also to develop more aware and mature social, moral, and affective behaviors.

In Figure 1.3 notice that in the zone of actual development for any particular task, the student can do the work unassisted and is therefore responsible for his own performance. The task that the student cannot do alone, but can do with help lies in the zone of proximal development. Here, the responsibility lies jointly with the student and the teacher, who must provide assistance to the student in the process of completing the task. That assistance can come explicitly and directly from the teacher, or from more expert peers, or the environment: the classroom activities or structures created by the teacher. The teacher lends the student strategies and language for approaching, controlling, and talking through the task behaviors. This process of talking through a task is *social speech*.

Over time, this social speech, lent by the teacher to the student, can become internalized as the student's *private speech*. This private speech allows the student to regulate her own problem-solving behavior with this task. Once that happens, the self provides its own assistance, and this leads to the achievement of a new zone of actual development. As expertise grows, the problem-solving language is abbreviated as *inner speech*. At this point, to keep students engaged and learning, teachers should introduce a new task, or a new facet of a task, that as yet lies beyond the student's independent functioning (ZAD) in the ZPD.

"When Work Is Play for Mortal Stakes"

It's worth mentioning that Vygotsky stressed the importance of playfulness and imaginary play to learning. In our own schools, there's an amazing split between teachers who believe that learning should be fun, and those who believe that learning should be hard work. Our interpretation of Vygotsky is that he would agree with both parties (though primarily with the first group): we think he'd maintain that teaching and learning should be play that does "WORK," by which we mean that the learning will have an immediate application, function, and real-world use.

Play was a major part of Vygotsky's theories, as the following quote attests:

Figure 1.3
A Teaching Model Based on Vygotsky

Student Responsibility ——→ Adult—Then Joint—Responsibility ——→ Self-Responsibility

Zone of Actual Development	*Zone of Proximal Development*			
What the student can on her own unassisted	Assistance provided by more capable others: teacher or peer or environment: classroom structures and activities	Transition from other assistance to self-assistance	Assistance provided by the self	Internalization, automatization
	SOCIAL SPEECH • Adult uses language to model process • Adult and student share language and activity	**PRIVATE SPEECH** student uses for herself language that adults use to regulate behaviour (self-control)		**INNER SPEECH** The student's silent, abbreviated dialogue that she carries on with self that is the essence of conscious mental activity private speech internalized and transformed to inner verbal thought (self-regulation)

Play creates a zone of proximal development in the child. In play, the child always behaves beyond his average age, above his daily behavior; in play it is as though he were a head taller than himself. As in the focus of a magnifying glass, play contains all developmental tendencies in a condensed form and is itself a major source of development. (Vygotsky 1978, 102)

Teaching and learning should be play that does work.

Representational play of all kinds offers a region in which new abilities and ideas can be safely exercised and experimented with inside the zone of proximal development.

We consider reading literature an advanced form of play. As Vygotsky emphasizes, all forms of imaginary or representational play contain rules for behavior that connect to meaning making and real-life situations. Vygotsky wrote, "Whenever there is an imaginary situation, there are rules" (1978, 95). These rules—and playing with them—prepare us for the rules of other, nonimaginary, conventional social behaviors.

It's our contention that literature is a kind of rule-bound play with high stakes of its own and a connection to real life. Kenneth Burke (1968) typifies the reading of literature as "imaginative rehearsals for living" and as the development through imagination of "equipment for living." If we value engagement with texts, then we must teach our students the rules and help them play and live through the game and we must help them connect literature to their current lives.

Vygotsky identified two fundamental capacities that are developed in play: "(1) the ability to separate thought from actions and objects, and (2) the capacity to renounce impulsive action in favor of deliberate and flexible self-regulatory activity" (Berk and Winsler 1995, 54). We would argue that these capacities can also be developed through the play of reading.

These are not insignificant capacities. Students who use characters and stories as objects with which to think, and who use texts to deeply consider and regulate alternative options for activity, are engaging in imaginative rehearsals for living. Through play, as Vygotsky (1978) tells us, a student can realize many achievements that "will become her basic level of real action and morality" in future situations (100). For example, drama-in-education strategies in which students become characters contemplating future decisions or asking "what if" about alternative courses of action show how this kind of literature and life connection can be achieved.

But what ways of being in the world are we imaginatively rehearsing with students? Because we believe such rehearsals are an important purpose of reading, this is a crucial question. We are rehearsing ways to develop more ethical, imaginative, critical, respectful, hard-thinking, possibility-seeing democratic living . . . and that's a mouthful worth working toward!

Our work around reading should be centered not only on educating the imagination, but also around the rehearsal, shaping, and implementation of actual behaviors that explore new possibilities. In other words, it should also be centered on how can we move from play to work.

In much the same vein, Seymour Papert (1996) argues that learning should be "hard fun." Seymour bemoans his finding that though the computer is the world's greatest construction kit, it is generally used in schools as an electronic worksheet (because it is used for teacher-centered vs. learning-centered instruction). A worksheet is not playful and does no real work, both features that a computer can deliver in excess. George Hillocks, too, finds that school is often boring drudgery that does not help students to apply knowledge. In *Teaching Writing as Reflective Practice* (1995), George makes a powerful case for the importance of playfulness and fun to learning. Using gamelike structures that are playful and purposeful can do work. So can framing reading as inquiry, because inquiring can be "hard fun." Drama, debates, questioning games, art, and the design of knowledge artifacts such as hypermedia and video documentaries are playful structures that can be about process as well as content.[5]

Hillocks draws heavily on the research on both student engagement and potential (see especially Bloom 1964, 1976, 1985; Cszikimihalyi and Larson 1984; Cszikimihalyi, Rathunde, and Whalen 1993; Heath and McLaughlin 1993) as he argues that:

1. The best learning is fun.
2. Engaged learning is fun because it is challenging, relevant, and purposeful but is supported in a way that makes success possible.
3. Almost all students can and will learn given supportive teaching and effective learning environments.

---

[5]See Wilhelm and Friedemann (1998) *Hyperlearning* for full discussions and examples of electronic knowledge artifacts.

Models of Teaching and Learning: Flowing from Theory

About a year ago, my colleague Paula Moore and I were both thinking about the issues of theoretical and instructional models. We were both interested and troubled by the well-documented problem that very little actual teaching goes on in American classrooms, particularly in language arts classrooms (Durkin 1979; Hillocks 1986; Nystrand et al. 1997; Tharp and Gallimore 1988). For example, readings are typically assigned and then quizzed. Typically, teachers provide little or no instruction or support in *how* to read. I had given Paula some things to read by George Hillocks, and she, in turn, had provided me with some articles by Barbara Rogoff.

In one of life's coincidences, we both came to the same conclusion on the same night: that the Vygotskian-inspired, sociocultural-based, learning-centered model that both of us were coming to adopt and espouse was so radically different from the two most dominant models of teaching and learning (teacher-centered and student-centered) that most people had never considered it. We both decided this was because our new model was two-sided and required mutual effort and responsibility on the part of learners and teachers, whereas the dominant models were one-sided and placed nearly complete responsibility for learning with the student. As a result, the two-sided model required a completely different kind of classroom and definition of teaching—one that may not look at all like what we have all experienced during our own schooling.

In one chapter Paula gave me (Rogoff, Matusov, and White 1996), the authors write, "It is difficult for people with a background in one-sided models of learning to avoid assimilating the community of learners [a two-sided model these authors espouse] to the adult-run/children-run dichotomy" (389–90).

In another quirk of fate, both Paula and I created charts to show the differences in these models, and brought them to school the next day to share with each other! The chart displayed in Figure 1.4 is a combination of the two charts, though Paula Moore must be given the majority of the credit for it (see Moore, 1997).

Because the dominant models of teaching and learning in our culture are linear, one-sided models, it's been typical to consider students responsible for learning: in the curriculum/teacher-centered model the teacher is an adult who runs the show and transmits information to students, whose job it is to "get it." In this transmission model the teacher provides an information conduit to the student, who is solely responsible for receiving and later retrieving this data. This model is referred to variously as a teacher-centered, presentational, curriculum-centered, or an industrial model of education.

Others argue that education should be "student-run." Proponents of this view often cite constructivist notions by arguing that learning is the province of learners, who must necessarily construct their own understandings. Knowledge is acquired by learners in the process of their self-initiated inquiries and personal investigations. Again, it is the student who is responsible. No one else can "do" learning for them, and their achievement of new knowledge requires active involvement and personal exploration. This progressive model is often seen in workshop types of settings in which teachers provide an environment full of opportunities and materials with which students may choose to engage. This model is often referred to as student-centered, participatory, exploratory, or natural-process learning.

An entirely different point of view is proposed by researchers, theorists, and teachers influenced by Vygotskian psychology, and to some degree by Bakhtinian notions of dialogism (Hillocks 1995; Rogoff, Matusov, and White 1996; Tharp and Gallimore 1988). Rogoff, Matusov, and White (1996) propose to call this a "community of learners" model in that, as Vygotsky suggests, it involves both active learners and more expert partners, usually adults, who will provide leadership and assistance to the less skilled learners as they engage together in a community of practice. In this model, it is the teacher who is responsible for students' learning, or their failure to learn.

Communities of practice attempt to create meaning and solve problems in a real context. Rogoff, Matusov, and White write that learning is not about "transmitting" or "acquiring" knowledge, but is about "transformation," namely about transforming the nature of one's participation in a collaborative endeavor. As the learner's participation is transformed, for example, he becomes a more active and expert member of the community of practice, often moving from observer to participant to leader of collaborative activity. But the more expert partner's participation will also be transformed as she learns

FIGURE 1.4
MODELS OF TEACHING AND LEARNING

	One-Sided Models		Sociocultural Model
	Curriculum-Centered	Student-Centered	Teaching/Learning-Centered
Historical Roots	Skinner, Pavlov, Thorndike	Piaget, Chomsky, Geselle, Rousseau	Vygotsky, Rogoff, Bruner, Hillocks, Dewey: *Child and Curriculum Experience and Education*
Theoretical orientation	Behaviorism	Progressivism Cognitivism	Coconstructivism Socioculturalism
How learning occurs	Transmission of knowledge: Teaching is telling	Acquisition of knowledge	Transformation of participation
Implications for instruction	Both teacher and student are passive; curriculum determines the sequence of timing of instruction.	Students have biological limits that affect when and how they can learn; teachers must not "push" students beyond the limits. Knowledge is a "natural" product of development.	All knowledge is socially and culturally constructed. What and how the student learns depends on what opportunities the teacher/parent provides. Learning is not "natural" but depends on interactions with more expert others.

	"Empty vessel"	Active constructor	Collaborative participant
Student's role			
Teacher's role	Transmit the curriculum	Create the environment in which individual learner can develop in set stages—implies single and natural course	Observe learners closely, as individuals and groups. Scaffold learning within the zone of proximal development, match individual and collective curricula to learners' needs. Create inquiry environment
Dominant instructional activities	Teacher lectures; students memorize material for tests	Student-selected reading; student-selected projects, discovery learning	Teacher-guided participation in both small- and large-group work; recording and analyzing individual student progress; explicit assistance to reach higher levels of competence
Who is responsible if student does not progress?	The student: He can't keep up with the curriculum sequence and pace of lessons or meet the demands of a prescriptive school program.	The student: He has a "developmental delay," a disability, or is not "ready" for the school's program. Often, family or social conditions are at fault.	The more capable others: They have not observed the learner closely, problem-solved the learner's difficulty, matched instruction to the learner, made "informed" decisions, or helped the learner "get ready."

about new ways to teach and new ways to participate and how to change her roles relative to the changing roles of others. Everyone is learning and working together to achieve a common purpose that will be useful beyond the world of school.

Rogoff and her colleagues argue that this two-sided model is a radical departure from the other two preceding models because both assume that learning is a result and function of one-sided action:

> The community of learners instructional model supersedes the pendulum entirely: it is not a compromise or a "balance" of the adult-run and children-run models. Its theoretical notion is that learning is a process of transformation of participation in which both adults and children contribute support and direction in shared endeavors. (Rogoff, Matusov, and White 1990, 389)

These authors and many others (Bleich 1998; Collins, Brown, and Newman 1992) have argued forcefully that the sociocultural context in which learning occurs, and the way in which something is learned, are necessarily a part of the learning. Therefore, students learning according to different models would learn in different situations and in different ways. This would affect how they come to understand and participate with different aspects of how information is represented and used. So, each model results in learning of a very different kind. Our ranking activity at the beginning of this chapter helped to demonstrate this.

Our goal is for students to develop a wide repertoire of reading strategies that they can independently deploy in a wide variety of situations with a wide variety of texts, and our ultimate purpose is that they use these strategies to participate democratically in their communities and cultures. We find that applying Vygotskian learning theory to our teaching is what best helps us to meet these goals.

2

A Theory of Teaching Reading

Help ME! A Reading Biography: A Reflection on Entering High School

Fifth through eighth grade came and went by,
And I came to hate reading and they didn't know why.

I expect high school to be the same,
To me, reading books is simply lame.

I did enough reading to just get by.
But I hated to read, and they didn't know why.

Teachers assigned me stuff day after day.
"We'll get him to read. We'll find a way!"

Not a day went by without a real try,
But I hated to read and they didn't know why.

Phonics, Textbooks, Grammar, Spelling.
Sometimes my teachers would end up yelling.

And look like they were about to cry
But I still hated reading and they didn't know why.

You see, no one helps me how to do it
And so I am frustrated all the way through it.

I just want to know the secret things
that readers do that make books sing.

And helps people love stories
And learn from them too

> *But no one has helped me,*
> *so sad and so true*
>
> *No one has taught me*
> *What I need to do*
>
> *And that is why I just don't get it*
> *So if you can't help me I'll just have to forget it.*
>
> *And give up interest in ever reading . . . and*
> *Believe me I'd rather be lying here bleeding.*
>
> —Jack

Cries for Help

All behavior has meaning. When students resist or avoid reading, this means something and could be a cry for help.

Jack's cry for help is one all three of us have heard over and over again during our careers as middle and high school English language arts teachers, if seldom so overtly and articulately. Usually such cries are masked by complaints that "Reading Is Stupid!" by heads down on the desk; by refusal to do work; by the pages written on or ripped from books; or by endless other forms of avoidance and resistance. But the cries are always there.

Not all students who are struggling act out negatively. Every so often a student like Jack voices the hidden need for competence and the stifled desire to be helped to know how to read—to learn new strategies and to find the best way to approach new and challenging kinds of texts.

Activity: Theories of Reading: Where Do You Stand?

What beliefs and theoretical approach to teaching reading hold the most promise for helping students like Jack to become more motivated and competent readers? Which is most consistent with Vygotskian learning theory? The following statements are composite statements from theorists expressing major views on reading. Read the statements and consider whether you agree or disagree with each one. Also consider which statements are consistent with each other and what these beliefs imply about teaching reading.

1. To read is to scan systematically from left to right across a linear sequence of letters, and then to convert the letters into sounds, and the sounds into words and those words into sentences . . . Phonic

unlocking is always the essence of reading, but it becomes particularly important when we have to read a word we have neither heard nor seen before.

2. Reading is a search for meaning. That is why aspects of the process and how it works cannot be isolated from the construction of meaning that is the ultimate goal. Learning to read involves getting the process of meaning construction together. Things become much harder if instruction takes this holistic process apart.

3. There is only one way to summarize everything that a student must learn to become a fluent reader, and that is to say that the child must learn to use real-life experiences and knowledge (nonvisual information) efficiently when attending to print. Learning to read does not require the memorization of letter names or phonic rules, or large lists of words, all of which are in fact taken care of in the course of learning to read, and little of which will make sense to a child without experience of reading. Nor is learning to read a matter of application to all manner of exercises and drills, which can only distract and perhaps even discourage a child from the business of learning to read. . . . The identification of individual words is at best only incidental to the reading process and is frequently not necessary at all. It can even be injurious.

4. The meaning of a text is found in the text. The text itself is the battle cry! Close reading, the scrupulous examination of complex relationships between a text's formal elements and its theme, is how the text's organic unity and meaning can be established. This kind of close reading is the essential task of the reader.

5. The special meanings—and more particularly, the submerged associations that the text's words and images have for the individual reader—will largely determine what the work becomes, because the work or "poem" is not in the text, but occurs in a transaction between reader and text. The reader brings to the work personality traits, memories of past events, present needs and preoccupations, a particular mood of the moment, and a particular physical condition. These and many other elements in a never-to-be-duplicated combination determine the response to and the meaning of the text. Readers must therefore be free to create and deal with their own responses to text.

6. It can only be through the subjective response that we are led to cognitive understanding. We define knowledge by how we continually respond to texts and how we collectively negotiate meaning in specific circumstances with others. We can only learn and dialogue from our own position and experience. And it is our emotional response that is the primary of all our subjective responses.

7. Good reading is more than a reconstruction of the author's meanings. Readers must relate what they read to what they already know. They must evaluate the new knowledge in terms of the old and the old in terms of the new. They must see and hear and move about in a story world that they create with the text. They must select and organize and make appropriate additions and be prepared to go beyond what the writer is telling them. They must be ready to create meaning, and this meaning is visual, auditory, physical, intellectual, and affective.

These statements[1] are meant to encapsulate various views from theorists and researchers that represent very different ways of thinking about learning to read and the act of reading. Though we are simplifying somewhat, there are three major theories about learning to read that have emerged over the years and that are still contending with each other in academic circles, and in the world of classroom practice. These are paralleled by three different literary theories regarding what happens when we read.

Theories of Teaching Reading

The ways these theories articulated above play out in classrooms line up with the teacher/curriculum-centered, student-centered, and teaching/learning-centered theories we discussed in Chapter 1. Taking a Vygotskian perspective of teaching and learning implies that we should adopt one particular theory of learning to read, and one theory of literary reading that can help us to assist student reading in the particular ways suggested by Vygotsky.

---

[1] I completed a similar activity to this as part of an English Centre workshop in London in the early eighties. I recognize #2 as being culled from Ken Goodman, and #3 from Frank Smith, I added #5 from Louise Rosenblatt, #6 from David Bleich, #7 from myself. I summarized the New Critical view in #4. If anyone knows who should be cited for #1, please let me know.

Here is a basic outline of the various major theories in play, exhibited in the above statements. The *bottom-up theorists* (statement 1) generally believe that students must learn to read from the "bottom up" or from "part to whole." It is maintained that students must first learn letter names, then phonemes and phonics rules, then words, phrases, sentence structures, and so forth until they can put these discrete elements together as they decode the parts of text into wholes as they read, or create the parts and meld them into a whole as they write.

This theory of learning to read is paralleled nicely by the *New Critical* theory of literature (statement 4). New Critics look to the text as the sole source of meaning, and seek to help readers do "close readings" that will help them understand the "unified coherence" and "single best meaning" of the text. The question they ask is "What does this text mean?" (Rabinowitz and Smith, 1998). Ironically, though New Criticism is a "dead" theory—that is, there are no longer practicing New Critics at universities or in critical circles—Applebee's (1998, 19) review of literature teaching in secondary schools shows that it is still the most widely practiced and widely embraced theory of literature when it comes to teachers. Also ironic is that most of the teachers who practice this theory are unaware that they are teaching from a theoretical orientation.

Many teachers are unaware of their theoretical orientations, although this affects how they teach and what the students learn.

Like bottom-up reading theorists, New Critics focus on decoding or unlocking the textual meaning—which, like Ragu spaghetti sauce, is "already in there!" just waiting to be discovered. Such approaches tend to be one-sided and teacher-centered since the teacher has the advantage of repeated readings, and the "critical" understanding that are necessary to discovering predetermined and organic textual meaning. The teacher's job, according to this theory, is to transmit textual knowledge to the student. The student's job is to know what the text means.

We have found that such an approach disenfranchises students because it focuses on the meaning someone else has gleaned from particular texts in ways that are disconnected from students' real-world concerns. Procedures of reading that students might master to make their own meaning are often lost.

Top-down theorists offer a view from the other end of the spectrum (statement 3). This general class of theories often goes by the names of *whole language* or *natural language learning*. These theories argue that meaning is made in the mind of the reader, who creates an emerging global sense of meaning that allows her to bring the "stuff" of reading—our experience—to bear in such a way that the parts begin to make sense. By moving from "the whole to the parts," reading becomes a meaningful and meaning-making activity.

Subjective reader response theorists (statement 6)—exemplified by the work of Stanley Fish (1980) and David Bleich (1978) mirror the top-down views in many ways. An excellent example of this approach, which Rabinowitz (Rabinowitz and Smith, 1998, 170) cites, is Fish's famous contention that "Lycidas" and "The Wasteland" are different poems only "because I have decided that they will be." Subjective theorists assert that meaning resides in the mind and in the activity of the reader, who brings his own meaning and associations to the text. There is no text, in fact, outside the minds of readers. According to Rabinowitz and Smith, these theorists ask, "What does this text mean to me?"

This approach is clearly student-centered. It is sometimes seen in workshop approaches to teaching that attempt to focus the reading activity around students, and to motivate aliterate or reluctant readers. We've already argued in the previous chapter that we find much to like about student-centered approaches, but that we believe the positive aspects of this approach can be incorporated into the much more powerful two-sided, "learning-centered" approach we are espousing. One example: expertise needs to be more actively shared than this model suggests. Workshop classrooms often allow students to work alone. Though they may share their reading or projects, these are not done together as "conjoint" or collaborative activity with the teacher—an aspect we feel is essential for student growth.

We are respectful of teachers who use such an approach in an attempt to get their students to read, and to empower them to begin seeing reading as personally relevant and meaningful. We know that matching kids to appropriate books and simply getting them to read is a very significant achievement that takes hard work and expertise and that is certainly worthy of praise. We, too, work hard to create a nurturing environment for reading. But we want to set the bar a bit higher. We want to help students (1) choose more complex books about topics they may not yet know about; (2) come to deeply understand the conventions of such texts and the procedures they need to make meaning with these texts; (3) grow beyond themselves as readers and thinkers and community members; and (4) take their place in ever grander social conversations about textual meanings and what these imply for how we should act in the world at large.

We think that all of our students, but particularly those students who are most disenfranchised as readers, benefit from the two-sided teaching/learning-centered model of teaching reading (Statement 2). This approach involves students and teachers reading texts together, with teachers lending their expert ways of meeting the demands of the particular text to the student. Students learn the codes and conventions that govern textual meaning. This kind of work is best done in contexts where the teacher and students are working together to answer a compelling inquiry question or explore a thematic issue of importance to all of them.

This theory of learning to read is paralleled by the transactional literary theory (statement 5) and the closely aligned reader response theory of engagement (statement 7). Another theory of reading that is consistent with these theories is that of *authorial reading*, which goes beyond these theories to add a democratic edge and energy to reading and learning. This edge promotes students' conversation with texts and the authors that created them, as we'll explore in the next chapter. For summaries of these theoretical perspectives, see Figure 2.1.

Let's now turn to the problem of how to know what it is that readers must do as they read and "transact" with particular texts. How can we make our own reading strategies in these situations visible and available to our students? These are the issues that we will take up next.

Teaching in ways informed by the transactional theory of reading is consistent with Vygotskian two-sided theories of instruction.

What It Takes to Join the Literacy Club

Jack's cry for help, like most pleas, seems to be a cry for connection and relationship. After all, these struggling kids know that they are being excluded from the literacy club—that they are outsiders, denied access to the secrets and pleasures and power of what Frank Smith (1978) calls "the club of all clubs."

FIGURE 2.1
THEORIES OF READING

	One-Sided Models		Two-Sided Model
	Curriculum-Centered	Student-Centered	Teaching/Learning-Centered
Reading instruction	Phonics Whole word Jeanne Chall	Whole language Natural and language learning Ken and Yetta Goodman	Reading recovery Guided reading Marie Clay
Theoretical orientation	Bottom-up	Top-down	Interactive
How learning occurs	Transmission of knowledge—teaching is telling	Acquisition of knowledge—learning is constucting understanding	Transformation of participation
Corresponding literary theories	Traditional New Criticism	Subjective reading response	Transactional reader response, particularly theory of engagement and authorial reading
Literary theorists	Warren, Brocks	Bleich	Rabinowitz & Smith, Rosenblatt, Wilhelm
Textual meaning	Correct meaning is IN the text and can be discerned through close reading and scientific analysis	Reponsibility for producing meaning lies with the reader; meaning is a private decision and subjective re-creation	Literary meaning results from conversation (transaction) of reader and author through the medium of text
Student's role	"Empty vessel"—receive meaning	Active constructor of individual meaning	Collaborative participant learning how to create meaning to participate in and create culture
Valid interpretation	Purely textual	Must account for reader perception, affective and associate response	Must account for textual coding but repond to this as interanimated with reader's needs, questions, experiences, and judgments

If we don't know or can't follow the rules, we can't play the game and are excluded from the club.

Reading is indeed a communal activity that has rules and socially agreed upon conventions for making meaning. Authors and texts share expectations with readers about how they expect to be read. Other readers also expect us to follow up on textual codes in particular ways.

The point is that, like any club, the reading club requires that we possess certain abilities and follow certain rules (cf. Hamel and Smith, 1997).

We want to explore some ways to make reading processes visible and available to students like Jack, and to assist all students in becoming more expert readers with the new, challenging, and more varied genres of texts that students are asked to read as they enter middle school and then high school.

At a recent conference here in Maine, Dick Allington (1999) reviewed a meta-analysis of several international studies. The analysis revealed that American students in the earliest grades rank second in the world in reading, but fall to the middle of the pack by the end of middle school, and twenty-ninth out of twenty-nine industrialized nations by the end of high school. There could certainly be various explanations for this. It is our contention that America's declining achievement relative to other countries, though certainly cultural, could also be due at least in part to these factors: (1) students are actively taught to read in elementary school and then are expected to read without further support once they enter middle school; and (2) reading is seen as the ability to decode words, and students are not provided further assistance in understanding or meeting the more sophisticated requirements of particular text structures. We argue that we must actively teach reading through all the grade levels by helping kids make meaning with the new text genres, textual conventions, and content to which they are being introduced.

As they enter upper elementary and middle school grades, these students are moving away from an almost exclusive preoccupation with narrative text to the reading of a wide variety of sophisticated literary and informational genres that place special demands on readers. Since these "task-specific" or "text-specific" demands (Smagorinsky and Smith 1992) go well beyond general processes of reading (like summarizing, predicting, monitoring, and questioning) and students are not taught how to recognize and respond to these demands, many middle and high school students find themselves lost in the sauce, and like Jack, terribly frustrated and feeling incompetent when met by their new reading challenges.

The most recent National Assessments of Educational Progress (see Campbell et al. 1998 for a review) show that high school students are very adept at decoding words and ascertaining the literal-level meanings of text. However, they do very poorly on more sophisticated tasks such as making inferences and drawing conclusions about text. In fact, only a very small percentage of students at the twelfth-grade level can identify and support an author's generalization—a thematic statement or point—from a piece of writing. This means that even though students have the ability to decode text, they do not have the ability to infer, critique, make meaning, converse with authors, or think with and about the texts they have read. This is quite an indictment of the lack of support students receive as readers once they enter the upper grades. It also indicates that students cannot converse about what they read, or use their reading as an object or tool with which to think.

The IRA Adolescent Literary Statement The International Reading Association's adolescent literacy statement (Moore et al. 1999) makes the same points. This statement argues that both the teaching of reading and the funding for teaching reading dry up by late elementary school. The statement posits that students need particular kinds of *direct instruction* throughout adolescence as they struggle to meet the demands of more sophisticated kinds of literary texts, a variety of informational texts and genres, and more substantial and complex content. The statement is a call to actively instruct adolescents at their current states of development, in ways that consider their current interests. The task this statement sets before us is exactly the one Tanya, Julie, and I have been attempting to undertake.

Teaching Ways of Reading

Early in my career, before I had encountered George Hillocks, Michael Smith, and other salutary influences, I was teaching the poem "Ozymandias" by the romantic poet Shelley. I was reading the poem aloud and really getting into it. "My name is Ozymandias, King of Kings, look on my works, ye mighty, and despair!"

"What a cool king!" Blake whispered.

"Ozymandias rules, the mighty drools!" responded Perci.

"But listen up," I told the class, "listen to what we hear next." I continued reading: ". . . NOTHING besides remains . . . DECAY . . . colossal WRECK . . ."

"What a king! Bigger than Elvis!" Blake continued to exult.

"But what about the desert, the wasteland . . ." I sputtered.

"He wasted them. He laid waste to everything!" Perci commented enthusiastically. "Wouldn't it be great to be that . . . well, GREAT!?"

They had missed the point entirely.

Like a New Critic, I eventually resorted to explaining to the students what the text meant, often going through the pieces step by step in a kind of formal exegesis.

I wasn't aware that I was making theoretical choices that weren't working, that I couldn't defend, and with which I really couldn't be too happy. For some reason, I thought my job was to automatically teach "the text"—or the various texts, anyway—that appeared in the anthology. My approach was a teacher-centered New Critical one.

In fact, the most helpful thing for me to do, after being slapped awake, would have been to guide the students over time to adopt "ways of reading" or strategies that would have helped them understand how to recognize and read ironic texts, or how to recognize, respond to, and critique arguments.

In such an approach the strategies we teach are not ends in themselves (as in the teacher-centered approaches), but a means to an end, so there must be a shared purpose and significant content that the processes help us to get after.

Isn't It Ironic?

When I was teaching British Literature and struggling with texts such as "Ozymandias," I resorted to an teacher-run, information-transmission model. As we've seen, this model implies particular instructional practices: namely, that teaching is telling. Through lecture and handout, I provided a brief introduction to the history of ironic literature, and through board work and worksheets I provided definitions and examples of kinds of irony. I asked students to identify different kinds of irony and to write examples of each kind. Although my students were engaged in activity, I was running the show to prove a point that I had already articulated. I did not solicit or use a larger purpose, interests, questions, or general input. I did not include procedures of learning *how* to read and write ironic texts as part of the lesson. In fact, when the kids did ask several questions along these lines, I saw the questions as interruptions to the task at hand, not as contributions to any communal kind of inquiry.

When I taught the kids in this transmission mode, they could transmit information back to me, but they had not developed an understanding or ability to *apply* the information. My students could define verbal irony and explain how "A Modest Proposal" was ironic only because I had given them the definitions and an exegesis of Swift's work, which they had more or less memorized. They could *not* recognize or reconstitute ironic meanings with unfamiliar texts. That was because the context in which they learned did not require or assist them in those processes.

I noticed that student-centered, natural-process learning didn't seem to work either. In another class with a workshop setting, several students who happened to encounter irony or ironic texts throughout the year were unable to understand the irony on their own. Usually they read the texts literally and without question. Sometimes they seemed slightly troubled, as if they sensed something was amiss, but then they continued to read the ironic text as if it could be taken on the surface level.

A few years later, I had another chance to teach irony to high school students. I had recently met and worked with Michael Smith. Michael had written his dissertation on teaching kids to recognize and read irony through careful sequences of activities and readings that helped them understand the codes of irony and the reading processes necessary to understand those codes (see Smith 1989, 1991). Michael's novel approach was "learning-centered": the teacher, who understood how irony worked, created situations in which the teacher and the students would work together to cumulatively learn how to deal with irony, and how to use it for their own purposes.

At the same time that I was teaching British Literature in high school, a demographic change moved most of my teaching load to the middle school, where I began work with the most ironic people on the face of the planet—the so-called hormone-geysering "transescents" and "tweenies." So I was able to use forms of Smith's irony sequence to teach both my high school students and my seventh-grade reading students to read irony. And amazingly, it worked at both levels!

As the British Lit class geared up to read some of the great satirists of the language, including Swift, I initiated a unit on irony. The unit was framed by the question *Can irony make us better people?* In other words, can irony work to change people for the better?

Following Smith's suggestions, I started the kids off with a variety of comics that used irony, and then we moved on to short vignettes, poems, and stories. As my students read these short selections, they discussed whether the irony helped them understand things in a new way, and whether that understanding might change their behavior. They examined whether there was a difference between sarcasm and irony. They wondered whether irony was cultural, and whether the British might make more and better use of it than Americans. As they worked, they wrote out their own rules for recognizing clues that a text was ironic and what they had to do as a result. (Here's an example: After reading several cartoons, a group of students wrote that "a clue to irony is when the speaker says or thinks something that conflicts with something else in the story, like what happens, or what other people do, say or think. If this happens, you have to figure out what the author is telling us through this conflict." The students could then apply this rule to "Ozymandias" by recognizing that the Big O's contention about being the greatest does not match the fact that his statue and his kingdom have been destroyed. The author is indirectly telling us that Ozymandias was not as great as he thought, and suggesting, perhaps, that his excessive pride led to his downfall.) It was a rich unit, we had plenty of fun, and it ended with the students not only understanding "A Modest Proposal" but making their own ironic music videos and skits that they showed to the school as Public Service Announcements.

My seventh graders, though not as adept as the high school students, equally enjoyed their unit. They also became very skilled at noticing ironic discourse and texts in their lives and in the media, and at being able to understand them. For their final project I asked them to create ironic public service posters for the purpose of improving our school, which they completed with gusto. (For example, one poster had text that read: "Cheating is cool! You can steal work from other people, get great grades without really learning, and nobody gets hurt! So don't be a fool—just cheat your way through school!")

When students become part of a community of learners, they are supported in taking on the concepts and tools of that community. In this case, they were able to explore the ironic discourse of artists, cultural and political critics, and the like, and they were invited to use this knowledge with others for real purposes.

Guided Reading

When I was working with those students, I didn't know that my instruction corresponded with Vygotskian theory and instructional models. Neither did I know my teaching was similar to what is called *guided reading,* an instructional strategy used with great success with emergent readers. I'll briefly outline some parallels here.

In guided reading, a teacher works with a group of students who have similar instructional needs. Because none of my students at either level really understood irony, it was appropriate to teach them all through the sequence of activities that built procedural knowledge about how to make meaning with ironic texts. Later in the unit, I worked with smaller groups of kids who had similar instructional needs, and we used different texts matched to their needs and interests.

In guided reading, students are prompted to develop sets of reading strategies that they can use to make meaning and to solve difficulties they might encounter. Because I was teaching older students, I was interested in the task-specific strategies required to read ironic text, instead of just the general processes of reading that teachers working with elementary school students might want to develop.

When you want students to learn something new, make sure everything else is easy! For example, make sure students already know how to meet all of the other task demands.

Guided reading begins with text selection, which is critical. Each text not only should help the reader learn more about the text, but it also should help the reader learn more about the process of reading for *all* texts. Texts must fit the students' interests, their prior knowledge, and their competence. If they do not possess the prior knowledge and competence, they must develop it before approaching the text. This is what we were up to with the cartoons and ironic anecdotes. I had to start with texts in which the text structure, the content, and the vocabulary were all familiar. The one thing that was unfamiliar was the procedure we were working on: recognizing and reconstituting ironic meanings.

FIGURE 2.2
WAYS OF ASSISTING READERS THROUGH THEIR ZONES OF PROXIMAL DEVELOPMENT: MODES OF SCAFFOLDING

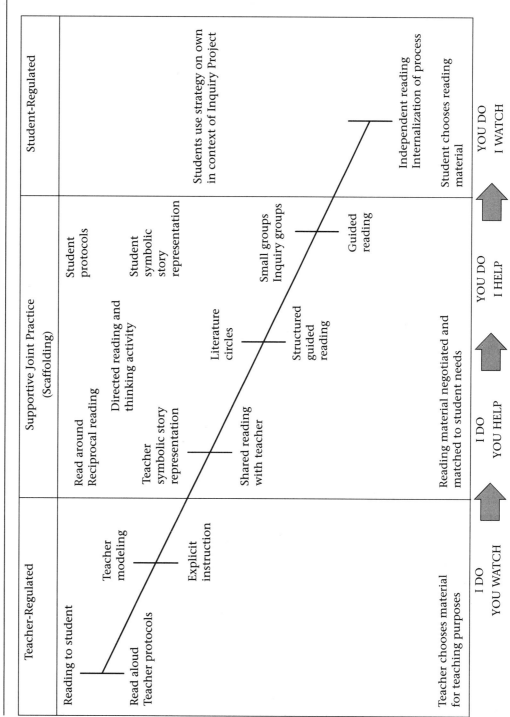

In guided reading, the next step after text selection is to highlight the focus. In this case, we knew we were trying to figure out how to read ironic texts, and that I would help scaffold the development of a repertoire or problem-solving scheme for doing so (problem-solving schemes for particular tasks are known as *heuristics*). The teacher first "frontloads" the text (or text set), and activates appropriate background knowledge, e.g., role-play a scene where a student says something ironic and ask them to brainstorm other examples. They can then try to explain how irony works in real life. Since the first texts I selected were short (e.g., cartoons), we reread them several times, focusing first on literal meanings of words, then on comprehension, then on making personal connections, and finally on understanding the text as it was coded to be understood. With each rereading, I focused on a particular strategy or idea. We named the strategies (e.g., "look for when the speaker says or thinks something that conflicts with something else in the story. . . .") we found useful and reapplied them in further readings. In this way, the students' reading was guided and reguided until they were able to successfully guide themselves.

The Inquiry Square: Knowing *How* to Teach *How*

The problem is that there are very few resources to help teachers understand the demands of particular kinds of texts or genres. We use Jonathan Culler's conception (1975) of a genre as sets of texts that use similar conventions and structures and that therefore make similar demands on readers. George Hillocks provides us with a very powerful heuristic (or problem-solving scheme) for thinking about what students need to know and do as they write and read particular genres or text types. And once we identify what students need to know and do to successfully meet and understand the demands of a particular text or genre, then we can assist them in this enterprise.

> Once we know what is required to complete a certain task, we can ask ourselves *how* to teach these specific processes.

George originally developed the following four-way classification to discern what kinds of knowledge teachers use in classrooms. We use it to argue that any time we read or write anything, we need to make use of these four different kinds of knowledge:

1. Procedural knowledge of substance (inquiry skills: knowing how to get the "stuff")
2. Procedural knowledge of form (knowing how to put the "stuff" you've got into an organized and coherent form)
3. Declarative knowledge of form (being able to name and understand the conventions of different genres and formats)
4. Declarative knowledge of substance (being able to name or articulate what the meaning or point of the text might be)

As you can see, procedural knowledge is to understand and know *how* to do something and declarative knowledge is being able to *name* and understand something.

We've dubbed this heuristic "The Inquiry Square" and its purpose is to help teachers think through what they must teach to students. George composed it for thinking about how teachers differ in what they emphasize in the teaching of writing, but we have found it tremendously useful for understanding how to teach both writing and reading.

First, I'll explain briefly how George used this to apply to writing. Step 1 (above) asks us to consider *how* we get the "stuff" to write about. In other words, what is the process we go through to access, find, or develop information to put in our writing? Once we have the stuff we can then proceed to Step 2, which asks us to consider *how* to put that stuff into a conventional text structure or genre-appropriate form. Step 3 asks us to help students *name* the form and articulate how a particular form works to fit their purpose. Step 4 asks us to help students *name* or articulate the meaning of their constructed text.

In Figure 2.3 you will see how we've adapted "The Square" to help teachers think about how to teach *reading*. This Inquiry Square is to help teachers prepare to guide students' reading of a particular piece of writing in a particular genre.

As you can see, we have added a step to George's heuristic: 1. *What is the purpose of reading a particular kind of text?* We did so because we believe that teachers should be "wide awake" about their teaching purposes. We also agree with Neil Postman (1999) that for a student who has an adequate *why* almost any *how* or *what* will do, so students need to understand and see a purpose, too. To help make purpose visible to students, we often brainstorm this first question with them:

FIGURE 2.3
THE INQUIRY SQUARE

1. The teacher must first consider the purpose of reading a particular kind of text, and the function it might play, the work it might do for students.

	Procedural Knowledge of	Declarative Knowledge of
S U B S T A N C E	2. The teacher must consider how to assist students to access background knowledge necessary for comprehending the text, or if the students do not possess the necessary background, how to build it. The teacher must help students learn HOW to access the information and strategies for reading.	4. Once students have brought their background knowledge to bear on the formal features of a text, then the teacher must consider how to *assist students to articulate* what meaning the author is communicating through the substance and formal construction of the text.
F O R M	3. The teacher must consider how to assist the reader to learn *HOW to recognize the form* of the text (genre or text structure) and its organization, conventions and expectations, and how to assist the reader to *appropriately respond to and interpret* these formal conventions so that the text constructed by the author can be realized by the reader. In this way, you actualize the author's virtual text structures, breathing life into them to make the text a reading experience.	5. Once students have an idea of the meaning the author is communicating (the thematic statement or authorial generalization), then the teacher must consider how to assist students to *name the structure and articulate* how the structure worked to help communicate the author's point.

Steps teachers must take when teaching a text:
1. Why write or read this kind of text?
2. How can we help students get the "stuff" to be able to read this? (Inquiry?)
3. What do we have to do with the "stuff" so that they can recognize the genre? (Satire, fable, etc.)
4. How can we assist students to articulate the meaning the text communicates to us?
5. How can we help students recognize and articulate how the text's structure and construction help to make this point?

"Why might an author want to write a fable (or a comparison-contrast essay, or any other kind of text)?" Once we have answered this question together, we know that our students see a new purposefulness, relevance, function, and significance to the task.

Notice that we start by asking why someone would want to *write* this kind of text. We start with writing because it is a more visible and accessible process than reading. During reading, the reader must be able to *match* the activity and codes of the writer; in other words, the reader must be able to discern what a writer does—the techniques or codes she uses—to compose a text in a particular genre and with a particular meaning. The text *tells* the reader how to respond to the text. Our job is to enable our students to "hear" what the text is telling them.

So, at the top of the Inquiry Square question 1 asks teachers to consider their purpose. Then, in the Inquiry Square boxes you will find steps 2 through 5 in which the teacher is asked to consider how to guide students' reading by addressing each of George's four types of knowledge. In step 2, the teacher's role is to access or build students' background knowledge so that they will be able to decode or comprehend the text (see Chapter 4 for specific methods for doing this). In step 3, students read and bring this knowledge to bear on the information presented in the text. The teacher's role is to teach the student *how* to put the information into a form—a story world or mental model that represents what they are experiencing and learning. This means assisting students' to respond to and interpret the formal conventions of the text. As they progress through their reading, they may be able to *name* the form, text structure, or genre of the piece they are reading (step 4), and eventually they should be able to *name* or articulate the main idea communicated by the text (step 5). In this way, the reader's activity parallels that of the writer.

George argues that all writing begins with what he calls *inquiry*, or "getting the stuff," as illustrated in step 2 of the Inquiry Square. We would add that this is also true for all reading. When we write, our first step is to find something to write about and gather information. When we read, our first step is to activate or build the background knowledge necessary to approaching the text. (See Chapter 4 for information on frontloading.) Thus the first and many subsequent steps in reading and writing situations are forms of inquiry.

If students do not know how to get the "stuff" by accessing their own background experience with life, information, or text, and if they do not know how to do the research and inquiry to procure that experience, then we must assist them in doing it. And we must help them understand that they must learn how to do so, eventually, on their own.

Until genre studies and research into various kinds of textuality provide us with more insight into how different kinds of texts work, and the kinds of demands these texts make on us as readers and writers, Hillocks' Inquiry Square is a powerful heuristic we can use to think about how to teach. Even when we do know more, the Inquiry Square will remind us that the root of all reading and writing is personal inquiry and the "getting of stuff." This key idea informs the instruction that we will discuss in the following chapters.

When we use the Inquiry Square with teachers during inservices and workshops, they are nearly always astonished at how much a student needs to know and to do to write or read what seems to be a simple kind of text like a fable. As one teacher remarked, "It's no wonder that [my students] couldn't write a decent fable. There is so much more to it than I realized, and I didn't help them to know what they needed to know or do what they needed to do."

Hillocks' Inquiry Square helps solve that problem for us. The Inquiry Square also sets up and organizes our teaching practice, which we share with you in the following chapters of our book. We give examples of frontloading (a way to "get the stuff"), demonstrate various strategies that help the reader fill in and actualize the structures of the text, name the structures and processes of reading, and explore social decisions, projects, and action. In Figure 2.4 we provide you with a blank inquiry square that you can use to guide your own planning.

Reading and Writing as Inquiry

We agree with Hillocks that all reading and writing begin with inquiry, and reading and writing can best be conceived of and taught as forms of inquiry. (We pursue this idea in more detail in Chapter 3.) A particularly powerful way of enacting two-sided teaching is through inquiry, and therefore an excellent way to teach reading and writing as

FIGURE 2.4
BLANK INQUIRY SQUARE

1. What is the purpose for reading or writing this kind of text?

		Procedural Knowledge	Declarative Knowledge
S U B S T A N C E		2. How can students be helped to "get the "stuff"?	4. How can students be helped to articulate the meaning of the text?
F O R M		3. How can students be helped to put "the stuff" into a conventional form (writing) or recognize the form or genre (reading)?	5. How can students be helped to name the structure of the text and how this construction helped communicate the author's meaning?

POINTS TO REMEMBER!
1. A reader or writer uses all four kinds of knowledge every time she reads or writes a text.
2. When teaching a new kind of text, a teacher must consider how to assist students to use all four kinds of knowledge.
3. A reader's activity parallels the writer's activity in reading any kind of text, i.e., everything a writer codes into the text, the reader should notice, interpret, and attempt to understand. What a writer encodes, a reader is asked to decode.
4. Though this is a recursive process, generally speaking a writer or reader must begin with a purpose to be achieved. Then meaning making begins with the next step of inquiry—with accessing background information with which to compose meaning. If the student does not possess the appropriate background, then it must be built, or the task must be given up.
5. All reading and writing begins with inquiry, is a sustained inquiry and meaning-making endeavour, and is best framed as a form of inquiry.

processes is through inquiry projects. George Hillocks (1995) draws on Dewey to argue, "we need a pragmatic inquiry that allows us to make sense of the world and to assess the sense we have made" (108). Reading and writing should create new meaning, connections, and relationships. Reading and writing, like all effective learning, is dialectical and social, and makes use of past and present materials to reach into the future.

We've already argued that teacher-centered instruction in the form of lecture and recitation is predominant in American education. Moreover, reviews that include other subject areas show this is true across the curriculum (Goodlad 1984; Hoetker and Ahlbrand 1969). This situation persists despite the compelling research that shows demonstrably greater gains for students learning in an inquiry-driven environment in which they are helped to know *how* to do things (Hillocks 1986; Nystrand et al. 1997). (We provide examples of inquiry projects in Chapter 3, and each following chapter exhibits work that was done in the context of an inquiry project.)

Learning how to do things is especially important for at-risk students. School will continue to particularly alienate many at-risk students until teachers value what they already know and help them put those skills to work as active inquirers and doers in the context of challenging collaborative projects (Cziksentmihalyi and Larson 1984; Cziksentmihalyi, Rathunde, and Whalen 1993; Heath and McLaughlin 1993). We've found the same results in our own smaller teacher research studies (e.g., Wilhelm 1997; Wilhelm and Friedemann 1998).

George Hillocks (1995) calls such teaching "environmental teaching." The teacher creates an inquiry environment with the following characteristics:

- Students exercise choice within certain parameters.
- There are clear goals.
- Students have a stake and an ownership in a project.
- The project is personally relevant and socially significant.
- The problems are challenging and complex.
- The project can be revised and made increasingly complex.
- Students are assisted as needed.
- Students have the opportunity to improve through practice.

- Students participate in problem-centered group interactions.
- Students have the opportunity to apply the learned skills independently in the project.
- The potential for success is great.
- There is a real-world application or performance that culminates the project.

Projects we have pursued with our students include one that inquired into the role of sports in American culture, and many that inquired into social justice issues in our school, town, and nation. We have explored whether the lobster catch should be curtailed, examined the issue of how Maine's forests can best be regulated, and attempted to define the nature of good romantic relationships, among countless other issues. Through such projects, reading and writing are purposeful and serve real needs. Students develop the dispositions, values, and strategies of problem solvers and researchers and become open to multiple possibilities. They learn the skills to review, revise, and critique one's own work.

Such projects allow students to construct meaning together and gain from the accumulated knowledge of others, including the teacher (who, in contrast, may have stepped out of the equation in natural-process-learning situations). All the relevant studies of such learning-teaching environments report that students were entirely engaged and that they experienced great fun (Cziksentmihalyi and Larson 1984; Cziksentmihalyi, Rathunde, and Whalen 1993; Heath and McLaughlin 1993). In our classrooms, during such projects attendance was up, homework was more complete, and evidence of new strategy use abounded.

Six Methods for Teaching Reading Strategies

Once we know what we need to teach students about reading particular kinds of texts, what methods can we use to help them recognize and internalize these strategies? The Vygotskian scholars Tharp and Gallimore (1988) identify six ways of teaching. These teaching techniques can be used in various ways to introduce, model, encourage, or support the use of new strategies. All these techniques can be used to teach reading strategies in the context of inquiry or thematic units and will be featured throughout the rest of the book.

1. *Cognitive Structuring* (environmental assistance)—this refers to the way classroom activity is organized to support learning
    a. Frontloading—the activating or building of background knowledge necessary to approaching a particular text. This may include the introduction of conceptual, procedural, or genre knowledge, i.e., knowledge about the content of a piece, about the strategies necessary to reading it, or about the text structure and the demands it places on the reader. (Chapter 4)
    b. Sequencing—the organization of activities and texts so that strategies are learned text by text and activity by activity. Knowledge is brought, forward and accrued over time during such a process. (Chapter 7)
    c. Directed reading and thinking activity—a teaching technique that guides student attention and strategy use throughout the reading of a particular text. (Chapter 3)
2. *Modeling*—ways of making reading, learning, and thinking visible and available
    a. Protocols—also known as think-alouds. The reporting out of what one is noticing, thinking, and doing as one reads a particular text. (Chapter 3)
    b. Drama—a set of enactment strategies that can make story content and reading strategies available to students[2] (Chapters 3, 4, 7)
    c. Art—visualization strategies that make story content and reading strategies available to students[3] (Chapters 6, 8)
    d. Symbolic story representation—a kind of text or story manipulative in which the content of a text and the processes used to comprehend it are demonstrated through found objects, cutouts, and other concrete devices. (Chapter 6)

---

[2]See *You Gotta BE the Book* (Wilhelm 1997) and *Imagining to Learn* (Wilhelm and Edmiston 1998) for rich descriptions of how drama strategies can assist reading and learning performances.

[3]See *You Gotta BE the Book* (Wilhelm 1997) for descriptions of how visual art can assist reading performances.

3. Questioning
    a. Question-answer relationships (Raphael 1982).
    b. Questioning circle (Christenbury and Kelly 1983).
    c. Questioning hierarchy (Hillocks 1980)—all of these schemes help students to articulate and internalize the different kinds of questions expert readers must ask and answer to comprehend different kinds of texts. (Chapter 5)
4. *Explaining/Instructing*—talking through problem solving; lending language to the learner
    a. Teacher and student think-alouds/protocols. (Chapter 3)
    b. Teacher and student symbolic story representation. (Chapter 5)
    c. Through other techniques of making reading visible, such as drama.
5. *Feeding Back/Naming*—providing explicit feedback and naming what the reader is doing or not doing, and explicitly naming what might be done
    a. Developing metacognitive capacity and self-regulation—this means that students are given the language and awareness to identify and manipulate particular strategies at the point of need. This capacity is developed through all of the activities mentioned here, such as in the think-alouds (Chapter 3) or Symbolic Story Representation (Chapter 5), or when students describe what they were thinking and doing when they created artistic or dramatic responses.
6. *Contingency Management*—this refers to the management of consequences and rewards of various learning activities, and managing the contexts that may provide these rewards
    a. Social/peer assistance through group work, reading buddies (see Chapter 8), literature circles (see Chapter 7)—such work is naturally motivating to students since the building of relationships is challenging and rewarding.
    b. Thematic, issue-oriented, or contact zone units—reading and learning about issues of personal relevance and social significance. Such work is motivating since it begins with student interests but leads to social action. (These are described throughout the book, see especially Chapter 3.)

Teaching involves assisting students with increasingly competent and complex performances of meaningful tasks. There are six ways to do this. Use them all!

c. Projects—designing and creating tools or knowledge artifacts for real use and real audiences. Such work is motivating because functional artifacts are created and used. (For an example of a relational social action project, see Chapter 8.)

Our following chapters exhibit the powerful contingencies of inquiry into relevant issues through group work, and focus on applying reading strategies and content learned to the students' lives.

3

Authorial Reading and Democratic Projects

The effective expansion of democracy . . . presupposes . . .
a process that will lead to its internalization. This seems to be
the key to saving today's global civilization as a whole.

—Vaclav Havel

Helping Students Develop Competence

I was modeling "think-alouds" for my students, a technique in which the reader reports out, or "thinks aloud" about what it is he is doing as he reads. This technique can provide a rich window into reading activity and is a powerful way to model particular kinds of reading strategies. (Think-alouds are also known as "protocols"; see the "Old Horse" model later in this chapter.)

One student exclaimed, "Wow, you make mistakes too!" And another added, "You just keep going because you fix things up later!" Like Jack, who wished someone had just told him or showed him what to do, these students need us to give them new ways of reading—and of thinking about reading—through active instructional strategies that help them understand what they have to do next to be better readers. As Margaret Meek (1983) tells us, our job as teachers is to make public those secret things that expert readers know and do.

Recently, I was moaning about my inability to reach some of my students. One of my colleagues said, "Do you think you are the UCLA basketball team?" (The juggernaut basketball team who once won eighty-three straight games.) He continued, "Do you want to win them all?"

The unanimous answer from Julie, Tanya, and myself is YES. We do want to win them all. We want all of our students to be the kind of readers who will become informed citizens and democratic participants in every realm of life. One of the most compelling features of Vygotskian theory, particularly as articulated and played out by Hillocks (1995), is the idea that given the right kinds of instructional support, nearly every one of our students can become powerful and motivated readers who can do humane and democratic work with literacy.

What is it, then, that we most want for our students? And what will our student readers need to succeed at meeting these goals? What do readers need to develop greater capacities and tastes?

To review, we believe that readers need a personally relevant and socially significant purpose. Readers need an understanding of the demands of the text they are reading and how to meet these demands. Readers need assistance to take on strategies and stances as they read new kinds of texts. And, we would now add: they need to see a connection between their reading, their personal lives, and the world they inhabit. They need for what they read to serve a higher purpose, to inform some kind of decision making and social action.

As Freire (1970) describes, we want to help our students become better readers so they can "read the world," and maybe, ultimately, begin to "write the world" as well, transforming it through democratic conversation and work into something new and better for themselves and for others.

Very helpful in working toward this purpose is the theory of "authorial reading" (Rabinowitz and Smith 1998), which is consistent with Vygotskian learning theory, and with the theories of transactional reader response and reading as engagement. But authorial reading goes beyond these and provides a political and ethical edge to reading that can help students work together toward democracy. This project will be theme of this chapter.

Working for the Future's Democratic Vistas

George Hillocks and Michael Smith have convinced us that we need to have a vision of where we want our students to land. To do this, we have to start where they are, but we are heading toward goals that we have identified for various educational and moral reasons. We ask: *Where is the best place I can get my kids to be when they are done with my class, and how can I get them there?* To us, this is what teaching is about. This is what literature is about. Teaching and doing literature are profoundly human and intensely moral pursuits. We don't hide from this nor do we hide our goals from students. We let them know where we are going and why and how we will honestly deal with the politics of the issues we will face. If we ignore the controversy and moral engagement teaching and literature offer us, then we have lost our chance both to engage our kids and to use literature (and any other kind of text) for its most powerful purposes.

To reach our own democratic vision, we must work together with students and have students work together too.

What Is Democracy? Democracy, like Vygotsky's vision of learning, looks to and reaches into the future. Michael Smith has convinced us that democracy is much less about governing and much more about associated living. For us, democracy means that tensions should be embraced and meanings should be negotiated, not controlled or preempted by the most powerful. Democracy is about learning to tap into and celebrate difference, which offers a wider array of visions and deeper pools of resources. Democracy is about sharing power instead of overpowering or being overpowered. Gordon Pradl (1996) argues that democracy is about the social act of becoming—of helping ourselves and those around us to continually grow and become more complex, of not being satisfied by the status quo.

If we want our work to help transform ourselves and others, then we must have a "constructive social enterprise" or a common project that we must negotiate and mediate. Democracy, as we'll use it here, is about undertaking common projects (see below) that require the complementary contributions of different perspectives and different people with different strengths, all of which will be considered and used with great respect for the completion of the project.

Louise Rosenblatt (1938) is perhaps most famous for both theorizing and popularizing the "transactional" theory of literature, which likewise posits that readers must bring meanings and strategies to a text to "converse with" and "come to understand" what the text is trying to communicate. Moreover, Rosenblatt makes an explicit connection between transactional theory and democracy. She critiques traditional literature instruction as decidedly undemocratic, and she announces her own intention "to demonstrate that the study of literature can have a very real, and even central, relation to the points of growth in the social and cultural life of a democracy" (v). As Pradl (1996) explains: "Such is the heart of Rosenblatt's formulation of literature education: a dialogic, back-and-forth movement between reader and text, and then a reaching outward to an ongoing social conversation with other readers and other texts" (77).

Transactional reader response theories that attend specifically to the ways in which readers should make meaning with text are the *theory of engagement* (Wilhelm 1997) and the *theory of authorial reading* (Rabinowitz and Smith 1998). These theories look specifically at the kinds of moves readers are expected to make and the responsibilities they are expected to fulfill as they read texts. The theory of engagement specifies ten dimensions of response that expert readers use to evoke textual worlds, elaborate on them, evaluate and use them. These dimensions include evaluating one's own reading, evaluating the construction of the text, and conversing with the author, the intelligence that constructed the text (Wilhelm 1997). The theory of authorial reading asks: "What does this text mean for the audience it was written for, and how do I feel about that?" This theory asks readers to grant the text and its author respect by reading the text as it asks to be read, i.e., responding as expected to all textual coding. But then it further asks that once the likely meaning of a text has been respectfully constructed, that we decide to what degree we will accept or resist the vision and ideas presented by the text (Rabinowitz and Smith 1998). Authorial reading thus includes authors and their texts in the conversations and debates about essential issues, and ensures that their views will be granted initial respect and consideration in terms of the social project being pursued.

We will work with these theories throughout the rest of the book precisely because they lend themselves to two-sided teaching and learning, ethical responsibility, democratic conversations, and community projects.

This is not the case with all reader response theories. Richard Beach (1993) describes five styles of reader response that differ in the relative stress each puts on readers, text, and context. What's missing from these five characteristic modes of reader response is the author. Engagement theory and authorial reading correct this omission.

I found in my classroom research with students that my most expert readers *did* consider the author, her message, how she had constructed a text to communicate that message, and what that message should mean for the way we live (Wilhelm 1997). I see a consideration of the author as totally consistent with transactional theories, because it emphasizes what a reader has to do to engage the text, the author, and the larger task (such as the issue or social project being pursued together in class) in meaningful ways. Rabinowitz and Smith (1998), who have powerfully influenced us through their recent book, *Authorizing Readers,* show that considering the author is absolutely necessary to the kinds of democratic work the three of us are promoting in this book.

If we are engaged in democratic conversations and work, then we have to construct the task of reading as conversing with authors so that we can converse with each other. We'll give a cursory overview of the ideas we will use the most, and throughout the rest of our chapters we will show how both of these theories have helped us think and play out various practical strategies and projects with our own students.

Rabinowitz and Smith argue, as we have, that reading literature is a highly conventional activity. In other words, there are rules and accepted ways of doing things, just like in any other social activity. Authors therefore count on readers who can recognize and respond conventionally when reading their text.

It's important to remember that just as phonemic awareness is essential to decoding text but is not sufficient for engaged reading, the strategies that kids need to learn in order to read texts conventionally (described in Chapter 2) are not an end in themselves but a means to an end: conversing with, respecting, and perhaps resisting an author to pursue our larger purposes. Students and teacher learn the strategies together so we can:

1. Communicate and engage with text as an expert (please note the Vygotskian transfer of expertise to the student)
2. Grapple with issues in new, vital, and important ways because we are entertaining a new point of view or a complication of a previously held belief.

Strategies for making meaning may be "foregrounded," as Michael Smith argues, but when students can use them independently, they are "backgrounded" in favor of the task at hand—deeply understanding and taking a stand on complex and highly debated issues. This means that we may provide instruction and practice that emphasizes the use of a particular strategy, but the students and we all understand that once the strategy is learned it will be put into use to comprehend texts that will be useful to us in pursuing our current project. At that point the text and our project will take precedence and be emphasized.

Authorial Reading and Democratic Responsibility

Rabinowitz and Smith (1998) argue that New Criticism asks, "What does this mean?" and subjective reader response asks, "What does this mean to me?" The New Critics' question requires that we devote ourselves to discovering a predetermined meaning. Yet democracy and democratic work, as Pradl (1996) tells us, does not determine results in advance! The subjective reader response question is based on an entirely personal reading, so there is nothing to resist or to build toward. As a student once told me, "You asked me what I thought so you can't say I'm wrong! I told you what I thought and now it's OVER!"

In contrast, authorial reading asks, "What does this mean for the audience the author was writing for—that is, a reader who would understand the conventions and coding of the text, as well as the cultural 'surrounding'—and how do I feel about that?" Once we have respected the text and its expectations of the audience it was written for, we should then ask whether we embrace this authorial vision or whether we would want to reject it, consider it in an adapted form, and so on. Rabinowitz and Smith point out that readers may not be able to play the authorial audience for particular texts—either because they do not possess the strategic knowledge to respond to the conventions employed, or because the content of the text is outside their experience and worldview—in other words, they are not the intended audience of the text. We need to make sure we can assist our students to be successful authorial readers of a particular text. If we cannot, the text in question is beyond their zone of proximal development and another text should be chosen.

Here's an example. A group of my students was doing a literature circle on Cormier's *The Chocolate War*. This was part of a larger unit on the question "What is essential to good political leadership?"

> In a democracy, meanings are negotiated, not predetermined.

When the group was discussing the author's thematic generalization, one boy volunteered that he thought the book championed standing up for yourself. A girl disagreed, and slamming her hand onto her desk said, "Jerry was crushed for standing up! He got smashed like a block of play-doh!" The boy rejoined, "That's what it means to me!" At this point I intervened and reminded the students, "Remember that our first job is to figure out what the author is saying to the audience he was writing for, then to explore in what ways we agree or disagree with that message."

At this point the group began to explore what Cormier expected of his audience. For example, they thought that he expected the reader to possess a knowledge of Catholic schools, a knowledge of fund-raising schemes and their purposes, a knowledge of bullies, etc. The discussion then considered whether the Catholicism was important or whether this could stand for any kind of doctrinaire authority. They disagreed about this, a couple group members arguing that the kids who weren't Catholic weren't going to "get" the book the way that they had. Two boys considered whether they were part of the authorial audience (not being Catholic), but decided that they were because they thought the story wasn't about Catholic authority but authority in general.

The group went on to agree that given Jerry's total humiliation and defeat, the textual coding led us to a message that a single person who resists an organized authority will be crushed. Then the group asked how they felt about that message. Two students who thought Cormier's message was specifically about Catholicism rejected the message and said he misportrayed authority, particular church authority. The others said they might agree that one cannot stand alone against an organized group of thugs, but they felt groups could organize to resist authority in most situations—perhaps even in repressive ones. This possibility resides outside the story, and perhaps because of that the conversation continued on to consider Nazism and the brownshirt thugs, and what possibilities for organizing resistance existed in Germany during the Third Reich. Through pursuing this analogy, several students indicated that perhaps Cormier was right about the power of an organized and abusive authority over individuals. The class ended with students continuing to argue as they gathered their books and walked out the door. The last comment I heard from one boy was, "Man, maybe that's why the Berlin Wall was up for so long!"

The most interesting and compelling parts of the conversation were made possible, I'd contend, by introducing the author and his message (embodied in his text and its construction) into a group conversation that negotiated meanings.

Vygotsky stressed the importance of working together in "everyday" activities. It's therefore important to connect the reading of literature to everyday life and to make it part of everyday activity. By organizing reading around "contact zones"—the salient issues in our culture and in our students' lives (in this case about what we should look for in a political leader)—we connect to the "everyday": to who kids are and what they are living through right now. In our classes, students learn real-world strategies such as how to be ironic, judge a narrator's reliability, or make an argument. They can apply these strategies to reading literature, and then use the literature to converse about and consider essential issues. In this way, strategy instruction is connected to life, and literature is connected to life. Strategies are taught as means to an end that is kept in immediate and future sight.

Motivated Reading: Curriculum, Contact Zones, and Projects

What kind of curriculum fits the theories of learning and reading we are espousing?

First, curriculum must be purposeful and connected to the students' current life needs and considerations. Neil Postman (1995) writes that for the student who has an adequate WHY, almost any HOW or WHAT will do. I always get a chuckle out of this quotation, even as I recognize the absolute truth of it. My students do not want to be taught for who they might be and what they might need to know several years down the road. *They want to be taught for who they are and what they need right now.* When students see the connection of what is studied to their own lives, they bring their life energy to the classroom project. They are able and willing to consider, learn, and converse around the relevant topic. And then they will be willing and able to use what they have learned.

Curriculum as Arthur Applebee (1996) argues that we should use "conversation" as
Conversation our curriculum model (notice the two-sidedness!) and place "conversation" at the center of classroom activity. He cites several practical benefits of doing so. First, conversation highlights that the intellectual

work of the class is to find meaning and construct knowledge. Conversation emphasizes that learning is an active, participatory pursuit. In other words, engaging in a conversation requires contextualized understanding, the application of meaning to real life, and a personal judgement of other people's thoughts and contributions according to certain critical standards for usefulness.

Conversation also requires integration of various subject matters and various language arts. When people have a significant issue to address or problem to solve they will not only bring to bear, but will also be willing and motivated to develop all relevant strategies and knowledge that could help. They will not arbitrarily divide this knowledge into subject areas as we do in school. Various "language arts" like viewing, writing, reading, speaking, and listening will be naturally integrated for the purpose of pursuing the group's goal of understanding the issue and undertaking a solution to it.

Third, the teacher becomes central to the learning project of the students by supporting students to learn skills they need to complete their projects, and by introducing relevant knowledge and skills from the larger community into the conversation.

Fourth, in conversation the task is not to guess what someone else knows, but to answer an open-ended question that affects us and that is worth arguing about. The curriculum is not a predigested set of knowledge for students to consume, but a set of issues for them to debate and evaluate and construct understandings about.

Finally, this kind of curriculum is consistent with the current theories of learning and reading that we have presented here.

Applebee also argues that such a curriculum "offers some straightforward criteria in evaluating a new or existing curriculum: Does it focus on conversations that matter? And does the structure of the curriculum foster conversation or make conversation more difficult to sustain?" (1999, 360).

Common In our book *Hyperlearning* (1998), my longtime team-teaching partner,
Projects Paul Friedemann, and I describe how we organized all of our middle school instruction around thematic units that were of interest to the kids, and that resulted in personal and group inquiry. We began by studying together a central concept, such as "What are the qualities of an effective leader?" or "What is culture?" We taught them basic concepts and procedures applicable to this study, such as identifying

cultural institutions and mores, understanding multiple perspectives, and reading for main ideas.

We started with content the kids were familiar with and looked at subcultures close to home, in the school and community, like gangs or the Missouri synod Lutherans.

Then we gradually released responsibility for these procedures and for content to the students as they asked research questions of their own about cultural topics a bit further from their experience. The students read about these issues (like did the Native Americans in Wisconsin deserve special "treaty rights" because of their cultural heritage?), conversed about them, invited informants (like a local tribal leader) to come and converse with them, and eventually made some kind of decision about where they stood on the issue. We then asked the students to create hypermedia or video documentaries to teach classmates about what they had discovered and what they now thought about the issue, and/or to pursue social projects that would address an issue or problem they had researched.

Student projects included developing and implementing a public service campaign about gender discrimination in our school, a project to clean up the lake in town to preserve its "cultural importance" to our community, building multimedia kiosks for a local history museum about immigration trends in our locality, and creating informational signage and guide sheets for local cultural sites. Our classroom was far from laissez-faire. The kids' questions drove their reading and composing, and their reading and composing drove the class. The context of a design-based classroom (meaning that we made things together that could be used)—and the problems and contacts that kids had identified—required them to read and interview and document what they were learning. (*Hyperlearning* contains a detailed description of how the instructional models of student-design learning and cognitive apprenticeship make use of Vygotskian notions of assistance.)

John Dewey (1944) thought of democracy as the pursuit of "conjoint activity," of working together to complete social projects that were of importance to diverse people. Tanya, Julie, and I have been working to reorganize all of our teaching around these ideas by using a variety of texts, including canonical literature, to explore ideas of personal relevance and social significance with our students. We hope that each of the units we create in our classrooms will become a project in itself, and we have been experimenting with guiding these units to end with social inquiry and social projects. Again, we present our teaching in this book as examples of our current thinking and struggles, not as end products, and we hope that they can provide a start for conversation and models to adapt in your own independent work.

The Contact Zone An idea that we all find attractive is that of a "contact zone" unit (cf. Bizzell 1994). A "contact zone" is a social space where differing perspectives on important issues meet, and therefore where imbalances in power can begin to be addressed. An example for us is the controversy surrounding groundfishing for lobsters off the coast of Maine where we teach, though this is part and parcel of the global issue of recklessly using any natural resource to the point that the resource may be used up or destroyed. Lobsters just happen to be a local version of this issue, and it is indeed a contact zone.

Several agencies and research groups warn that lobsters are overfished and that the industry is on the verge of collapse. Lobstermen, coastal residents, and other researchers dispute this position and point to record catches of lobsters in recent years and data collected on lobster boats. The geographical ground of the coastal waters and Gulf of Maine is at stake, as is a way of life; this is the social, intellectual, and geographical space of the debate.

Our students bring strong opinions to the table and can be highly motivated by such a close personal issue with clear stakes and immediate local implications. They read the environmental saga *Cod: A Biography of the Fish that Changed the World* (Kurlansky 1997), *The Hungry Ocean* (Greenlaw 1999), folktales and fiction about Maine coastal life, informational texts, databases, and research reports. They also listen to invited speakers and search for data on the Internet. Through this work, they become engaged in a democratic conversation that is much bigger than themselves. They see authors and their texts as voices to consider and converse with, to respect, and perhaps ultimately to resist as larger purposes are considered and contended. In such a way, reading takes on a motivated and higher WHY that can do immediate work and have clear consequences. And what they learn about lobster and the environment is connected to a myriad of other environmental issues. What they are learning is transferable and can be used in new debates and situations regarding the environment.

Louise Rosenblatt (1938) refers to Dewey, who "reminded us that in actual life constructive thinking usually starts as a result of some conflict or discomfort, or when habitual behavior is impeded and a choice of new paths of behavior must be made" (267). Pradl (1996) likewise tells us, "Yet, as Dewey and other progressives have shown, every area of the curriculum can be organized democratically in terms of problem solving, active learning, agenda negotiation, and interpersonal cooperation. The reading and writing of literature offers a primary opportunity for developing these social abilities" (107–108). Difficult situations are prime opportunities for valuing controversy and learning how to deal with them, converse about them, and learn from them. Pradl reminds us that "democracy does not determine results in advance" (128). By making our units of study "real"—that is, by pursuing issues to which we do not know the answer—we energize our students' reading and writing. Our teacher research shows that we still teach them everything *we* want them to know (the processes of reading and writing) by helping them work through the content and problems that *they* want to know about.

As Michael Smith points out, most kids see literature and textuality as foreign—separate and apart from their own lives and concerns. They also see authors as mythic figures and unquestionable authorities. As students read authorially in the context of democratic projects, they cast authors as part of a larger conversation that helps us think about and do our work. As we read authorially and reflect on the issues addressed in texts, we can work hard to make conceptions of reading, speaking, and engaging in social action part of the class.

Our beliefs about what happens when we read, and what good reading entails, has a great effect upon how we teach, and therefore upon what our students learn and may believe. If our instruction centers on prompting students to remember isolated details, then that is how kids will conceive of reading, and that is what they will do when they read. In *"You Gotta BE the Book"* (Wilhelm 1997), I describe Marvin, a very poor reader who did not even know silent *k*. As I tried to get Marvin to use new strategies, he signaled over and over again: "I'm doing what I've learned reading is, so leave me alone!" When we teach authorial reading in the context of inquiry, we provide a bigger and more energized vision of what reading can be, and how it can contribute to empowered democratic living.

Overcoming Our Expertise

I tell the preservice and inservice teachers I work with that they have a *very big* problem that keeps them from understanding the kids who most need their help, and it keeps them from providing the help that is needed. The problem is that they are expert readers. This means, in my experience, that they are probably not aware of the things they automatically do as readers. These strategies are seamless, under the level of consciousness, automatic. As a result, they do not struggle as our students do, don't experience the ruptures and difficulties, and don't have the same reading experiences as students do.

Peter Rabinowitz (Rabinowitz and Smith 1998) points out teachers are usually "reading against reading": reading and teaching a text for a third or fourth if not twentieth time as students read it for the first. And we also read against an intertextual grid of previously read texts and critical literature that our students cannot hope to match. We always read a particular text as a kind of text, and we know what kind of text it is in relationship to other similar or differing kinds of texts that we know. As experts, we easily locate the kind of text it is and what texts we've read that are like it. Therefore, we can know how to get started with it. We know what the text expects us to know and do as we read through it. Most of our kids don't have that kind of experience and have trouble getting into the game and sustaining their involvement. In fact, some can't even hope to get to the same ballpark.

If we teach in a way that pretends that our students bring the same resources to a task as we do, or if students come to think that they should be able to read as we do, great damage can be done. Students who believe they should immediately be able to read like experts often retreat into the belief that "I'll never be able to read like my teacher." These students don't understand the strategies and processes that are available to them, or that time and practice will make it possible for them to improve their reading.

Activity: Reading Pictures

Because teachers are usually expert readers, we need to disrupt our own reading in some way to gain awareness of how we proceed as we "read" or make meaning with text. These disruptions in turn can help us think of how to help students. The Inquiry Square is one tool teachers can use to prepare themselves to do this. There are other ways we can achieve this as well.

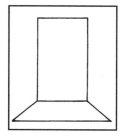

What do you see when you look at the picture to the left? When we ask this question to colleagues and students, we get an array of answers: a graduated cylinder (from a science teacher); an empty cereal box (from someone who didn't eat enough breakfast?); an Abe Lincoln hat (someone from Illinois?); an empty doorway (Freudian analysis, anyone?); a trapezoid with a cube on top (must be Ms. Math?); and many other answers.

The joke of course is that what we have is none of those things; it's just a bunch of lines. But if we expand this activity and think of the picture as a text, then we can consider how the mind wants to make meaning of symbolic text. A story is really just ink on a page, but a reader takes that text, infuses it with meaning, and creates a full and complete secondary world that can be lived through, deeply experienced, elaborated upon, enjoyed, used to think with, and much more.

What the reader brings to the table is essential. It is only by "transacting" with a text, by bringing ourselves and our interpretive abilities to bear, that meaning is made.

When we ask people whether the bottom horizontal line or the vertical lines are longer, most everyone answers that the vertical lines are longer. In fact, the lines are the same length. So, why do we perceive the vertical lines as longer? Because the meaning we have imposed on this "text" organizes how we see it. And a doorway or graduated cylinder is longer than it is wide.

Now, the question we want to ask is this: *Where does meaning reside?* Totally in the text, as the bottom-up theorists would argue? If so, how can we have so many different meanings that we all agree could be good readings?

Or does the meaning exist totally in the mind of the reader, as the top-down theorists believe? A seventh-grade student told me that this was a picture of a Green Bay Packer helmet. I used my standard reply: "OK, prove it to me . . . convince me." The student then had to refer to the "text," and his argument quickly fell apart. Why? Because all of the other interpretations respected the text itself and fit the explicit features of the text. According to Rosenblatt (1938), any interpretation that does not violate the explicit codes of the text can be seen as valid. But those that do not account for the explicit text features must be seen as invalid. This exercise demonstrates that textual meaning is created transactionally—through a give-and-take between a reader—her purposes and life experiences—and the text and the codes it offers for communicating.

Activity: Reading Let's try another picture reading exercise, which you have probably al-
Pictures, Part Two ready seen in an educational psychology text somewhere.

In this illustration, we are expected to see two pictures: one of a young woman, turned slightly away from us, who has a feather boa hairpiece coming out from her forehead; and one of an older woman, with a large nose, whose face is much larger and who is turned to us.

More than 90 percent of the time, younger readers, like my seventh graders, see the older woman first, whom they label as a "witch" or a "hag." They have great difficulty seeing the young woman.

This can be explained several ways. First, they do not have the background knowledge of Gibson Girls and the Gay Nineties to bring to the text. In fact, they do not possess the knowledge to perceive the young woman nor to understanding what her image "means." Witches and hags, however, are close to the kids' experience and the cultural myths they know and play with, so this is easy to see and label. (For the pedagogical implications of this phenomenon, associated with schema theory, please see the next chapter on frontloading.)

Second, the genre conventions of portraiture lead them to expect a face turned toward them. The young lady subverts these conventions (much like ironic literature subverts typical narrative) and is therefore much more difficult to notice and understand.

Third, the older lady not only fits the conventions of portraits, but her face is bigger and more noticeable, so the kids see her first. As students organize the codes of the text into this more salient pattern of meaning, they are unable to see any other pattern. They have organized the text into a meaningful whole by using their "schema"—their organized background knowledge of the world. They must suspend this schema to see another possibility because the text cannot be organized and perceived in two ways simultaneously. (If you think you can do so, please have a checkup with your nearest educational psychologist!)

Now what if that seventh-grade student insists that he sees a Green Bay Packer helmet here? I would reject this interpretation as violating the explicit codes of the text, and therefore of being disrespectful to the author, who created this text the way it is. Or what if that student, as some do, sees an eagle regurgitating into her nest? If an interpretation is supported by all the codes of the text (and this one nearly can be), then we must recognize it as a valid interpretation. Now what if a student can see only one of the two pictures? Is the student wrong? Has she achieved the richest possible reading? Should we help her achieve a richer reading by helping her to see both pictures? If so, how can we best provide the necessary assistance?

All right. Here is a final twist. The title of the picture, when it first appeared in *Punch* in 1915, was "My Wife and Her Mother." I would maintain that this changes everything. Now we know that we are expected to see both pictures, and that they both must be women (not eagles regurgitating!). And we know that we must compare the two women and draw some kind of meaning from the comparison. Given the coding of the title, this is what the text clearly expects of us, and to do less would be to not honor the author and the expectations of his text.

This is an example of how authorial reading requires us to attend to the text in the way that its construction asks us to. (In this case, the message would be to understand the joke about the differences between women and their mothers, or the implication that one who is beautiful today can be a "hag" tomorrow.) Once we have respected the text and its expectations of the audience it was written for, we should then ask whether we embrace this authorial vision, or whether we would want to reject it, consider it in an adapted form, and so forth. Do we believe, for instance, that wives are beauties to be admired, and mothers-in-law are hags to be avoided? Do we believe that women become like their mothers with the passage of time? Only by first understanding the text can we then meaningfully reject or embrace its meaning.

Many students, as well as adults, need assistance to see both pictures. If we want to promote a successful authorial reading, then we must give that assistance. This assistance may involve providing necessary background knowledge (for instance, by showing my seventh-grade students photographs of Gibson Girls, they were immediately enabled to see the young woman—they simply hadn't known enough prior to that to be able to perceive her), widening genre expectations (reminding kids that portraits can be subverted by a turned face), or sharing strategies for making meaning with that genre or structure (helping students see that when elements are juxtaposed that we are asked to notice similarities and differences and attempt to explain them).

Directed Reading and Thinking Activities (DRTA)

A Directed Reading and Thinking Activity (also known as a DRTA or a DRA) is a perfect way for guiding reading in the Vygotskian sense. A DRTA is a highly flexible technique that guides students to attend to certain textual features and to make certain interpretive moves before, during, and after their reading of a particular text.

Activity: Getting Horsey

The best way for me to explain to you how a DRTA works is to show you one that I discovered many years ago and adapted for my own use. The story that it is based on, "Old Horse," works particularly well for a DRTA aimed to develop student's authorial reading skills because, as you will see, there is a clear opportunity for the reader to resist the author's generalization or theme. The complete text of the story is shown in Figure 3.1. In Figure 3.2 you will find the DRTA that I adapted for use with this story (CRISS 1986). The DRTA consists of the *purpose*, *goals*, and *activities* for reading this story with students. Suggested guidelines and criteria for completing a DRTA of your own for a piece of literature that *you* select appear in Figure 3.3. These general criteria,

FIGURE 3.1
PROTOCOL FORM FOR GUIDING READING WITH "OLD HORSE"

OLD HORSE

Old Horse was the algebra instructor at
the school where I teach. I don't remember his
real name any more. But he had a long face
with big, square teeth, and so the students
called him Old Horse.

Perhaps they would have liked him
more if he hadn't been so *sarcastic*. With his
cutting remarks Old Horse could force the *most
brazen student* to stare at the floor in silence.
Even the faculty had a healthy respect for his
sharp tongue.

One day a boy named Jenkins flared
back at Old Horse. "But I don't understand
this," Jenkins said, pointing to a part of a
problem on the board.

"I'm doing the best I can considering
the material I have to work with," said Old
Horse.

"You're trying to make a jackass out of
me," said Jenkins, his face turning red.

*"But, Jenkins, you make it so easy for
me,"* said Old Horse—and Jenkins' eyes
retreated to the floor.

Old Horse retired shortly after I came.
Something went wrong with his liver or
stomach, and so he left. No one heard from him
again.

One day, however, not too long before Old Horse left, a new boy came to school. *Because he had buck teeth and a hare lip, everybody called him Rabbit.* No one seemed to like Rabbit much either. Most of the time he stood by himself chewing his fingernails.

Since Rabbit came to school in the middle of October, he had make-up work to do in algebra every day after school. *Old Horse was surprisingly patient during these sessions.* He would explain anything Rabbit asked. Rabbit, in turn, always did his homework. In fact, he came early to class if he could manage it. Then after the lesson he would walk with Old Horse to the parking lot.

One Friday because of a faculty meeting Old Horse didn't meet with Rabbit. This afternoon I walked with Old Horse. We were passing the athletic field when suddenly he stopped and pointed. "What's the matter with that one?" he asked. He was referring to Rabbit, standing alone chewing his fingernails while watching some boys pass a football.

"What do you mean?" I asked.

"Why doesn't he play ball too?" Old Horse demanded.

"Oh, you know how it is. He came in later than the others, and besides—"

"Besides what?"

"Well, he's different, you know? He'll fit in sooner or later."

FIGURE 3.1
(*CONTINUED*)

*"No, no, no. That won't do. They
mustn't leave him out like that."*

Then we had to break off the
conversation because Rabbit had hurried over
to join us. With a smile he walked beside his
teacher, asking him questions.

Suddenly one of the boys from the
athletic field called out, "Yea, Old Horse! Yea,
Old Horse!" and then he threw back his head
and went, "Wheeeeee!" like a horse's whinny.

*Rabbit's face reddened with
embarrassment. Old Horse tossed his head but
said nothing.*

The next day the students from my fifth-
hour class came to my room awfully excited.
*Old Horse had gone too far, they said, he ought
to be fired.* When I asked what had happened,
they said he had picked on Rabbit. He had
called on Rabbit first thing and deliberately
made him look ridiculous.

Apparently Rabbit had gone to the board
with confidence. But when he began to put
down some numbers, Old Horse said they
looked like animal tracks in snow. Everyone
snickered, and Rabbit got nervous.

Then Old Horse taunted him for a
mistake in arithmetic. "No, no, no. Can't you
multiply now? Even a rabbit can do that."

Everyone laughed, although they were
surprised. They thought Rabbit was Old
Horse's pet. By now Rabbit was so mixed up
he just stood there, chewing his fingernails.

"Don't nibble!" Old Horse shouted. "Those are your fingers, boy, not carrots!"

At that Rabbit took his seat without being told and put his red face in his hands. But the class wasn't laughing anymore. They were silent with anger at Old Horse.

I went in to see Old Horse after my last class. I found him looking out the window.

"Now listen here—," I began, but he waved me into silence.

"Now, now, now look at that, see?" He pointed to Rabbit walking to the athletic field with one of the boys who complained about how mean Old Horse had been.

"Doesn't he have a special class with you now?" I asked after a moment.

"He doesn't need that class anymore," said Old Horse.

That afternoon I walked with Old Horse to the parking lot. He was in one of his impatient moods, and so I didn't try to say much. Suddenly from the players on the athletic field a wild chorus broke out, "Yea, Old Horse! Yea, Old Horse!" *And then Rabbit, who was with them, stretched his long neck and screamed "Wheeeeeee."*

Old Horse tossed his head as if a large black fly were bothering him. But he said nothing.

"Old Horse" was printed in *Luther Life*, Vol. 71, November 1959 and reprinted in *How to Read a Book*, by Eileen E. Sargent, published by International Reading Association, Newark, Delaware, 1970.

considerations, and questions will show you *how* to come up with a DRTA, and are the questions that help guide my thinking when I create a DRTA. Below I will explain my thinking about the purposes, goals, and activities included in the DRTA for "Old Horse."

When I was teaching seventh and tenth graders, I used the "Old Horse" story with both groups for several units I taught on the topic of "What makes a good relationship?" People of all ages care about relationships and it's a significant issue to think about, with clear implications for behavior. We know that the success of our relationships has a lot to do with our happiness in life, how we are regarded, and the good we are able to do in the world for others. It's also a great unit for teaching kids procedures of understanding other perspectives, for constructing and understanding character, and for doing authorial readings on the topic. After all, everybody has plenty of experience with relationships, and has probably considered what makes a relationship good and fruitful, or negative and painful. So students can bring background and knowledge from "home institutions" (Goldblatt 1995) to the table.

I now use this story each year when my methods students begin to consider how they want to relate to the students they are teaching and will teach in the future.

As you can see in both Figures 3.2 and 3.3, the first step in composing a DRTA is to set your teaching goals. With "Old Horse" mine are to assist students to notice and interpret what characters do, and to support them in understanding the author's generalization (which is dependent on characterization and how the two major characters change). By the end of our work, I also want students to consider whether they embrace or resist this message about relationships.

The next step is to "frontload" their reading by activating background knowledge. I ask students to talk about nicknames and inform them that names are important to characterization and story meaning. Names are something authors expect them to notice and interpret.

Because my research (Wilhelm 1997) shows that students usually give up on a story in the first few paragraphs, my third step is to set purposes and to assist students through the first few paragraphs. I remind them that our purpose here is to explore this author's vision of effective and ineffective relationships. I get them on their way by modeling how I read the first few paragraphs, thinking aloud for them

1. **My Teaching Goals**

   a. To help students personally connect to the text.

   b. To use character clues to understand characters and their contribution to story meaning. I will particularly focus on character change and how this contributes to the meaning an author communicates to us through a story.

   c. To explore the nature of good and poor relationships as part of our inquiry unit on What Is a Good Relationship?

2. **My Frontloading Activities**—for the purpose of activating background; building personal connections; activating strategic reading processes—in this case, rules of notice about characters.

Assignment to students:

Write briefly in your journal about these two questions. Then I will ask you to share your responses in small groups. We will then share some of the important insights from your group discussion with the whole class.

   a. What are or were some of your nicknames, or those of your friends? What do nicknames indicate about people? How can nicknames be both postive or negative? Predict why the students in this story might call their Algebra teacher "Old Horse"?

   *You will want to pay attention to nicknames in this story and what they indicate about character. Authors use names and nicknames to reveal character. This is a rule of notice!

   b. When was a time that you were positively or negatively surprised by an action of someone you knew? Why did the action seem out of character? How did it change how you felt and thought about that person?

   *You will want to pay attention to surprises in this story. Authors use surprises to draw our attention to hidden features of characters. This is a rule of notice! When something surprising or unexpected happens, we are supposed to notice this and figure out what it means!

   c. What is someone like who is "sarcastic"? "brazen"? "patient"?

   *These are words that are used to describe characters in this story. You will want to pay attention to how characters are described and what they are doing when they are first introduced. This is a rule of notice! Authors expect you to notice how characters are first introduced!

   **All of these: names, surprises, and introductory descriptions fall under what we call "rules of notice," things an author expects you to pay attention to.

FIGURE 3.2
(*CONTINUED*)

3. **My Previewing and Purpose Setting**—These activities are designed to help kids achieve story entry, an appropriate reading stance, and to begin meaning construction with the codes of the text—particularly those codes having to do with characters.

Assignment to students:

   a. I will read the first few paragraphs of the story and provide a think-aloud of everything I am thinking, feeling, noticing, and doing as I read. I'll pay particular attention to the characters, and I'll ask you to do the same when you take over and read the rest of the story on your own, doing your own think-aloud protocol.

   b. Now that I have read the first few paragraphs, let me ask you: What is your intial impression of Old Horse? Would you want him for a teacher? Why or why not?

   c. What do the names Jenkins and Rabbit suggest about the two boys in the story? How do you think these two will get along with Old Horse?

   d. Do you think we will be exploring positive relationships, negative relationships, or both through our reading of this story?

4. **My Guided Reading Activities**—This written protocol activity is designed to help students create meaning and monitor their meaning making. I am going to assist and cue them to pay attention to codes about characters and character change.

Assignment to students:

   a. As you read the rest of the story on your own, you will complete a written protocol. As you read, write down things you are thinking, feeling, seeing, doing, connecting to on the lines next to the place in the story where you are doing these things.

   b. Respond to the italic phrases. All of these phrases have to do with character. How do these phrases help us to understand the characters and illuminate story meaning, re: relationships?

   *I have italicized phrases that I believe the author wants you to notice. We will discuss later how we should know what to notice. We'll discuss what clues help us to notice such details. In a later protocol you'll underline the cues about character that you think the author wants you to notice.

   c. As you read, try to build meaning about the following:

   How is this story about relationships? What is effective and ineffective about Old Horse's relationships with his students?

5. **After Reading: My Plan for Encouraging Student Reflection**

   a. My plan for small-group discussion and rereading

Assignment to students:

1. Go through your protocol comments and try to characterize your reading. Were the things you wrote down mostly about "seeing" or visualizing the story? or were they mostly questions? or connections to your life or other stories you've read? Were there a lot of feelings in it? Or was there something else that typified your reading? Pick out some typical "moves" you made and share these and your assessment of how you read this story with a partner.

2. With your partner, revisit guided reading questions.

3. Now consider why you think Old Horse changed his treatment of Rabbit. How does this demonstrate new information about Old Horse? What points are being made by the text about the theme of relationships and ways of relating to each other? How do the characters and their relationships help to make these points?

b. My plan for large-group discussion

Questions for students:

1. How does the text's coding encourage us to feel and think about Old Horse by the end of the story?

2. What does this suggest about the nature of good relationships and perhaps teacher-student relationships in particular? What is the author trying to communicate to us through this story?

3. How do you feel about this message from the author, and do you accept, adapt, or reject this vision of relationships?

4. How can your thinking be applied to the relationships in your own life?

6. **My Follow-up Plan**—I will engage in some drama activities to assist the students to elaborate on the story, and to consider what might happen to these characters in the future.

Assignment to students:

a. Correspondence drama. Imagine that you are Rabbit. As a 28-year-old adult, write a letter to Old Horse—tell him how he influenced who you are today and how you now think about him. Now exchange letters with a partner. Imagine you are Old Horse receiving this letter. How do you feel? What would you like to say or explain to Rabbit? Write a note back and give it to your partner.

b. Hotseat drama. In groups, we will brainstorm how Rabbit feels about Old Horse and how Old Horse feels about Rabbit. We might also consider what the other teachers and students think about both of these characters. I will then ask for volunteers to "sit" on the "hotseat" to be interviewed by the rest of us, who will play reporters researching the influence that teachers have on students.

c. If we have time, we may use some of the comments from the correspondence letters and hotseat interviews to create choral montage poems.

When using a Directed Reading and Thinking Activity to guide students through a text, you should provide active instruction and assistance at several points before, during, and after reading. In this way, you can assist students to recognize conventions and use particular interpretive strategies. When you create your own DRTAs to teach particular strategies, you may find the following considerations will help guide your design.

Before Teaching: Setting Goals: Set your teaching purposes.

___ 1. Set goals for your DRTA.

    a. Affective goal—what emotional goal might you address through this activity?

    b. Conceptual goal—what content knowledge do you want students to gain through this reading? What issue do you want them to inquire into?

    c. Procedural goal—how are you helping students to know HOW to do something new as readers? What interpretive strategies are you assisting students to use?

Before Reading: Frontloading Activities: Consider how to motivate your students to read this text. Also consider how to access or build background knowledge necessary for supporting their successful reading.

___ 2. Design a frontloading activity.

    a. How will you prepare students to make personal connections during their reading?

    b. How will you activate personal background information and schema that will be useful during reading?

    c. How will you build background knowledge of important contexts, concepts, and vocabulary necessary to understanding?

Beginning to Read: Set a Purpose: Consider how to preview the text and build positive expectations of it. Consider how to help students set a purpose that will motivate their reading and how to help students achieve entry into the text.

___ 3. Support student entry into the reading transaction.

    a. Preview whole text—get sense of structure and length.

    b. Read first section together or in small groups.

    c. Consolidate important information and textual cues that need to be "carried forward" during the reading act

    d. Make predictions about future action

    e. Set personal (and academic/theme) purposes for the reading—what do we want to find out?

    f. Continue to encourage the making of personal connections to the text.

During Reading: Guide Students' Reading: Consider how to encourage a deeper and fuller experience of the text.

___ 4. Guide students' reading by helping them to notice details and use particular strategies.
   a. Guide and support students to notice key details, stated and implied relationships, structural demands, and textual conventions.
   b. Help them to continue to make personal connections.
   c. Guide them to notice and learn content.

After Reading: Consider how to encourage students to reflect on their experience of reading the text, what the text means, and how the construction of the text by the author contributed to textual meaning.

___ 5. Take students back into the text.
   a. Alone and together.
   b. To reflect on constructedness and meaning of the text and reading experience.

Follow-up: Consider how to extend student understanding by asking them to go beyond the text, elaborate upon it, think how its meaning might apply to them in the context of their lives.

___ 6. Design a final assignment to synthesize a coherent view of the text as a whole and consider thematic generalizations that go beyond the text.

   a. Student inquiry projects or writing that encourage further connections, motivates further inquiry, goes beyond the known to what may be known.
   b. Explore textual implications for students' own lives.

about my reading. As I do so, I show how I notice the title, make predictions, consider how the characters are introduced, visualize the characters, and make judgments about them.

In step four, I asked students to continue their own "protocol" of their reading of the text, not by "thinking aloud" as I have just done, but by "writing down" everything they are thinking, feeling, noticing, and doing as they read. I tell them that I have italicized textual codes about characterization and character change that I think the author wants them to notice. I ask that they pay particular attention to why the author wants them to notice these codes and how they should interpret them. This is my way of guiding their reading.

After students have completed their written protocols, I ask them to go through and characterize how they read and responded to the story (step 5). For instance, did they do a lot of visualizing? Judging? Comparing the story to other stories or movies? Were they emotional? Did they compare people and situations to their own lives? I ask them to share how they read and compare it to how other kids in their group read. Then I ask them to consider follow-up questions in small groups that ask them to consider the author's generalization and how this theme was coded into the text.

Finally, I ask the students to consider the questions in 5b1 and 5b2 (Figure 3.2): "How does the text's coding encourage us to feel and think about Old Horse by the end of the story? What does this suggest about the nature of good relationships, and perhaps good teacher-student relationships in particular?" This question encourages authorial reading: what is the text supposed to mean for the audience for whom it was written? There is generally unanimous agreement that the text is coded to make us understand that Old Horse is really a good guy, and a teacher who only has his students' best interests at heart. It is also coded to make us understand his own life troubles and how they parallel those of Rabbit. This is why he understands Rabbit and acts on his behalf. After all, he gives up his one close relationship with a student and exults when Rabbit's peer group then accepts Rabbit.

Then I spring the second half of the authorial reading question: (question 5b3) "How do you feel about that? Do you accept, adapt, or reject this vision?" In other words, do you agree with the text that Old Horse is a good teacher, and that his relationship with Rabbit brought positive results? Many of my students, including preservice and practicing teachers, are knocked off kilter by this question. Some of them are genuinely moved by Old Horse's sacrifice. But when I pose the question, various points of view emerge about what Old Horse has really taught Rabbit, what Rabbit has really learned (check out Rabbit's last actions in the story), and whether this was admirable or positive in any way. Once students converse about and stake their own claim, we can then consider what this claim should mean in terms of how we engage in our own relationships.

DRTAs generally conclude by asking students to reflect on the story and to extend their understanding beyond the story in this way. In this DRTA, I also provide some additional follow-up activities.

In Chapter 1 and the scenario ranking activity there, we maintained that reading was not accepting other people's interpretations, but constructing one's own understandings. The authorial reading questions here encourage the students to do just that.

Another story that I use during this unit is Shel Silverstein's *The Giving Tree*. A masterful story, *The Giving Tree* is constructed so that the selflessness and sacrifice and love of the tree emotionally move us. But as a father of two daughters, and as a teacher of many young women, I'm concerned about accepting an authorial vision that celebrates a female presence (the Giving Tree) that is so nurturing she gives everything she has and is to an unappreciative and abusive (male) partner until there is nothing left of her but a stump. I want my own daughters to say, "That was stupid! I would never do all that for some guy!" And if they do make a different choice, I want them to understand that it is a choice that exists among other alternatives.

Authorial reading allows us not only to learn from authors, but also to converse with them, to interrogate them, and ultimately, if warranted, to resist their visions and offer our own alternative. It levels the playing field because it requires that we help kids read and understand the rules and conventions of what they are reading, and it allows them to offer political and moral critiques of an author, her text, and her vision. This kind of critique, as Michael Smith emphasizes, does not depend on literary knowledge but on knowledge based on student experiences and home institutions. When we welcome and require this kind of knowledge in the classroom, everyone can be engaged in the democratic pursuit of sharing and making meaning. No longer is the teacher or author someone from whom we unquestioningly accept information.

Student Attitudes and Beliefs

Last year, I surveyed more than one hundred fifty middle and high school students and more than sixty adults about their attitudes toward reading and I found an amazing congruity in their beliefs.

Since most of the informants were either college-bound students or successful and literate adults, it's not surprising that the follow-up interviews revealed that they generally felt that school reading has instrumental, if not intrinsic value. (Subsequent research in which Michael Smith and I interviewed boys indicates that even lower-track boys seem to regard school reading as instrumentally valuable. But none of these informants could tell WHY or HOW the reading they did in school would be valuable. They simply accepted that it would be.) However, it is striking that almost all informants differentiated between school reading, which they deemed as largely unpleasant, and real-world reading, which they found much more on point, personally relevant, and enjoyable. Two major themes emerged. First, school reading is unpleasant because:

- The material comes from textbooks.
- It has no immediate function or use outside of school.
- The material isn't connected to personal interests and current needs.
- The reading is pursued individually.
- The reading is done under duress and sometimes in uncomfortable situations.
- The reading is disjointed (you read one thing, and then you read something else that is unconnected).
- The reading is work being done for someone else.

In general, readers felt they were in over their heads with school reading. They felt incompetent and that they were often asked to proceed without much help or guidance. *Remember that these are the feelings of* ***successful*** *students!*

Second, and in great contrast, respondents felt that real-world reading can be pleasant for the following reasons:

- Readers have no time limit and can read at their own pace.
- Readers can choose their own material, at their level of interest and competence. Readers can choose materials, like magazines or websites that may not be privileged in school.
- The material fulfills a current interest or need, answers urgent and immediate questions, and may have an immediate physical, psychic, or emotional function.
- The reading is used to DO or THINK about something.
- Readers can pursue the material in more comfortable surroundings and situations.
- The reading is often social and shared.
- The reading often follows a similar theme or idea over time.
- The reading is work done for the self.

While we were surprised that these successful students seem to value school reading as instrumentally useful, we were not surprised that they did not understand its usefulness. Nor were we surprised at how they differentiated between the pleasures and uses of personal reading versus that of school. We propose that if we make school reading more like the successful reader's home reading—more pleasant, more supported, more functional, and more part of a larger social project—then we have a chance to motivate nearly all of our student readers.

Students want to connect personally to what they read, so we can help them choose books that match their interests and needs and that will lead them to more complex ideas and texts. Since we must start where students are before we can help them outgrow their current selves, we argue for the wide use of young adult literature, and for the bridging of this literature—both as themes and genres (conceiving of genre as texts that make similar demands on readers)—to more canonical text. Since students desire challenges and the competence to meet them, we can motivate them by providing challenges in the zone of proximal development and instruction over time that helps them meet those challenges and develop and name their competence. We can assist their competence by providing our own expert procedural assistance and by creating a classroom environment and instructional assistance that will be supportive for learning new things.

Students also want reading and learning to be social, and we can provide various group structures that will in turn provide peer assistance. We can make reading functional by organizing our reading around the creation of knowledge artifacts (e.g., the video or hypermedia documentaries, websites, or public service announcements our students create) or the pursuit of social action projects that have personal relevance and social significance. This is what the kind of instruction we propose throughout the rest of this book will be designed to do.

Roll of Thunder, Hear My Cry!

Using authorial reading in a classroom helps us engage in democratic work. It also serves as an entry point to inquiry and democratic innovations in the students' lives. First we consider what we've learned together, and the various positions that the group, or individuals within it, have staked out. From there we can then ask: So what? What do we do about it? How can we inquire further about this or related issues? How can we figure out what to do as a result of the issue and our beliefs about it? Then we can move on to socially relevant inquiry and/or social action projects.

Several years ago, I was teaching *Roll of Thunder, Hear My Cry* to my seventh-grade classes. The book, a moving story of the Logan family, details their struggles as people of color living in Mississippi during the Depression. They suffer the effects of racism, humiliation, and physical danger unto death, and they are threatened, pressured, and also humanely assisted by both people of color and whites. Various forms of resistance to their oppression are offered throughout the book.

The book concluded our group study in an integrated language arts/social studies unit on civil rights and social justice. As such, it also served as the entry point to an independent inquiry project into the topic of social justice. The class had already made a civil rights time line and had brainstormed civil rights issues in our own community and at the national level. Now small groups were readying themselves to identify a research question for the inquiry project.

Right after we completed the book, I distributed some snippets from six reviews. I expected students to use these reviews to get the conversation going in class the next day. I had chosen these reviews specifically to prompt them to think about issues of authorial reading—namely, who the story was written for, what it would mean to that group, and what the class felt about that. Though most of my students were white, we did have group members who were Chicana, Asian, Arab, Hmong, and some new Eastern European immigrants. Several religious groups were also represented.

The third reviewer maintained that the story was written for and would resonate with African American students, but that more mainstream populations would have little to relate to and would not comprehend the issues or struggles of the Logan family. The next day, before the kids were settled in their seats and I could get the attendance slip to the door, Josh, a normally reticent boy, called out to the class, "Hey, what did you guys think of that third review?"

The class erupted. Even kids who hadn't opened their notebooks and didn't have the reviews available instantly knew what was up. Everyone, it seemed, took issue with this reviewer's contention that they were not part of the intended audience of this book. I remember chuckling as kids passionately began to talk with each other about "how wrong" this reviewer was, how "totally out of the loop!"

Before I could say anything to calm the kids or guide the discussion, Josh took over by asking who had something to say about this to the group. I quietly sat at my desk in the back of the room and began taking notes. For nearly seventy-five minutes of a blocked period I did not utter a single word. It is the only time in my whole teaching career, before or since, that I can remember this happening.

This is what I witnessed: twenty-six seventh graders engaged in a discussion about *Roll of Thunder,* about what the text had to say, about who it was written for, about what it meant to them, and how it served as a lens on their own lives. My Arab student spoke movingly about how Arabs are depicted in movies and treated in the shopping mall, and about how she was certainly included not only in the audience of the book, but also in the group for which this book advocated. A student named Lisa told us how her parents spoke very passionately about fighting anti-Semitism and prejudice, yet exhibited intolerance or colluded with it in quiet ways. She drew a parallel between her parents and the character of Harlan Granger in the book.

Several students spoke about their older siblings' dating experiences, and how the issue of dating seemed to galvanize racial, religious, and class prejudices. In this regard, a long discussion ensued about whether Papa Logan was making the right decision by forbidding his son Stacy to "hang" with the white boy Jeremy Sims.

Each of my twenty-six students had at least two conversational turns to speak to the whole group. Occasionally the conversation fragmented into small-group discussions, but they always came back to the group. As one small-group discussion began, Lisa yelled, "I want to hear what everybody is saying! I don't want to miss anything!" and a whole-class discussion resumed. The discussion, though very personal, never strayed too far from the book, and the book was clearly used as a lens to consider their own lives and what they wanted them to be. The author was clearly a conversant in their discussion. For the most part, there was no leader. Various students took charge at different times. At other points, the group regulated itself.

Toward the end of the period, which I could hardly believe had passed so quickly, the students began to consider how the book should inform both their upcoming inquiry projects and their future lives. One girl said she wanted to study dating rituals among different groups in town, and interview elderly people to compare their views to those of her own peer group. She wondered aloud whether these rituals would express any kinds of prejudices. Two other girls and a boy asked to join her. (They eventually created a wonderful video documentary that contrasted interviews with middle schoolers, high schoolers, parents, and several folks from the town's senior citizen center.) Another boy said he had never understood gun control advocates until he read this book, with its "night men" terrorizing innocent people. He proposed to look at both sides of the gun control issue. This was a hot topic. The case of Native Americans and treaty rights, another hot issue, also became an inquiry topic. And on it went.

I can hardly begin to describe my emotions at the time, or even now as I look back. I had worked very hard throughout the unit to develop the students' procedural skills at questioning and discussion. I saw these skills played out here with great independence. Obviously, a further purpose was to understand others distant from us in time, place, and situation, and to develop respect for their situation. This kind of understanding was exhibited over and over as well. Further, I had wanted them to consider the author as someone with whom they could converse, and I wanted them to take the reading of the book out into the world with them, as they interrogated, evaluated, and made decisions about how they wanted to be in the world and how they would work as agents of change in that world.

I didn't get up when the bell rang. A few kids said good-bye, and I remember giving them a wave. As Lisa and another student walked by my desk, totally oblivious to me, they exclaimed, "What an awesome class!"—which proves they also have a fine sense of critical standards!

I can't pretend that this event is typical of my classes. But I also don't want to pretend that it was an accident. I think it happened because I assisted the kids to read and talk about books in ways that they found personally rewarding, that were socially significant, that included the author's consciousness, and that were connected to the world they inhabited at that time.

I think democracy was achieved that day, and in a big way. The kids sustained a respectful way of being together that served significant practical, moral, and psychological purposes for them all. They were using the tools and processes we had worked together to develop to do their own mutually satisfying work that met their own purposes. I stayed out of the way, and I was very proud of them. I was also proud of myself—proud that I had become, even if only for a day, totally obsolete. The kids had reached a new zone of actual development.

4

Frontloading
Teaching Before Reading

[Frontloading can be viewed as] a function of the individual searching for similarities between new problems and old ones, guided by previous experience with similar problems and by instruction in how to interpret and solve such problems.

—Rogoff and Gardner, *Everyday Cognition*

*W*aterskiing. If you've never done it, the very word strikes fear in your heart and makes your mouth go dry. You have never even strapped on a pair of skis, and now you're about to learn to ride the waves. You're nervous. You are pretty certain that you're destined to fall and break a limb. You have no idea what to expect. Your bottom lip trembles and your knees shake as the cool lake water laps against you. Your ill-fitting life jacket holds you up while you struggle to keep your skis from crossing. Your mind wanders to the beach, where your friends and family are munching hot dogs with their feet planted firmly on solid ground. Their safe haven beckons you—how you envy them!

Suddenly, the spotter on the speedboat yells, "Hit it!" Your lifeline, the huge umbilical cord of a rope, jerks you forward. There is a brief lag in speed as the boat pulls you up out of the water, but that lasts only momentarily. The speedboat takes on a life of its own; like some insidious beast it sneers at you as it picks up momentum. Your legs admit defeat as you go crashing into the water. You feel the pressure from the water as it slams up your nose, and you gasp for air, belching up the remnants of what was inadvertently taken in by your lungs. You wonder if there might have been a better way to prepare for this new adventure.

Frontloading is a way to prepare, protect, and support students into the acquisition of new content and new ways of doing things. Frontloading is the use of any prereading strategy that prepares students for success—and in Vygotsky's view, students must be able to be successful with challenging tasks if they are going to truly learn something and cultivate a continuing impulse to learn.

Let's revisit the waterskiing scenario to look at how frontloading— the advanced preparation and activation of one's prior knowledge, both conceptual and procedural—might have alleviated all of your waterskiing difficulties. Here's how it would go.

After you read a waterskiing brochure, your instructor helps you put on your skis to be sure that they are fitted properly and comfortably. She demonstrates how to position your skis with the backs in the sand and the tips out of the water, and she explains that you should hold the rope in place between your legs. She listens to your concerns and tells you to imagine yourself sitting on a porch in a nice, comfortable rocking chair. The water is like that rocking chair, she says. She reminds you that when the spotter hollers "Hit it," you should imagine that someone is tipping you forward in your rocking chair.

She goes on to say that once you feel as though you are actually capable of balancing yourself, you should slowly straighten up your body and balance your weight evenly on both skis. Most important, she reminds you to stay away from the wake behind the boat until you get used to being on water skis. She explains that the way to do this is to keep your knees slightly bent and to apply an even amount of pressure on your skis.

The spotter signals with a "thumbs up" that the driver of the boat is ready. Your instructor asks you if you feel prepared. Although a bit anxious, you nod your head. She tells you to signal to the spotter when you are ready to come back in by tipping your head back. Your instructor reminds you to picture yourself in that rocking chair. You have a good idea of what to expect. The instructor has provided you with a framework to help you know how to instruct yourself or to monitor your own performance. All learning is based on something,

Students must be assisted with challenging tasks if they are going to be successful and truly learn something.

If we do not activate students' prior knowledge, prepare them for the challenge ahead with appropriate strategies, and help them monitor their own performance, then we are not assisting them into new and more complex learning performances and experiences.

and that something is prior knowledge. We can only learn the new by building on the known.

As the spotter hollers "Hit it!" you remember the instructor's words about the rocking chair tipping forward. You visualize yourself in that rocking chair. Before you know it, you are moving behind the boat on both skis. You are in a semi-crouched position, and you remember that the instructor told you to get your balance and slowly stand up. Your legs are as wobbly as a new teacher's during her first day on the job, but you manage to stand erect and to ski behind the boat. The wake looks huge to you, and you chuckle to yourself about your instructor's warning to stay out of the wake. You aren't going to venture near it anyway.

After two laps around the lake, the excitement and anxiety wear you out, and you tip your head back so the spotter knows you want to go into shore. When you are even with the point of the cove, just as the instructor told you, you lean back slightly and let go of the rope. You glide effortlessly into shore and sink slowly down into the water. Your friends and family are on the beach cheering for you. You did it! You finally waterskied!

What and How

In life we are presented with many challenges similar to this. Think of your first day of school, college, or your first day on the job. At one time, these experiences were new to us. Without preparation of some sort, it would be, at the very least, intimidating, perhaps even frightening, if we did not know what to expect in any of these situations. At worst, we would be totally unprepared and set up for failure. The same holds true for students who are reading an unfamiliar kind of text for the first time, or who are reading about unfamiliar content, or who are asked to use unfamiliar strategies. If we give students no framework or schema for approaching new information or for using new strategies, then, as in the first waterskiing scenario, it is likely that they will fall flat on their faces.

In addition to activating or building content prior to reading activities, it may also be necessary to learn a set of procedures for doing a task (if new procedures are required). In the waterskiing example, the instructor was clear about WHAT to expect and HOW to approach the task. Not only did she provide information about waterskiing (novices should stay out of the wake), she explained what it would feel like to be lifted out of the water (imagine that someone is tipping you forward in your rocking chair). To successfully teach students how to read, we must remember to provide content or information about the text that they will read, and specific strategies to use when they are reading the text.

Once the WHAT (content) and the HOW (processes) are introduced, the learners will have a sense of the task purpose and expectations, and can then become "novice experts" of sorts so that they can engage in real activity and take on, to some degree, the stances and strategies of the pros. As with any task, reading and waterskiing make new task demands on the learner. Knowing how to snow ski, for example, has transfer value to waterskiing, but because "getting up" is unique to waterskiing, newcomers will need to learn this "task-specific" skill.

Remember that George Hillocks maintains that "what is learned must be taught," and our waterskiing instructor explained "getting up" by comparing a person's body position in a rocking chair to the position needed to water-ski. We need to prepare students for reading experiences in the same way by offering analogies and frameworks to assist in their reading, understanding, and learning.

In an effort to prepare students for a particularly challenging expository science text, I recently observed a middle school teacher employing successful frontloading strategies of his own. Mr. Davis was teaching a unit on chemical bonds and photosynthesis, and he wanted his eighth graders to understand and visualize what happened with these bonds when they connected. Prior to assigning the reading of the text, Mr. Davis used a dramatic tableaux technique called "mental modeling." He had Jennifer and Melissa stand in front of the class to represent the "oxygens." The rest of the students were told that they would be "carbons." Dustin, a carbon, was instructed to link arms with Jennifer and Melissa, oxygens, as they walked by.

As Dustin locked arms with Jennifer and Melissa, Mr. Davis explained that Dustin was much more interested in Jennifer and Melissa, the oxygen, than he was in the other carbons in the class. He then explained that if given a choice, the carbons would always link up with the oxygens, and by linking together, the three had formed the chemical bond "carbon dioxide." The concept of chemical bonds is a highly abstract and difficult concept, particularly if no background information had been provided. Mr. Davis' frontloading technique prepared students by introducing students to a new concept prior to their reading of the science text. This helped them to bring prior knowledge to their reading, which in turn helped them to comprehend it.

Necessities for Understanding Texts

What kinds of attitudes, knowledge, and processes do we need to bring to a text to be successful with it? There needs to be a sense of purpose and motivation, for starters. There also needs to be knowledge of content (we can only learn about something we already know something about), and there should be knowledge of the necessary processes—in other words, knowledge of the particular genre and the processes this text type expects us to use as readers. George Hillocks argues that we need to have five things: a purpose and use four different kinds of knowledge whenever we read anything:

1. Purpose: knowing why one should read a particular text and how one might use what will be learned by doing so
2. Procedural knowledge of substance: knowing how to activate and find background knowledge necessary for comprehending (inquiry skills)
3. Procedural knowledge of form: knowing how to organize what we are reading into a coherent pattern of meaning
4. Declarative knowledge of form: knowing how to name the structures of the text we are reading and how they contribute to communicating meaning
5. Declarative knowledge of substance: knowing how to ascertain and articulate main ideas or theme.

(For a more detailed explanation of the above, see the Inquiry Square in Chapter 2. See Chapter 7 for a sequence that leads from frontloading to the internalization of a strategy set for understanding main ideas or themes.)

In order for students to understand the conventions of different genres and text formats, they must be able to access or develop the appropriate interpretive strategies related to procedural knowledge of substance and form. By making textual expectations explicit, we can help students learn *how* to access the background they need (procedural knowledge of substance) to get started, and we can help them learn what conventions to notice and how to interpret them as they create a mental text structure (procedural knowledge of form). If we teach specific procedures for reading, then the reading experience is no longer a complete enigma for our students, and readers will be able to concentrate more on what the text is actually saying and what that means to them.

To illustrate this point, imagine that a student has never been exposed to an acrostics poem. You show your student several examples of acrostics poetry and point out that you not only read the poetry from left to right, but you are also expected to read the poem vertically, paying special attention to the first letters in every line. After you show him a couple examples, he is able to tell you what word the acrostics poem is spelling out vertically in the next example. Finally, he writes his own poem after he decides to use the first letters of his last name. Without your assistance and guidance, it might have taken this student a long time to figure out that acrostics poetry contains a secret code of sorts—or he might never have figured it out. Teachers should actively assist students to engage with *all* types of texts with which students may have difficulty or be unfamiliar.

Students have difficulties when they have no prior knowledge to bring to bear on a text, or when they have no sets of procedures for dealing with specific tasks required by a text. As a prereading strategy, frontloading prepares the reader to approach a text, so that she may build from her current knowledge to move toward a deeper, more expert reading.

Consider this very text that you are reading now. Not only was the waterskiing scenario provided as an analogy to define frontloading, it was also written as a frontloading technique to prepare your mind for the reading journey that you are about to embark upon. If you tap into the knowledge and skills necessary to be successful in any new learning situation (whether it's waterskiing or something else), and then you transfer that knowledge and skill appropriately to understand its connections to teaching, you understand what frontloading means and how it can be used. Frontloading helps to familiarize the reader with material and concepts that might otherwise be foreign.

Research in the cognitive sciences indicates that most comprehension problems are probably due to a failure to activate background that students already possess. If we attend to this issue, and build back-

---

Frontloading is a technique used by teachers to help readers access or build their prior knowledge (both conceptual and procedural) so they can better comprehend and approach a new text or kind of task.

The most powerful time to support reading is before students begin to read.

ground that kids don't have, chances are that we can alleviate most of the comprehension problems in our classes.

Schema Theory: Barriers to Comprehension

Research provides evidence that a reader's experience with a text is enriched when prior knowledge is activated before engaging with a new and unfamiliar text. One way to understand the need for frontloading is to explore schema theory. A *schema* is a rich set of understandings around a particular topic. If students do not possess or do not activate the appropriate schema, they will not comprehend a text. For example, as we discussed in Chapter 3, most middle schoolers are unable to "see" the young woman in the picture "My Wife and My Mother-in-Law" because they don't have the schema, or background knowledge, about the Gay 90s and Gibson Girls to even perceive that picture. In order to comprehend a text, we must use past experiences as we enact our interpretive processes. New knowledge or new kinds of texts can sometimes be like the slick backside of Scotch tape—unless there is something to attach new knowledge to, unfamiliar concepts probably won't stick!

Another problem associated with a lack of schematic knowledge may be an insufficient level of vocabulary or labels for the new information. In one study, researchers replaced the words *municipality, site,* and *hamlet* with the words *town, place,* and *village* in a passage, and students' scores on a standardized comprehension test were markedly improved. The students were entirely equipped to understand the meaning of the passage except that they did not know these three words.

And how about understanding the processes essential in the successful interpretation of a particular genre? I worked at length with my students to frontload their knowledge of expository texts when it became apparent to me that they continuously avoided this type of reading. In our literature book there was often an expository or an informational piece of writing that prefaced each unit. Our unit on *Julius Caesar* began with an informational piece on Shakespeare, the Globe, and Elizabethan times. Included in this expository writing were graphs, diagrams, and headings, all of which (according to their own testimonies) "bored" my students "to death."

With George's Inquiry Square still new but ever present in my mind, I began to ask myself how much I had done to prepare students to read texts of this type. The answer to the question was embarrassing—I hadn't done a thing to prepare my students. I started thinking hard about ways to make up for lost time and to better assist them in their reading of expository writing. I began by doing work with my students on identifying main ideas, both in paragraphs and in sections of reading. We created a list of things to notice that would guide our reading: headings, bold print, diagrams, and captions. Then I cut out headings from expository texts and asked students to create their own headings for sections, which they then compared to the headings that other students created. We then explored how headings expressed topics, and the information that followed expressed key details and explanations about that topic.

I taught my students how to "read" visuals or graphics by using examples to show why graphics were important, what to look for when encountering one in the text, how to relate the graphics to the written text, how to ask questions about the graphic, and how to incorporate new understandings of graphics into one's overall textual reading. Then, once we had explored several ways of noticing and interpreting key features of expository texts, we read some in groups and on our own. These frontloading strategies helped my students see the task expectations of expository text. It also helped them to see how to "get the stuff" and get started with reading expository texts. This knowledge helped them feel more competent. They knew how the text expected them to use its various features and what they needed to do to make meaning with these features. This changed, to some degree, their negative attitudes toward this type of reading.

> Some students fail to use what they already know in order to link it with what they are about to learn.

Students Fail to Use What They Know

Some students fail to use what they already know in order to link it with what they are about to learn. A great example of this comes from a story that one of my students shared with me. Kevin said that his social studies class had been studying the White Star Lines and the shipwrecks that had occurred in the early 1900s. They had previously discussed the sinking of the *Lusitania,* and more recently, the sinking of the *Titanic.*

One weekend, not long after the unit on the shipwrecks, Kevin and a classmate, Steve, went to the movies. During the preview for coming attractions, there was a long, dramatic, and suspenseful clip about the movie *Titanic.* When it was done, Kevin turned to his friend and said, "Awwww! And the ship sank!" Steve, who had been quite caught up in the previews, turned to him angrily and said, "Yeah! And thanks for spoiling it for me!"

Kevin found the story comical because they had just discussed the sinking of the *Titanic* at great length in their class; in fact, they had even read primary sources that chronicled eyewitness accounts of the tragedy. During Kevin's uproarious laughter, Steve said that he remembered some of what they had covered in class, but that he didn't think of that stuff as "real life" (interesting that many of my students tend to think of movies as such!). Steve had failed to use what he already knew about the sinking of the *Titanic* in order to make sense of the new information that he was assimilating during the previews.

Words with Multiple Meanings   Other hindrances to reading comprehension occur when students encounter words with multiple meanings. Words like *capital* have different meanings in geography, economics, and regular conversation among English-speaking people. Also, new organizational structures of a text (e.g., argument, comparison-contrast, cause-and-effect, classification) or genre conventions (coding for fables, irony, or satire) can confuse students. In addition, students do not always know the meanings of "signal words" (e.g., *as follows, consequently*), and it is essential for educators to make signal words and organizational structures apparent and explicit to students.

Given all the potential barriers to reading comprehension, it is important to remember that active strategies are not only helpful, but are necessary for improving the reading experience of our students. In Chapter 7 Tanya poignantly describes a frustrating experience she had with a math problem as a child. While she was studying her math text in despair, her father walks behind her and gives her the answer to the problem that she has been battling. When she demands to know *how* her father has arrived at the answer, he is unable to explain the steps he has taken to come up with the correct choice. Little good it does to give our students the "answers" (declarative knowledge of substance) to reading a particular text when what students need is assistance in how to do it themselves (procedural knowledge). We need to make the hidden demands of learning and reading known to our students to prevent frustration and to welcome them into the world of the informed.

Connecting

I was never introduced to a prereading experience other than a traditional summarization of a text until I was nearly thirty. My English teachers might have directed us to look for a certain feature in the text, such as foreshadowing, but I was never prepared in any other way for any text that we read. In my own teaching experience, I would prepare students for their reading by referring to the first page in any unit. I cringe to think about the lack of preparation I gave my students during a poetry unit from *Questions and Form in Literature,* a sophomore text. Instead of asking students to play the role of the characters in Robert Frost's "The Fear," or engaging them in some similar frontloading activity, I reminded them to reread the introduction to poetry at the beginning of the unit and to take note of the figurative language definitions I had written for them on the board.

Why had I thought that knowing the definition of a term like *alliteration* (declarative knowledge of form) could prepare students to use procedures to understand something as complex as poetry? Like so many other times throughout my teaching career, I was simply going through the motions and instructing in the same manner that I had been taught. I never thought about ways to better prepare my students for reading because I had never questioned HOW to go about truly teaching my students what they needed to know. I hadn't realized there was a better way—I hadn't yet read the work of Michael Smith or George Hillocks.

By sharing the structures of a text and the demands or expectations the text has for a reader, I might have helped my students unlock some of the secrets to becoming expert readers. Instead, I left them to fend for themselves against the impenetrable texts that they could rarely conquer on their own. Finally I began to familiarize myself with textual structures and genre expectations for reading to assist both comprehension and aesthetic readings, and then I was able to begin passing these strategies on to my students. My teaching eventually progressed to include teaching students HOW to read in a certain way by frontloading the ways to engage in authorial reading, such as using opinionnaires or scenario rankings to test their beliefs, or by identifying hidden structures and features of texts they would need to notice. (I will describe these methods in more detail later in this chapter.) We

> By sharing the structures of a text and the demands or expectations the text has for a reader, I am able to help my students unlock some of the secrets to becoming expert readers.

have people like George Hillocks to thank for advocating that the un-written rules of the exclusive "literacy club" be made accessible to all our students.

Drama: One Method of Frontloading

In George's book *Teaching Writing as Reflective Practice* (1995), he refers to prewriting strategies as "gateway activities." These gateway activities serve much the same function as the frontloading activities that are discussed here. In his book, George discusses his observation of a student teacher named Marjorie Hillocks, who just happens to be his daughter. While teaching a racially mixed fifth-grade class, Marjorie exposes her students to a "gateway activity" or prewriting experience that informs their writing.

Marjorie is teaching her class about Ellis Island, and wants to place special attention on the immigrant experience. She knows that students may need help in the procedures of understanding a perspective different from their own. So she and her students take part in a role-playing activity. While in character, students are on a "ship," which is really just a section of the classroom marked by masking tape that is roughly in the shape of a ship. Marjorie is the "ship's captain," and the students are immigrants. They are pleading with Marjorie for food, water, and basic needs. While in character, Marjorie impatiently sends each group away.

Once all twenty-six students have taken part in this activity, they return quietly to their desks and write from the point of view of an immigrant. The products that result are astoundingly sophisticated for fifth-grade students. No doubt this prewriting strategy or "gateway activity" was essential to adding detail and depth to their work. Such an activity would also give these students an experience that they could use when reading about immigration.

Marjorie's story is a great example of a gateway activity because her role-playing exercise moved students to another level of thinking. The role-playing was Marjorie's way of opening the door to a new world for her students—a world far removed from their own experience. If these students had not participated in an activity that helped them envision and feel what it was like to be an immigrant, then their first-person narratives would probably have been poor depictions of the immigrant's

It is important to frontload generative concepts or procedures that can be used throughout a unit, and into the future. Frontloading activities that prepare students to read only one particular text are helpful but are of limited usefulness.

plight. By becoming immigrants themselves, Marjorie's students were engaged in a frontloading strategy that produced a "wide-awakeness" that could not have been achieved with a traditional textbook reading. Marjorie returned to and developed the skill of entering another's perspective throughout the unit.

Drama strategies provide a flexible set of techniques for activating or building background knowledge and for developing new procedures. Drama can help us personally understand experiences distant to us in time or place, and it might also help us prepare for first-person writing, as we saw with Marjorie's class.

Though frontloading techniques can emphasize teaching kids how to attend to a particular feature or features of a text (procedural knowledge of form), the emphasis of drama here will be to focus on activating or developing special content (procedural knowledge of substance) that will aid reading.

At first glance, drama might seem like an easy approach to pre-reading, but the success of this strategy depends on the attitudes and efforts of your students, as well as your own commitment. Dramatic frontloading isn't easy, and it didn't take me long to realize that I played a key role in the success of this activity.

My first attempt to use drama as a frontloading technique was not totally successful, but I had resolved to give it at least three tries, and I solicited feedback from my students. My students reminded me to select a more interesting and age-appropriate text for drama next time—something that mattered to them right now. They also asked me to abbreviate the alloted time in class to prepare for the drama. According to them, the preparation time (40 minutes) gave them a serious case of stage fright. Their insightful responses helped me develop questions to guide my thinking about frontloading in general. For example:

1. How might I organize this reading experience to make it personally and socially relevant? How might this text lend itself to exploration of a contact zone or lead to social action ("something that mattered")?
2. What do my students probably already know about the text that we will read? (If you do not have any idea how to answer this question, you may want to use the "quick-write" strategy discussed later in this chapter.)

3. What background information do my students need to know prior to their reading of this text? How can I help them "get" this stuff?
4. What procedural knowledge should they have to help them in this reading? How can I alert them to the importance of this skill and begin to help them develop it?
5. What knowledge or skills are most "generative"? That is, what will have the most transfer value and be most useful as a touchstone to return to throughout our unit and beyond?

Serving a Larger Purpose

Frontloading must serve the larger purposes of your unit. Once you have designed the type of frontloading activity that best suits the needs of your students, consider the following questions to guide your thinking about the usefulness of the frontloading activity that you are considering:

- How is the unit theme purposeful and of relevance to your students?
- How does your activity activate or build the students' prior knowledge or background information regarding your unit theme?
- How does the activity work to motivate students for reading and inquiry regarding the theme or driving question of your unit?
- How will the frontloading activity work to organize inquiry, set purposes, and consolidate learning about the theme throughout the unit? That is, how will it help students set purposes for their reading, focus their learning, clarify what they are coming to know, and help them monitor their learning progress?

Our purpose frames and drives our reading. Reading is a purposeful and meaningful activity and must be framed as such.

"In the Blink of an Eye"

I frontload my own teaching on the first day of class when I ask students to write me a letter including three things I should know to be able to teach them. I may also ask them to tell me about their favorite interests or activities. I do this to get to know my students—to build my own background knowledge—so I *can* meet them where they are and assist them from this point to becoming more. It also introduces me to the more silent and struggling students in my classes, so I can pay special attention to them and try to integrate them into the work of our class. I believe, along with Vivian Paley (1992), that the classroom must belong to every child. The classroom is a public space for growing through collaborative participation.

A year ago, I was concerned about several students, including Annie. Annie was a freshman in my reading class, and students seemed to be having difficulty relating to her. Annie wasn't your typical freshman—she was witty, humorous, full of questions—and pretty much confined to a wheelchair, at least during her time at school. Although Annie is semi-mobile, she has cerebral palsy, and she is essentially unable to communicate without the help of her Liberator, a technological device that allows her to type in symbols and phrases. When Annie pushes the right button, her Liberator vocalizes these phrases for her listeners.

Students in my class were cordial to Annie, but they were polite to a fault. I wanted Annie to fit in and have the same experiences that other students had. I wanted the other students to be comfortable with Annie and to learn to value her differences. Although I wanted respect for everyone in my classroom, the respect that students afforded Annie was superficial, and she was not a part of the community to the degree that I had hoped. Students were cautious and appeared to be uncertain of how *they* should act around Annie.

Not knowing exactly how to deal with this challenge, I continued with the status quo. I asked Annie to demonstrate how to use her Liberator, and I had her speed the voice up, thinking this would get a chuckle from my students. (Annie had shown me this trick before.) The otherwise rambunctious group just smiled politely while Annie and I had a good laugh. Not willing to quit just yet, I knew that there had to be another way to connect Annie with her classmates.

I decided that the best way to help students relate to Annie was by structuring a unit around the subject of understanding the perspectives of people with whom we can't communicate in normal ways. I thought a possible contact zone might be the issue of whether we can really understand people who do not have a voice, or who are silenced in some way. We could explore whether we have a special responsibility to protect people who cannot speak fully for themselves. We could ask about who has a voice and who is silenced in particular situations and with what effect, and what ways we might try to overcome the lack of communication. I could imagine several highly contended, real-world "contact zones" that revolve around this issue: the rights of people in comas, the rights of unborn children or newborns, the rights of children in society, the rights of students in school, and so forth.

The problem with this contact zone was that I had no idea what texts I would use to accomplish my democratic and reading goals. "Shaving," a short story in our literature book, was a text that I thought might tie in tangentially to this thematic study. This story is about a man and his father who are unable to communicate with one another because of their own personal hang-ups and because of the traditional expectations that society has imposed on them. In this short story, the author explores the strained relationships that sometimes exist between fathers and sons.

The man and his father finally really communicate their love for one another in a unique way when the father becomes ill and disabled and is unable to shave himself. The father never asks the son to help him, but the son realizes that his father needs help, so he takes it upon himself to assist. The author poignantly depicts the communication that exists between father and son during the shaving episode. Although the two never utter a word to one another, the son's gentle hands and his father's trust communicate volumes. I liked the idea of using this text in my contact zone because it showed that barriers to communication come in many different forms, and my students would more than likely encounter communication problems throughout their lives. But what other stories could I use to get at this subject?

I was flipping through an ancient *Reader's Digest* one afternoon when I came across an interesting article called "In the Blink of an Eye." The catchy title grabbed my attention, and I began skimming through the text. The nonfiction story was about a man who had been a soldier and had been so badly wounded in a war that he was placed in a full body cast. He was unable to communicate in any way, and merely stared out of the small opening that his doctors had left around his eyes so that he could see. The doctors and nurses were unable to identify the man, so his only support was the hospital staff.

One very dedicated nurse saw something in the man's eyes that made her believe that he understood more than the doctors gave him credit for. The nurse, trying desperately to communicate with her patient, told him to blink his eyes if he understood what she was saying. Much to her delight, her patient blinked in response. As days wore on, the nurse's communication efforts became more sophisticated. She asked the man to talk to her by blinking his eyes. She instructed him to blink once for the letter "A," twice for the letter "B," and so on.

Although this was an extremely time-consuming process, the two communicated on a regular basis.

I couldn't wait to share it with my students. I was just learning about the importance of frontloading to facilitate reading, and several ideas were percolating in my mind. Armed with the two texts that I had discovered, I was finally ready to address an immediate concern—the discomfort that students had with Annie's condition—and a generative concept about silencing and voice. In addition, I could teach them something about the process of reading.

A Frontloading   Carrying my short stories and a heart full of missions, I began my class
Exercise   with a frontloading exercise. I had planned two sets of frontloading. The first was for the whole unit, and the rest was to build on the generative concepts to frontload particular stories.

First I asked students to brainstorm a list of things that give people power over their lives. We then shared lists and debated the relative importance of wealth, social situation, physical strength, intelligence, family and friends, access to computers, and the like. Interestingly, neither language nor the ability to communicate was directly stated. I planned to keep returning to this ranking as the unit progressed.

Now I wanted to involve my students in a drama activity that would help them understand—and more important, *feel*—how difficult it is to be silenced in some way, whether through a handicap or through social and political situations. I hoped my students would begin to see Annie's struggles through the struggles of the man in the full body cast and the struggles of the father and son in "Shaving" and realize that all of us experience communication barriers. The only difference was that like the main character in "In the Blink of an Eye," Annie's communication problems just happened to be more obvious or pronounced compared to the ones that most of us faced.

I told my students that we were going to read a story about a man in a full body cast who couldn't communicate in any way. Without giving too much detail, I discussed how the man had the good fortune of having a nurse who believed in him. I explained the nurse's communication experiments and asked if they would like to give the experiments a try. I knew that my students would, on a superficial level, be able to comprehend the story "In the Blink of an Eyee" without the help of a sophisticated frontloading activity. However, like Marjorie's students who role-played the immigrant experience, I knew that a similar role-playing activity might help them develop new capacities of empathy for those who have difficulty communicating by way of speech, and it might help them connect this to other forms of silencing because of gender, race, class, or politics. Furthermore, whether it was stated or not, I wanted students to make connections between Annie's situation and her difficulty with communication in order to understand her better, to alleviate their discomfort with the unknown, and to come together as a group to function more as a democratic classroom community.

Students who could yawn their way through a Disney theme park were sitting up and taking notice. I asked them if anyone was willing to play the role of the nurse and the patient. Hands shot up all around the room, but my eyes focused on the first two hands to go up—Annie's and Jason's. I asked each of them what role they would like to play. Annie typed into her Liberator that it might be easier for her to play the role of the "interpreter" or nurse, and Jason, a shy sophomore, agreed to play the role of the patient. Looking around the room at the intense faces of my students, I could tell that they were interested.

Students circled around Annie and Jason. Students who were whispering messages to "send" to Annie surrounded Jason. Jason finally said he was ready, and he leaned back against a desk and began "blinking" out his message. Jason blinked eight times, and Annie typed an "H" into her Liberator—one blink, an "A," and so on until Annie had an entire message. Students crowded around Annie, buzzing with comments. "Oh, I know what it is! I know what the message is!" Finally Annie was ready to "speak" her message. A computerized voice filled the room, and the Liberator spoke, "Have a nice day, Annie."

After asking Annie to play the message several more times, students "blinked" out their own messages to their nearest classmate. This role-playing developed naturally and without my direction. I then asked my students to write a diary entry from the perspective of the man in the cast. What was it like not to be able to communicate? What was it like when communication was finally established? After this writing, my students wanted to know more about the man in the cast: how he came to be in a hospital and what his fate would be, if his communication with the nurse allowed his views to be known and considered. Students understood the context and were motivated to read.

"Shaving"   After we had completed the frontloading activity and read "In the Blink of an Eye," we then read "Shaving." This text is a much more complex exploration of communication, and I hoped that reading "In the Blink of an Eye" would frontload the reading of "Shaving" by activating knoweldge and strategies that the kids would need to bring forward with them to a reading of "Shaving." (This is a principle of sequencing, explored in Chapter 7). But since this story does make more complex demands on readers, I decided to also prepare for this text an explicit frontloading strategy. (I had assigned this short story in the past to another class during my Pre-George Hillocks Era without engaging students in frontloading or situating the text into the context of inquiring into a contact zone, and their response was always a frustrated, "What's the point of this story, anyway?") After all, the communication breakdown in the story of the father and the son was much subtler—not at all as readily apparent as the communication difficulties characterized in the former story.

Before we began reading "Shaving," I asked students to think about a time when they had difficulty communicating with someone. I gave them five minutes to complete a quick-write (described in more detail later in this chapter) by describing the communication problem and their accompanying thoughts, feelings, and emotions about the situation. After they had completed their quick-writes, I instructed the students to pair up and discuss their difficult communication experience. Next, we came together as a large group and discussed common themes from our experiences with communication difficulties.

One girl spoke about a time when she thought she had an eating disorder and didn't dare tell for fear of disappointing her mother. Someone else mentioned a time when her grandfather was battling cancer, silently suffering in a morphine-induced coma, and how she was unable to say "good-bye" to him because she was afraid that he couldn't hear her and that she would have to face reality. A male student spoke about a fight he had with his brother and how difficult it was to reconcile because both they each felt they were right. Each was angry and unwilling to admit that he did anything that contributed to their fight; their pride got in the way. Students noticed that the majority of communication problems that were brought up in class involved a self-imposed hold on expressing one's feelings.

This frontloading activity was the perfect way to begin talking about the short story "Shaving." In contrast to the man's ordeal in "In the Blink of an Eye," which involved physical communication difficulties, the communication difficulties in "Shaving" were much more common to us. The quick-write and the follow-up discussion helped me prepare my students for the text they were about to read by providing a purpose for the activity: to explore the communication issues of others in order to better understand ourselves.

While students read "Shaving," they worked on a think-aloud/protocol (see Chapter 3) to make visible the thoughts that emerged during their reading. The protocol that we used was simplistic in form, but produced excellent results. I simply photocopied each page of the "Shaving" story on to half of a piece of legal-sized paper. On the other half, students were instructed to write what they are thinking, seeing, feeling, and questioning as they read. Becky, the girl who had written about and discussed her eating disorder during our frontloading activity, mentioned how she was reminded of the look that her mother gave her when she finally told her that she thought she had an eating disorder. According to Becky, her mother didn't say a word; she just gave her a hug and "a look that said, 'I am here for you—everything's going to be OK.' " Becky said that she thought about her mother's look when she noticed how careful the son was to shave his father the way he liked to be shaved. She mentioned that the son's careful attention showed how much he loved and admired his father.

Other students in the class mentioned specific connections between their quick-writes and the text, which indicated to me that the frontloading technique was useful in obtaining a deeper, more personal, and meaningful reading of the text. One student even mentioned "In the Blink of an Eye" in his protocol, saying that of the two communication problems proposed in each story, the difficulties in "Shaving" were much more deep-seated and difficult to overcome.

We proceeded through the unit, reading newspaper and magazine articles, surfing the web for political sites, considering the issues of animals rights, and ending with free-choice readings that included *Shabanu,* the story of a girl silenced by the Islamic culture in which she lived; *Johnny Got His Gun,* a book about a boy who cannot communicate due to injuries suffered in WWI; *Life as We Know It,* a story about a family with a child who has Down Syndrome; and many others that our librarian helped us find.

Synthesizing
Learning After we had completed our work, I asked students to revisit our original lists and to make a representation that synthesized their learning about what gives us power in our lives and about the importance of voice and silencing. Students created collages, music videos, poems, and many other projects. One student, Michelle, wrote a children's book about two five-year-old girls. In the story, Emma is afraid of Sarah because she has a strange, squeaky voice. Throughout the story, Emma does everything to avoid Sarah. Then one day, Emma falls on the playground in a remote area. Sarah, who always played alone because she had no friends, sees that Emma is hurt. Emma has twisted her knee and is crying too hard to holler for help. Sarah greatly admires Emma because she is so outgoing, and she wants to help in any way that she can. Sarah yells her loudest, squeakiest yell until the teacher comes to help. Emma declares that this is "the sweetest-sounding voice I have ever heard in my life."

In a follow-up interview with Michelle, I learned that Annie had been the indirect inspiration of this story. Michelle recognized that she had been afraid to get to know Annie because she didn't want to say something that might offend her. She was unsure about whether or not she could even understand Annie, and if she could, she didn't know what else to talk about other than her Liberator. Through this story, Michelle—placing herself in Sarah's shoes—certainly shows that she understands how it would feel if she were unable to communicate freely or in a normal way.

The frontloading activities and the discussions surrounding the contact zone helped create a community of learners. Topics that are purposeful and have relevance to your students' lives will naturally support a more democratic community. The selected topic for this contact zone in concert with an existing issue in the classroom served as an even greater bridge to establishing an atmosphere of social learning.

At the end of each year, I require students to complete a reflective final that chronicles their progress as learners. One of the questions asks students to discuss their greatest learning experience in the class. We had completed the "In the Blink of an Eye" activity in September, so you can imagine my surprise when several students wrote about that experience on their final in early June. Many students saw this as a unique and interesting activity that stood out among the rest of our literary endeavors. I saw it as an opportunity to assist students in making imaginative leaps and as a way to celebrate diversity, unify my students, and nurture a democratic community.

Annie, like the majority of the other students in this class, became more confident and eager to participate. She volunteered frequently in class, and felt safe enough to attempt oral communication to the best of her ability. Her peers were patient and considerate of Annie's feelings, but no longer polite for the sake of being polite. If Annie had a thought about a particular text that students disagreed with, they finally felt secure enough to challenge her opinions and present their own beliefs.

Other Frontloading Techniques

Quick-Writes One of the most expedient ways to assess the prior knowledge of individual students is to ask the class to complete a *quick-write*—a free-write with a focus. The frontloading occurs when the class reflects on this exercise.

Simply tell your students, "You have the next three minutes to write the most important things you know about the following topic." (Depending on the topic, you may want to give more time.) Earlier in the chapter, I assigned a quick-write to focus my students' attention on communication issues. You might also assign a quick-write to check students' knowledge of a particular genre. For example, if you are about to start a unit on satire, you might want to assess what your students know about satire and how to read one in order to plan and prepare for the unit.

If you are using the quick-write as a diagnostic tool, the information you gather from students might be invaluable. If all the students seem to have a working knowledge of satire, then you might decide to focus your energy elsewhere or to create a contact zone around satire. You might plan to help students understand how satire is used to influence people in a political way. Conversely, if you haven't received much data from the quick-writes to indicate that students are aware of the elements that characterize satire, then you know that those are areas you will want to address while teaching this unit.

New terms and conversation may also arise as students discuss this writing. In a reading class with students from ninth to twelfth grade, we recently completed an extensive unit on the Holocaust that centered around the issue of whether it has or could happen again. As a frontloading activity, I asked students to complete a five-minute quick-write on what they knew about the Holocaust. Notice the differences between the quick-writes written by students in the same class.

Laurie wrote:

Saddam Hussein led many Germans to kill Jews, gays and some other people I can't remember.

Heather also confused the details of the Holocaust:

Well, I don't know that much about the hollocoust, but what I do know is that the white people were very mean to to black people. I think that is really bad. Everyone should be nice to everyone.

On the other hand, Greg did a remarkable job of summarizing the details of the Holocaust:

The Holocaust happened during World War II. Hitler used Jewish people as scapegoats, and he blamed all of Germany's problems on them. He had Jewish books burned, Jewish homes and businesses destroyed, and people killed. Other countries knew that this genocide was going on, but didn't let Jews migrate to their country. Jewish people were opposite of the aryan race and were murdered in large death camps. These death camps were called concentration camps, the largest being Auswitch. More than 6,000,000 Jews suffered a horrible death of being gased, shot, starved to death, and buried alive. Gettos sprang up due to the holocaust. Large cities were walled in to hold Jews.

When I first planned my contact zone around the topic of tolerance and how we need to use the lessons of our past to direct us in our future decision making, I assumed that students might need to learn more specifics about WWII. I suspected that they *might* need a refresher of important dates, events, and people involved in the Holocaust. What I did not bargain for was that students would struggle with the very term *Holocaust,* or that they wouldn't really have an understanding of Hitler's role in the tragedy. In fact, my initial assumption was that much of the material I would cover in my Holocaust unit would be "old hat." Actually, I had hoped that students would understand the Holocaust to the degree that Greg did, so I could focus more on tolerance on the contact zone that I had planned. Greg ended up being the exception rather than the rule, and I revised my plans to accommodate the individual needs of my students. In this way I could address the lack of background knowledge of most students and provide special advanced opportunities for Greg.

An advantage of the quick-write is that I could quickly identify students with prior knowledge of the topic. Quite obviously Greg has a good sense of the events surrounding the Holocaust. His use of terms like *genocide, Aryan,* and *Auschwitz* indicate that this is not a new subject for him. Since I discovered this in advance, I was able to enlist Greg in the early stages of instruction for this unit by having him assist the students who were struggling with the topic. This lending of Greg's "novice expertise" shows that there is a democratic component at play here, too. Students were able to use the strengths of individuals like Greg to help the group do their work. Later, Greg engaged with more advanced information sources and texts about the Holocaust so he could extend his own knowledge.

Once students had completed their quick-writes, I asked them to share with each other in small groups, and then to report to the larger group. Although it became readily apparent that the knowledge base was not the same for all students, they realized from the discussions that the Holocaust was an important subject that had somehow been overlooked. Like me, perhaps many of my students' former teachers had considered teaching a unit on the Holocaust but had changed their minds, thinking that this material had already been covered. Whatever the case, the quick-write was a simple, expedient way to determine that more work needed to be done on this subject.

More pertinent to this chapter is the fact that the quick-write activity assisted students in their preparation for reading by helping them build a framework to attach to the new knowledge that would be encountered in the texts. By sharing the misinformation included in the quick-writes—such as the notes about Saddam Hussein and racial discrimination against blacks—students were able to help each other correct the information and gain a better idea of the topic in general. When Laurie's partner recognized that she had information in her quick-write that was inaccurate, he immediately asked others in the classroom for clarification. Coincidentally, her partner could not remember that Hitler was the impetus for the Holocaust, either. As mentioned earlier, Greg's detailed quick-write offered many new terms and concepts that students might not have been exposed to prior to their reading of the text that followed.

K-W-L Chart   A great visual expansion of the quick-write, and another effective frontloading technique, is the K-W-L chart (Ogle 1983). In Figure 4.1, Katie's creation of the K-W-L (Know-Want to Know-Learn) helps organize and focus her attention on the Holocaust texts.

Before we started reading any texts on the Holocaust, I asked students to list what they knew about the subject in the "K" column. Next, I asked them to make a column labeled "W" to represent what they *want to know* about the topic. As we progressed through our contact zone based on the Holocaust, students were then able to fill in the "L" column, which represented what they had *learned*.

Because knowledge of the Holocaust was limited, we worked as a group to complete the "K" and "W" columns for this contact zone. As

FIGURE 4.1
KATIE'S K-W-L CHART

K-W-L (Know - Want to know -Learn) 1st quarter

K	W	L
Killed many Jews 6 Million	– Why were religious groups targeted? (And minorities)	
America wouldn't let Jews come here.	– Why didn't other countries intervene more quickly?	
Hitler wanted an Aryan Race (blond + blue eyes)	– How come he wanted an Aryan race if he wasn't himself?	
During World War II.	– How did Hitler persecute victims?	
Hitler used Jews as scapegoats.		
Not just Jews - Gypsies, Communists, Jehovah's Witnesses, minorities, homosexuals, Catholics.		

we progressed throughout the unit, students would add individual comments to this chart under the "L" column indicating what they had learned. Throughout our contact zone on the Holocaust, I found that students had many similar questions about the Holocaust. However, because there were lots of questions that were unique to individual students, I assigned mini-inquiry projects to adequately address them. One student did an extensive inquiry project on Mengele focusing on the question, "For what purpose did Mengele conduct his experiments?" This was a great way for students to learn about aspects of the Holocaust that were intriguing or had personal significance to them, and it was a great way for students to teach one another.

Good frontloading must:

- activate background knowledge (which is precisely the goal of the "K" column)
- help the reader set purposes (which Katie's group did when they considered the "W" column)
- serve as a template for what is being learned during the reading (the "L" column does just that).

The following steps explain how to help students complete a K-W-L chart.

Creating a K-W-L Chart with Your Students

1. Ask students to make three columns on a sheet of paper.
2. Students write down the topic of a story or selection at the top.
3. Ask students to contribute what they know (or think they know) about a topic. These contributions will be recorded in the first column, "K" (What We *Know).*
4. As this information is shared, encourage students to raise questions. These questions should be recorded in the second column, "W" (What We *Want* to Know).
5. Ask students to categorize what they know and want to know. You may instruct students to prioritize their "W" column. This then becomes a list of "categories of information we expect to use."
6. Let students read the story or selection, or conduct their independent research. As they read, encourage them to look for information that helps answer their questions or expands their understanding of the knowledge categories and general topic.

7. After the reading, have students place the new information they have discovered under the third column, "L" (What We *Learned*). Students can then code the new information according to the cited knowledge categories. New knowledge categories may then emerge.

8. When the K-W-L grid is complete, ask students to create a concept map that organizes the information. *For example, students might have listed information in the "K" column about Jewish people being persecuted. Throughout the contact zone, they might also have learned that Catholics and others were also victims during the Holocaust. Each of these facts could be categorized under the heading "Victims of the Holocaust."* All information on the K-W-L grid can be categorized in this manner. This organizes the information for student writing or other projects. Unanswered questions can serve as the basis for independent projects and research.

Character Quotes   Another good way to prepare students to read is to provide them with a number of different quotes by one character in a story. This helps them infer personality traits of a character. This is particularly useful with more challenging texts because it helps students become interested in characters and make predictions about them and their relationships to one another. In addition, this activity highlights quotes and passages that are important to story meaning (and we can discuss later how such quotes contribute to story meaning) and is a wonderful way to engage students in lively discussions. The strategies of prediction and inferencing are also introduced and supported through this activity.

Steps for the Character Quotes Activity

1. Preview the selection to be read, selecting quotes from a particular character (or characters) that reveal important issues or personality traits.

2. Give small groups of students different sets of quotes from different characters. Each group has the responsibility to generate as many words as they can that might describe this character, based on the information from the quotes. Ask students to predict what this character's problem might be, and how this problem might be similar to issues facing students in our school.

3. Ask groups to report to the class by reading their quotes and sharing their list of predicted character traits, predicted issues, and possible connections of the character to our own lives. These inferences must be justified based on the textual cues from the provided quotes.

4. Ask students to make some generalizations about the character and predictions about what may happen in the reading selection involving the character.

5. Since each group has a different character from the story or unit, ask them to predict what the characters might have in common, or what they might have to do with each other. Again, ask them to justify their inferences based on textual cues.

6. Let students read the selection and then ask them to return to their generalizations and predictions to discuss what should be added or changed.

The Tea Party   Another similar frontloading activity is referred to as the "The Tea Party."

Steps for The Tea Party

1. Each student gets a quote from a character. All quotes come from the same text.

2. Students rehearse their quote, sharing it with other members of the class.

3. Students write a response to or explanation of their quote.

4. The whole class brainstorms their communal ideas about the plot, setting, characters, character relationships, purposes, and arguments of the text. If the quotes are numbered in the sequence they appear in the text, students can read them aloud in the correct sequence and make predictions about plot sequence or cause-and-effect relationships. Students may also explore how the author uses particular techniques, such as appealing to the senses. Students are then ready to read and test their predictions.

Opinionnaires,   The frontloading technique of opinionnaires or surveys requires stu-
Scenarios, and   dents to articulate their own beliefs about a certain topic. The opin-
Role Play   ionnaire is in the form of a survey that asks students to agree or disagree with particular perspectives on the issue they will study. The

FIGURE 4.2
FRONTLOADING WITH SCENARIOS

Frontloading for *The Crucible* and The Inquiry Unit: What is the American character? And why are we the way we are? And should we be different?

Read the scenario that you have been assigned. As you read, think about the situation, and then write about what you would do and why. Afterward, you will get into a group with other classmates who had the same scenario and discuss your decisions. You and your group members will then present the scenario and your answers to the rest of class, so that we can all discuss it.

1. There has been an increase in the number of terrorist attacks on the U.S. Airplanes have been hijacked, and buildings have been bombed. Most of the attacks have been attributed to Middle Eastern terrorist organizations, and most of the attackers happen to be Muslim. The fear of Muslims is growing in the country, and the government decides to take action. The government says that the U.S. needs to "hunt out" its enemy before they have a chance to strike, and it encourages citizens to report any suspicious activity that might be related to terrorism. In the past week, thirty Muslim-Americans have been reported, arrested, and sent to trial.

   You live on a quiet suburban street. Your neighbor, Ali Jahd Barak, has lived next door to you for almost fifteen years. Mr. Barak is Muslim, but was born in the U.S. Lately, you have noticed Mr. Barak spending a lot of his free time in the basement and garage, tinkering with some project. You know that several other people in the neighborhood are talking about reporting him to the police, and have asked for your support. You are becoming very suspicious about Mr. Barak's activities too, but you're not completely sure if you and your neighbors should report him to the authorities (they will probably arrest him). What will you do? Why?

2. You are a high school teacher. Two students in your class have asked you to write them college recommendations. They both want to go

to the same school, and it is known that this school usually does not accept more than one student at a time from your small rural school district. One student, Emily, is a well-dressed, bubbly girl who plays softball, is on the yearbook committee, and plays in the school band. The other student, Tony, likes to dress in what some people call "grunge" and is much more quiet and reserved. Tony doesn't participate in any extra-curricular school activities, but he spends most of his free time volunteering to work at the homeless shelter. Both students get the same grades in school. You want to be fair, but you just don't understand Tony's appearance, personality, and priorities. You don't think he'll fit in at the college that he wants to attend, but you think Emily would be perfect there. What will you decide to do? Why?

3. You are a high school student. John is a friend of yours from your neighborhood. You don't hang out with him a lot anymore, but the two of you grew up together, and you've always thought he was a nice guy. Sometimes you still get together to study or go to a ball game. A few days ago, John decided to "come out" and let a few of his friends know that he's a homosexual. You never would have expected it, and it's kind of weird for you to think about, but you respect him as a person, and you don't think it really matters. Today, however, you heard a group of your classmates talking about John behind his back. They were laughing and ridiculing him and calling him very nasty names. You overheard that they are planning a horrible prank. You don't think they'll hurt him physically, but you know that he'll be extremely upset and humiliated in front of the whole school. They ask you to join in. What will you decide to do?

opinionnaire form itself can then be used to compare their beliefs to those of others who take the opinionnaire, and eventually to those perspectives of authors and characters who we will read about. In this way, an opinionnaire helps students to see that various views exist about important issues, and that they must converse with these perspectives and stake their own claim among the various views.

Opinionnaires are easy to create. I often go to Bartlett's Quotations to find comments about particular topics. I also find brain-

Figure 4.2a
Frontloading Through Role-playing

"Some Play Before the Play"

Directions: You and your partners must prepare for a short presentation in which you dramatize one of the following scenes. Think about how each character in the scene would act and what he/she might say. Be ready to defend the choices that you've made based on your knowledge of the world and human behavior.

Situation A:

two people: high school principal, daughter

You are the high school principal, and a somewhat controversial figure. Some people in town don't like how strict you are. You find out your daughter has been at a keg party this weekend, and some people in town know or suspect that she was there. She is denying being there, or at least denying drinking. What do you say to her? How does she respond?

Situation B:

four people: friends who are in trouble

As athletes you have all signed the athletic code. You've all been to a keg party this weekend, and the athletic director and the assistant principal have some evidence that suggests that you were there, but haven't been able to prove it yet. You are meeting to discuss what you should do. One of you (who has all *A*'s and is a "goody-two-shoes") wants to admit everything, one of you (who has been in trouble before, and is pretty "tough") wants to admit nothing at all and wait this out. What would each person say? What do you decide to do?

Situations C:

six people: athletic director, principal, parents, students

You have been called before your parents, athletic director, and principal. They know you were at a party where people were drinking, and they know it was a big party and that some people were also using drugs. They are willing to let you off the hook for your part in the issue, if you will tell them who else was there. What do they say to convince you? What do you say in return?

Debriefing: Were the scenarios realistic? In each, which person was right?

storming with friends about typical cultural attitudes around a topic to be very helpful in getting me started on creating on opinionnaire.

Opinionnaires prepare, guide, and inform the student's reading of a text because they not only activate background knowledge and beliefs students can use during a reading, but because they motivate students to read and converse with views different than their own. Further, they can be used as a template to think about and record authorial and character views because later students can be asked how the characters and the author would respond to the opinionnaires. In this way, students can be helped to play the narrative audience as they understand character experience, and play the authorial audience, contrasting their own point of view with the author's and engaging the author in conversation about the meaning of her text.

In Tanya's assignment sequence during a unit on dreams (Chapter 7), she frontloads with an opinionnaire that students can return to as a touchstone throughout the various readings in the unit.

In the next chapter she explores how questioning strategies can assist students to richer and more complex reading in the context of inquiry around the American character and why we are the way we are. She begins this unit by asking students to respond individually and then in groups to scenarios that describe real-world issues concerning her topic of conformity and difference to certain cultural standards. Before reading *The Crucible*, the central text in her unit, she has students role-play scenes that touch on these issues. By engaging in these activities, students activate and build background knowledge that they can bring to their readings of particular texts and to their inquiry into what it means to be an American, and how far the definition of being an American is allowed to be stretched.

5

Loving the Questions
Fostering Student Questioning and Discussion

It is better to ask some of the questions than to know all of the answers.

—James Thurber, "The Scotty Who Knew Too Much"

Critical readers—in the best sense of "critical"—need to question the ideology of the texts they read. . . . Critical reading involves questioning the values of the texts you engage.

Peter Rabinowitz, *Authorizing Readers*

It's the second Sunday of the month, our book club Sunday, and ten of us lounge comfortably around Jeff and Peggy Wilhelm's kitchen table, mugs of hot coffee before us. We've enjoyed a great meal, but now we're ready to get down to business. Five or six people pull out copies of Graham Swift's *Last Orders*. Some copies look pristine, and we tease their owners about just how much they've actually read. Others are dog-eared and clearly marked, ready for discussion. Still, the talk starts slowly, tentatively, with safe and easy questions: "Did you like it?" "Couldn't you just see it?" As things warm up, we get to the meatier discussion: "Are these admirable characters?" "Is their adultery at all justified?" Points are made, counterpoints offered. The text is opened again and again; passages are read and commented upon. The discussion is lively, comfortable, engaging. No one stares out a window or wishes they were somewhere else.

We talk first through various events, then how they might be connected. We spend considerable time discussing the "last orders" and how this is connected to the secret events many years ago. Were the last orders a form of atonement? What point was the author making about marriage, the importance of certain acts, the possibility of forgiveness? Do we buy his message?

Then, just as things begin to wind down, Jeff, the most outspoken person of faith among us, asks the last question, "Was this book morally satisfying?" It stops us for a moment; we want clarification. "What does that mean, _morally satisfying_?" "Does a text HAVE to be morally satisfying?" "What does it mean if a text is not?" Several people argue that no, this text is not morally satisfying. Some say it is not, but that this doesn't matter. I listen for a long while before I speak; I have not considered the question before now. Then, suddenly, I am surprised to hear myself weigh in against them. I argue that the quiet character of the undertaker shows us how to lead a happy and moral life, that we have missed him in our earlier discussion, that we need to look at him more carefully, and that, yes, this _is_ a morally satisfying text. I had not known that I thought this until I heard Jeff's question and other people's answers—indeed, I had not ever even considered the question.

As we drive home, my husband, Jamie, and I continue to consider the book and our discussion of it. I had enjoyed the actual reading of the book, but I am more content with my own reading of it now. I know more about the book and indeed about myself than I had before. I say to Jamie how some of the most important and pivotal moments in my life have come about while discussing books. There are things that I have learned in such discussions that I think about and make use of every day.

Nancie Atwell (1987) has said it, Leila Christenbury (1994) has said it, and many people believe it: Our goal for classroom discussion should be to replicate that "dining room table" discussion. But aside from the fact that this kind of reading is enjoyable to us (and I'm remembering that George Hillocks and Vygotsky would say that such enjoyment is important to learning)—why is this what we want for our students? People who read for their own purposes read to understand themselves and the world in which they find themselves right now. Such expert readers often read "authorially" to understand an author as an "intelligence that created the literary text" (Rabinowitz and Smith 1998, 31)—a voice, as it were, to be heard, considered, agreed, or argued with. The multiple perspectives that the members of our book club "bring to the table" provide other intelligences, enriching and challenging our discussion and our construction of meaning. I want to replicate that "dining room table" experience for my students because it allows them to read as members involved in a democratic discussion with an author and with their peers. Through conversation students can come to understand that the task of reading is not simply to ask, "What does this text mean?" but rather to ask, "What would this [text] mean for the audience the author was writing for and how do I feel about that?"(Rabinowitz and Smith, 31). And as they do so, I would argue, they are developing the dispositions for granting others initial respect for their opinions and work, for democratic conversation, thinking, and action.

One large "umbrella" goal I have for students in my classroom is that they become better citizens. And what do we expect of citizens in a democracy? That they will be thoughtful and well informed; that they will listen carefully to all sides of an issue before deciding where they stand. That they will hold opinions about which they care deeply and on which they are willing to act, but that they will always listen respectfully to dissenting opinions, weighing new evidence carefully. Teaching literature allows me to work with students at developing these democratic skills in a safe, consequence-free zone. Through authorial readings students can listen to the ideas and opinions of characters and authors and decide what the author meant and how they, as readers, feel about that. They can try on new and scary ideas and opinions in the context of the made-up story world before carrying their opinions and actions out into the "real world." In all of the units of study in my American literature classes, I try to allow students to try on new ideas in this "liminal" world of literature—that space on the threshold between the real and the imaginary.

But how do we achieve this with students who have little experience with "dining room table" chats, or with reading itself? Like learning to write about literature, learning to engage with texts the way these texts ask to be read and learning to talk about literature in complex ways are skills that must be modeled, explicated, supported, practiced, reviewed, and revised. If we analyze my book club experience, we should notice several things:

If we want students to ask better and more powerful questions, we need to realize it won't happen automatically. We must push them in that direction.

1. No one person dominated the discussion or asked all the questions.
2. People talked about what interested or concerned them—not only about the book but about their lives.
3. Most of the time people's contributions were voluntary.
4. Everyone was engaged: first, with trying to understand the book as deeply as possible, and second, with weighing in on how we felt about the book's construction and message, and how we might apply understandings gained from the book to our own lives.

How can we support students to develop and internalize skills so that we might replicate this environment in our classroom?

A way to start is to consider the types of questions that we ask about literature and about life problems, the power and importance of different kinds of questions to "do work," and the manner and contexts in which particular questions are most fruitful. Then we can consider how to help students internalize questioning and discussion strategies so they can engage independently both in group discussions and in internal discussions with texts and authors.

It seems to us that most influential reader response theorists ignore the importance of questions, maybe because they see questions as a device of New Criticism. We think this is a mistake. We need to ask ourselves, "When does questioning aid in the understanding of a text, its construction, and its message? What kinds of questions aid in this kind of understanding? When is questioning useful? What kinds of questions are not useful?" If we ignore the fact that questions support and assist students to understand life and literature, we undermine our power to teach and help students. We are using two-sided teaching in line with the work of both Hillocks and Vygotsky when we assist students to use questions to achieve better textual comprehension, develop discussion skills, and learn how to self-question in a kind of "inner speech" and dialectic with text.

Questioning

As a beginning teacher, I broke just about every rule I now know about questioning. I asked too many questions, I didn't wait long enough for answers, and if a student didn't answer fast enough, I moved to someone else. My questions often jumped to author's craft and style before students had a chance to discuss what happened and why, and who cared. As a result, a "class discussion" in my early days of teaching resembled a quiz bowl, or a manic recitation, but certainly not a discussion. Some students learned to anticipate what sort of questions I would ask (often those included at the end of a selection in their anthology). These students "played school" with great success, reading only to find the answers. Others never said a word. None of the students was reading for himself or herself or because he or she cared. They were reading to answer my questions, or they weren't reading at all. Unfortunately, George's research (Hillocks 1999) shows that many teachers who say they have class discussions really don't—they are doing most of the talking, and students merely recite and fill in the blanks that teachers leave for them.

Questioning Schemes

Things changed for me when I asked myself why I was asking questions at all. After deep consideration, I decided the following: (1) I wanted to use questions to find out what students understood about what they were reading; (2) I wanted to use that information to lead and support them into new territory to create an even richer engagement and understanding of the text. In other words, I wanted to use questions to gauge my students' zone of actual development as readers so that I could design activities to support them in their zone of proximal development as readers. Ultimately, I wanted them to internalize questioning strategies that they could use independently to meet textual expectations, problem solve, self-monitor, and converse with texts and their authors through their own reading.

There are three questioning schemes that Jeff suggested I might use to help me achieve this goal:

1. Question-answer relationships (Raphael 1982)
2. Hillock's questioning hierarchy (Hillocks 1980, 1984)

3. Questioning Circles (Christenbury and Kelly 1983) and other schemes that help students move beyond the text and that promote student engagement.

Each of these questioning schemes did *some* of the work I hoped to do with questioning, but none did all of the work by itself. Therefore, in my teaching I now use different questioning schemes depending on what my goals in questioning are. Also, I work with each scheme to help students internalize the question types and the work that the questions do for a reader, so students can question texts and their own readings independently of me.

Question-Answer Relationships

Question-answer relationships (QARs) are a powerful technique created by Taffy Raphael (1982) for elementary school readers. Jeff came upon this technique when he was doing research for *"You Gotta BE the Book"* (Wilhelm 1997). His data made him realize how essential inferencing is to reading of all kinds, but particularly to literary reading, and he was looking for a way to support his reluctant readers to make various kinds of inferences.

Question-answer relationships highlight that readers must ask different kinds of questions, and that these different kinds of questions require different kinds of work (or interpretive moves) to answer. Raphael identifies two kinds of text-based questions:

Text-Based Questions
1. Right-there questions
2. Think-and-search questions

Right-there questions are literal questions that can be answered by finding directly stated information. *Think-and-search questions* are inference questions that require students to bring information forward from one part of the text and connect it to new information later in the text. By putting the various pieces of information together, students can make a connection and an inference. Literary theorists call this "reading along indices," and Jeff realized that few of his students could do this. Jeff reframed this kind of question as "Finding the Puzzle Pieces" (Wilhelm 1996).

Jeff also recognized that another category of inference questions would help his students. Jeff calls this kind of question "filling the gaps." Students need to recognize places where information is missing or withheld and fill it in. For example, in *The Great Gatsby* there is a flashback scene in which readers find Daisy drunk and crying in her bathtub, holding on to a piece of paper that has disintegrated. One of our major jobs as readers is to use the action of the book to fill in this gap. Students sometimes need help making the inference to understand that the paper is a letter from Gatsby.

Raphael goes on to describe two other classes of questions that she calls "in my head":

In My Head Questions
1. Author-and-me questions
2. On my own questions

The answers to *author-and-me questions* are not in the story; readers need to consider the story and their life experiences to answer the questions. Jeff likes this kind of question because it highlights how an author and her text can help kids think about a contact zone or theme that they are studying together in class, and how what the author has to say can inform the students' thinking and action around this theme. For example, one unit we sometimes cover in American literature asks students to consider and write a position paper on the death penalty in America. We use Truman Capote's *In Cold Blood* as the central text in this unit. An *author-and-me question* students are asked to consider is, "What does Truman Capote think about the death penalty and how do I feel about that?"

To answer "on my own" questions, students don't need to have read the book at all. The story may have stimulated such a question, but is not linked to answering it. An on my own question in our "death penalty" unit could be "How do I feel about the death penalty?" or "Is capital punishment a crime deterrent?"

Jeff found that his students could easily internalize QARs (Wilhelm 1996). He modeled the questions with questioning games. Before students answered a question, they needed to identify the kind of question asked and how to answer it. Eventually, Jeff asked them to come up with their own questions as they read. He often had students place their QAR questions in a coffee can at the beginning of class and he pulled them randomly to fuel class discussions. Jeff focused not only on how to answer each kind of question, but on the usefulness of each type.

I use QARs successfully in my own classroom. They are easy to use, and students do internalize them quickly. However, I did not find this scheme to be a panacea. It did not help me assist my students to meet all the textual expectations necessary to achieve authorial reading and the full democratic conversation I wanted, one that would more fully consider the author and his construction of text. A much more specific heuristic was available to me in Jeff's second suggested scheme: George's questioning hierarchy.

Hillocks'
Questioning
Hierarchy

In "Towards a Hierarchy of Skills in the Comprehension of Literature," George Hillocks (1980) presents a "questioning hierarchy," a carefully constructed set of question types based on the idea that "before students can deal with the abstractions . . . they must be able to deal with the literal and inferential content of the work" (306). The hierarchy is not intended to be exhaustive. It examines the relationship among frequently asked questions *about the text*, which must be answered *before* students can consider questions about the relationship of their personal experience to the text, or about their evaluation of the reading experience. Students need to answer textual questions of one kind before they can answer textual questions of the next kind; one kind of understanding is the foundation for the next kind. The questioning hierarchy is a set of seven question types. The first three questions are literal; the last four questions are inferential. The explanations that follow are taken from George's article. The questions are mine; I use them to assess students' comprehension levels while reading the first two chapters of John Steinbeck's *Of Mice and Men.*

Level 1: *Basic stated information*
Example: Who are the two characters introduced in Chapter 1?
Purpose: These questions are used to determine if a student can read and comprehend literal and repeated information.

Level 2: *Key details*
Example: Why, according to Lennie, are George and Lennie different from other guys?
Purpose: These questions refer to something important to the plot and its development. They are used to determine if a student comprehends a detail that is stated only once but must be noticed and brought forward throughout the reading.

Level 3: *Stated relationships*
Example: Why does Curley pick on Lennie?
Purpose: These questions are used to see if the reader has located the relationship said to exist between two pieces of information.

The relationship is often causal and must be directly stated in the text.

Level 4: *Simple implied relationships*

Example: Why did George and Lennie leave their last job? (This question is based on a single paragraph in which students must recognize what Lennie did in Weed, and then infer how that is connected to them being in Salinas.)

Purpose: Like questions at level 3, these questions determine whether a reader has recognized a relationship, but these questions address a relationship that is *not* directly stated in the text. Rather, the reader must make an inference based on a few (two, three, four) pieces of information close together in the text.

Level 5: *Complex implied relationships*

Example: There seem to be many reasons why George and Lennie travel around together. Give at least three reasons and explain which is the most important.

Purpose: These questions determine if students can infer an answer from a large number of details. In order to answer such a question, a student must be able to "identify the necessary details, discern whatever patterns exist among them, and then draw the appropriate inference" (Hillocks 1980, 308).

Level 6: *Author's generalization*

Example: What might Steinbeck say about the pluses and minuses of having and committing to a long-term friendship? Give evidence to support your idea.

Purpose: Questions in this category go beyond those in Level 5 to determine what students believe the work implies about the world or human beings. These questions deal with what English teachers generally refer to as "theme." However, whereas the "theme" is often described in one word, such as "the theme is war," this question demands a more sophisticated response. Students must consider "the proposition(s) that the story might be said to represent" (Hillocks 1980, 308).

Level 7: *Structural generalizations*

Example: How does Steinbeck use the bunk house and the guys in it reinforce the major themes of the novel?

Purpose: "Questions in this category require the reader to explain how parts of the work operate together to achieve certain effects" (Hillocks 1980, 308). They are used to determine whether the student can explicitly explain how the structure works to create a central meaning rather than interpreting some aspect of the structure (which would fall into level 5).

It's important to note that you may have to ask several questions at one level before proceeding to the next. Students must deal with local and more limited meanings before "putting the puzzle pieces together" to explore more abstract and global meanings.

Because of its hierarchical nature, the inventory is a great diagnostic. It is an invaluable tool to assess students' comprehension achievement with a particular story and to plan the next necessary step in instruction. It has also given me a general sense of what students can and cannot do and how I might help them. For example, using it in studying *Of Mice and Men* showed me that my students were having great difficulty with inferencing. And this in turn explained why they could not identify or defend an author's generalization, which made it impossible for them to understand how a text was constructed in a particular way to communicate that generalization. Learning activities that focus their attention on extracting information and seeing relationships between pieces of information helped them to be ready to move on. An evidence extract exercise, in which students must list all of the negative things that George says about traveling around with Lennie and then all the positive things he says about traveling around with Lennie, helped students who were having trouble answering the question at level 5. Understanding this information is then key to being able to answer the question at level 6.

Using the hierarchy helped me see my students' zone of proximal development and how to move them through it so that we could work on another question type in another ZPD. Internalizing the hierarchy helped me to recognize more quickly where and why my students' readings are breaking down.

Finally, using the hierarchy has helped my students understand and internalize the different kinds of questions they must ask and strategies they must use to fully understand a text and to read it authorially. As a result, the hierarchy has helped many of my students to monitor their understanding, and to self-correct when their reading breaks down. These are big achievements.

I developed the questioning hierarchy that follows for Herman Melville's "Bartleby":

> Question 1: *Basic stated information.* What does Bartleby do for a living?
>
> Question 2: *Key detail.* Where is the narrator's office located?
>
> Question 3: *Stated relationship.* Why is the narrator, at first, glad to hire Bartleby?
>
> Question 4: *Simple implied relationships.* What causes Turkey's personality to change so drastically each day?
>
> Question 5: *Complex implied relationships.* Although the narrator's response to Bartleby is somewhat suprising, we see several indications of his own personality earlier in the text. Why is the narrator is so accepting of Bartleby? Give at least three examples from the text to support your answer.
>
> Question 6: *Author's generalization.* How might the author explain people's attitudes toward and treatment of people who behave in surprising or upsetting ways?
>
> Question 7: *Structural generalizations.* How does Melville use walls to reinforce the major themes of the story? Give evidence to support your idea.

Bartleby is a difficult text and is dated, yet students, when helped through discussion to understand WHAT the story says, are very interested in discussing Melville's ideas about "otherness" and "isolation," both themes with which most teenagers struggle. It has also helped me prepare instruction as we tackle longer and more difficult works from this time period such as *The Scarlet Letter.* I try to organize my instruction around the theme of "the American character" with the following question as our guide: "What is an American, and why are we the way we are?" This is our macro-question of the course; smaller micro-questions are used to organize shorter inquiry units that tie loosely to this major theme. Readings that address these kind of questions and how the answer changes (or doesn't) over time make the class and our readings inquiry driven even as we fill curricular mandates.

Hillocks' hierarchy really helps me think about what I want students to know about how to read and converse with literature, and it helps me determine what students are able and unable to do. It allows me to see what students need to attend to and do to play the authorial audience, engaging in discussion with each other and with an author (remembering always that such discussions, promoting a sense of the skills and attitudes required to be a good democratic citizen, are an "umbrella" goal of the course). As a diagnostic tool, it lets me design activities or insert questions into classroom inquiry that help students "get the stuff" of the text, because it shows me where their readings have broken down. Most important, the questioning hierarchy helps me know and be able to name what students are doing, and then assist them with the readerly things they cannot yet do without help. As Michael Smith argues in *Authorizing Readers* (1998), "Our students can only make a political commentary on a literary text if they understand the codes and conventions that text invokes" (32).

> For questioning strategies to be useful, students must internalize them so that they will drive their own future reading and discussions.

At first I could not see how to give the power of the hierarchy to my students so that they could use it to ask their own questions of a text. To make the hierarchy more student-friendly, Jeff simplified it to four essential kinds of questions:

1. What, literally does the text say? (first three types of questions)
2. What can we infer that it says? (next two types of questions)
3. Why was the text written (i.e., what is the author trying to say)? (author's generalization)
4. How is the text constructed to say that? (structural generalization)

This started my quest to help students formulate their own questions. I began to look for other ways to get students asking and answering questions about the texts they read. As enormously helpful as the hierarchy is, I wanted to find some other schemes that would help me move them from asking textual questions to asking questions about themselves and the world.

Moving Beyond the Text: Questions to Promote Student Engagement

Personal Response   I discovered an article by Kris Myers (1993) called "Twenty (Better) Questions." The article discussed the difficulty of getting students to read. It suggested replacing pop quizzes with response journals, in which students responded to one of Myers' "twenty (better) questions." I was struck by the fact that all of these questions honored students' responses to the selections they were reading. I photocopied Myers' list immediately and began to use the questions and my students' written responses to them as a springboard for discussion. Suddenly, my students were engaged; they wanted to talk about their own responses to what they were reading, how they felt as they read, which characters they liked or didn't.

When I began to use such questions to build and go beyond textual understanding, students suddenly came to class with things to say, often beginning the discussion before I had a chance to throw out the first pitch. Even better, students did not necessarily look to me to see if they were "right," or to direct their questions and responses. Myers' questions, which focus on a reader's response, democratized the discussion, in that everyone had an equal chance to participate, to have a personal response to the text. However, by itself, such "reader response" questions don't require students to respectfully listen to the author and what she is trying to say.

Questioning Circles   Questioning circles (Christenbury and Kelly 1983; Christenbury 1994) are extraordinarily useful in helping students combine textual and critical reading with personal connections (see Figure 5.1).

This strategy provides an alternative to traditional scope-and-sequence or hierarchical questioning strategies, and it is still more structured (and therefore more supportive) and organized than a free-for-all, "anything goes" reader response questioning strategy. In Christenbury's words, "The questioning circle provides a logical, yet flexible, format for questioning" (1994, 206). It also offers readers a chance to connect their own knowledge and expertise to a reading by covering areas of personal response that are not addressed in the questioning hierarchy.

The questioning circle consists of three overlapping areas of knowledge that expert readers bring to bear when reading: knowledge of the matter, personal reality, and external reality. For literature, these three circles represent the text being read (matter), the reader (personal reality), and the world and/or other literature (external reality) (1994, 207). As the figure shows, these areas of knowledge also overlap in the center, the area Christenbury and Kelly (1983) refers to as "dense." Although this "dense" center represents the highest-order thinking, assimilating three domains of knowledge, the diagram represents Christenbury's idea that how and when students get to the dense question is flexible.

FIGURE 5.1
CHRISTENBURY'S AND KELLY'S QUESTIONING CIRCLES

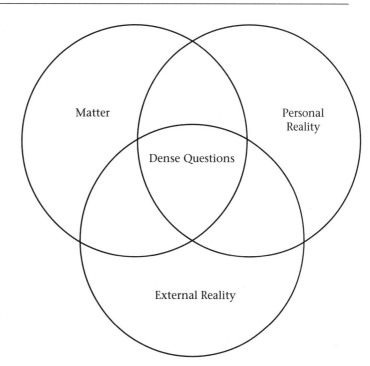

The questioning circle has really helped me devise questions about literature that are interesting and engaging to students, but which also help them think more critically and carefully about what they have read and about how that relates to their own lives and the world in which they live. Further, as I think carefully about the dense question and devise questions that lead students' thinking toward the "big question," the questioning circle helps me consider how discussions build and develop.

Figure 5.2 shows one use of questioning circles, a set of questions I devised to lead a class discussion of "Bartleby the Scrivener." As I stated earlier, "Bartleby" is tied directly to our inquiry into a uniquely American kind of character.

Real Discussion   In order to establish an atmosphere of respect for student discussion, we must sometimes allow for our best laid plans to go

FIGURE 5.2
QUESTIONING CIRCLE QUESTIONS FOR "BARTLEBY"

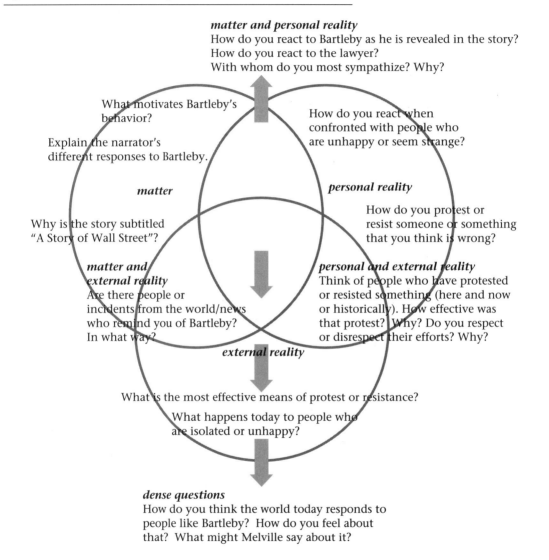

matter and personal reality
How do you react to Bartleby as he is revealed in the story?
How do you react to the lawyer?
With whom do you most sympathize? Why?

What motivates Bartleby's behavior?

Explain the narrator's different responses to Bartleby.

How do you react when confronted with people who are unhappy or seem strange?

matter

personal reality

How do you protest or resist someone or something that you think is wrong?

Why is the story subtitled "A Story of Wall Street"?

matter and external reality
Are there people or incidents from the world/news who remind you of Bartleby? In what way?

personal and external reality
Think of people who have protested or resisted something (here and now or historically). How effective was that protest? Why? Do you respect or disrespect their efforts? Why?

external reality

What is the most effective means of protest or resistance?

What happens today to people who are isolated or unhappy?

dense questions
How do you think the world today responds to people like Bartleby? How do you feel about that? What might Melville say about it?

awry and to know when it is better to let this happen. If our students understand the strategies for making textual meaning and the ways to go beyond this (the order), then we must then give them a chance to flex their muscles by letting them use these strategies to forge their own discussions (the adventure).

One day, as we were using the questions in Figure 5.2 as a basis for discussion of "Bartleby the Scrivener," the class took a thrilling and dangerous turn. I was sitting in a circle with a small group of students (seven boys, three girls), and they were expressing what I have come to view as the typical teenage inability (at first) to come to terms with Bartleby. In order to help them see his circumstance more clearly, I asked them to focus on two passages: one that described his work environment, and one that described his boss' behavior toward him. Here is the latter:

> One object I had in placing Bartleby so handy to me behind the screen, was to avail myself of his services on such trivial occasions. . . . I abruptly called to Bartleby. In my haste and natural expectancy of instant compliance, I sat with my head bent over the original on my desk, and my right hand extended with the copy, so that immediately upon emerging from his retreat, Bartleby might snatch it and proceed to business without the least delay.

After we read the passage, I asked the class a question connecting personal reality to the matter, "Now, who would you treat this way? In other words, from whom do you expect 'instant compliance' with your wishes?" Imagine my surprise when one boy answered "my mother"—and another and then another concurred. Mothers, the boys went on to explain, at least the ones who stayed at home, did so in order to be available for "instant compliance" with requests for clean clothes, repaired baseball uniforms, and late dinners. As several boys agreed, the girls' faces contorted in disbelief and then anger. Suddenly, another boy quietly said, "No, you're wrong. No one should be expected to 'instantly comply' with your wishes, except maybe your dog." A hot discussion ensued about the personal value of human beings; about how and when we show respect; and about how we should treat our mothers and why.

The girls in the group were irate, at first just looking at one another, raising eyebrows, and moving uncomfortably in their seats. Soon, though, although they were outnumbered, they couldn't resist the temptation of this hot discussion. They also jumped in, attacking the boys' position as indefensible: "How can you treat your mother like that?" "Don't you have any respect?" I sat back, refereeing occasionally, but mostly letting the discussion take its course. At one point, clearly agitated, Joe, the first speaker, looked at me and said, "You're judging me on how I treat my mother. That's not right!" I pointed out that I hadn't said a word in more than ten minutes. When the bell rang, the class broke up slowly, and as I left for lunch, a little shaken myself, I heard the discussion spilling down the corridor toward the cafeteria. The bell may have rung, and class might be over, but the discussion was not finished. The students were doing their own work.

Before the Bartleby discussion, I used the questioning circle to devise the questions that helped students move on to do their own work. However, the ultimate goal is to have them ask and internalize their own questions using these various schemes, so they are enabled to do textual work that is completely their own. Then it's not just "something" that's working, it's something that is made to work by and—most important—for the students!

My Rules for Questioning   Here is an overview of my own "rules for questioning," which I have developed in large part by learning from my own mistakes and paying attention when something works:

1. *Consider the purpose of your questioning, and choose questions accordingly.* Don't try to do everything at once. Do you want to diagnose your students' reading comprehension? Do you want students to engage personally with the text? Do you want them to discuss the major themes? Do you want them to focus on the structure of the text? Probably all of these cannot be accomplished in a one-period discussion.

2. *Involve as many students as possible.* Although I believe ideally that participation in discussion should be voluntary, do not allow your classroom to become a place where a few students dominate and the rest check out.

3. *Ask follow-up questions.* Don't allow discussion in your classroom to become a ping-pong volley of question and answer. Challenge students' responses. Or leave room for them to challenge one another. Can they support their responses? Is there evidence in the text? Is there a reason they feel that way? Ask others if they agree.

4. *Allow for wait time.* This is the simplest rule to state and the hardest to follow. Silence feels deafening and awkward, but it doesn't mean that nothing is happening. It might mean students are really thinking about your question and how they want to answer it.

5. *Listen to all the answers, not just for the one you are expecting.* When I began teaching, I was so worried about controlling the class and getting to the "right" answers that I passed over answers that weren't what I had expected. As a result, I missed many great opportunities for discussion and for involving students. If you want students to listen to you and to each other, you must model by listening to them.

6. *Teach students to ask their own questions,* of the texts, of each other and of you. Helping them to internalize the questions from the questioning schemes introduced here helps them to see the kinds of questions readers ask and the work these questions can do to understand texts and converse with authors.

Teaching the Skills of Discussion

Although something had worked in the Bartleby discussion, I knew that much of what took place had not. Students had not been completely respectful of one another or of their rights to hold differing opinions. The girls had been reluctant to join in. One student had not spoken at all. Jan Duncan (quoted in Allen 1995), says "Reading and writing should float on a sea of talk" (113). Of course, sometimes that sea is choppy and dangerous, and sometimes it's dead flat calm; nothing is going anywhere. So how do we develop an environment friendly to "floating," and how do we teach students to navigate the waters of discussion no matter what the weather?

If students don't engage in much civil talk at home, and if they don't have much personal experience with literature, these questions become even more difficult. Further, my many years of teaching juniors in high school has convinced me that, for the most part, school has not helped develop my students' discussion skills. This view is corroborated by the research of Hoetker and Ahlbrand (1969) and Nystrand et al. (1997).

There's a lot of research to indicate that high school students spend most of their time in school tuned out and totally unengaged (Csziksimihalyi and Larson 1984; Csziksimihalyi, Rathunde, and Whalen 1993; Goodlad 1984). Because they have learned "the rules of school," it takes many students little effort to "get by." My students know how school works, and they have taught me that for much of their time in school, answers have been a lot more important than questions. Early discussions each year show this as I throw out a question, some "smart kid" answers it, and silence ensues. I offer another question, I get another quick answer, and no one else speaks up. When I offer another question, the tennis match is on. Those who aren't looking out the window or sleeping in the back corner watch the volley between me and two or three "smart kids"—kids who then sit a little taller in their chairs and puff out their chests a little more because they "know the answers." Sometimes in these early days, just to see if I can shake things up a little, I might challenge an answer, ask for an opposing opinion, or loudly ask, "Do you all agree with that?" The "smart ones" seem to wilt as if I've let the air out of their sails.

This is not the way school is supposed to work. It's where I start, to see what students know about and are able to do in a discussion. But I believe that the skills of discussion must be broken into component parts that must be taught, practiced, reviewed, and practiced some more. At the same time we must always keep our eyes on the big prize, knowing that what we are doing will be quickly put to practice in democratic discussions where we all will have a responsibility to collaborative meaning making.

I often begin with a description, like the one at the beginning of this chapter, of a healthy, living discussion. We talk about all of its component parts: asking; listening; answering; following up (with questions or development of an answer, or a counterpoint); referring to the text; and soliciting others' opinions and ideas. Then we practice. The next section reviews a few of the activities I use in order to teach and assist students to take on expert skills of discussion.

Silent Discussions   In order to encourage participation, I often begin with a "silent discussion." In this activity, I give students a blank piece of paper and ask them to sit in a circle. I ask each student to write two questions about the text. Though one question may be literal (e.g., "What happened?"), the other must be written to promote discussion. (I might encourage them to use a particular kind of hierarchy or circle question, depending on what we are working on.) Students then pass their papers to the right, and I ask each student to write an answer to one of the questions and add a new question to promote discussion. Students then pass their papers down the line and I ask them to read everything on the paper, answer one question, write one more, and pass the paper again. On the next turn, I ask them to read everything on the paper, answer one question, and respond to one answer with either an agreement and support, disagreement, or a follow-up question.

Generally, I will ask students to take approximately five turns. At the end of those turns, I ask them to report one interesting thing from the paper they have in their hands. The silent discussion helps ease students into vocal discussion by allowing them to participate without putting themselves publicly on the line. After all, they are reporting from the paper what other people wrote, not necessarily what they think. It also gives them plenty of time to think about what they want to say and a chance to privately weigh their own thoughts and understandings against what other people are saying before "going public."

The Three-Index-Card Discussion

Occasionally, it seems that no matter what you do to promote democracy, you end up with a class that is somehow unbalanced in a way that affects discussion. Too many boys and not enough girls (or vice versa), a group that is heterogeneous in social power, or simply a group with some introverts and some extroverts. In order to promote more equal sharing in these groups, I sometimes use a method I found in NCTE's "Teacher's Notes" called the "three-index-card discussion." In this activity, the students each receive three blank index cards as they enter the room. Students place their desks in a circle, and they understand that for each turn they take, they must throw an index card in the center of the circle. All students must use all of their index cards, but once they've used three, they're done. Not only has this increased participation, but it has made discussions richer and more focused, as those students who just love to talk must be careful about what they say since they only have three turns. Students who would normally not participate seem to develop more comfort after a number of "index-card discussions" as they see that no one is allowed to dominate.

Encouraging Students to Listen and Follow Up

Although it sounds simple enough, active listening is difficult. To encourage listening, I may start with something as simple as a game of "Telephone," the children's game in which one student whispers a sentence into the ear of the next. The sentence is passed around the room that way, until the last person reports what he or she heard. After a good laugh about the discrepancies between the original message and

Vygotsky has insisted that learning is social. Teachers must therefore listen to students to be able to teach and peers must listen and observe to help each other learn.

the final one, we talk about the importance and difficulty of listening carefully and about the effect of poor listening on discussion. I also like to use taped radio interviews or speeches and ask students to take notes on what they hear. We then use the overhead projector to list and compare notes. I emphasize the importance of listening carefully to each other, and of listening to the authors we invite into class through our reading.

I like to begin the year by having students interview one another in order to introduce each other to the class. To get them thinking about listening and following up, I explain that the interviews must fulfill the following criteria:

1. Students may not prepare more than five general questions for the interview.
2. The interview must last five minutes.
3. They must keep the interview rolling by asking follow-up questions after each general question.
4. They may not introduce any completely new topics.

After the interviews and introductions, we make a list of opening questions and the follow-up questions associated with them. We talk about the uses of follow-up questions and what we learned from them. I then tell students that we must often follow up on initial questions as we study characters, or interrogate texts and their authors. Following up in this way leads us deeper into texts and deeper into understanding.

As we move into literature discussions, I will often encourage follow-up by asking students to work in groups with a transcript that I provide of the previous day's discussion. Each group must analyze the transcript for possible places where follow-up could have occurred but did not. Each group must include one redirecting question, one supporting statement for an answer that was given but underdeveloped, and one counterpoint to an answer they feel could have been argued. This activity, which recognizes students' competencies and names the skills used, has been most useful in helping students understand the dynamics of group discussion as well as all the possible ways a person can participate.

The following transcripts represent three conversations from the same group. In each transcript, the group is pursuing self-directed discussion (after the support of questioning and discussion instruction) on *The Great Gatsby*. The conversations occurred over the course of a four-week unit. Note the development, away from skill-and-drill sort of questions and answers, toward deeper thinking about a few key questions.

Discussion clip, *The Great Gatsby,* Chapters 2 and 3, February 10

Joe: Dr. T. J. Eckleberg is not a real person in the book; he's a billboard.

Melissa: Eyes in the sky, Eckleberg's like God.

Alex: T. J. Eckleberg's eyes, then later on someone else's nose. Does it have any purpose or is it just in there?

Stephen: Do they really look like that or is that the way our narrator sees them because of something else he's thinking or feeling?

Joe: What did Gatsby and Miss Baker do in there?

Marie: In Chapter 4 there's a meeting between Nick and Gatsby that reveals something about what they were doing. We're not supposed to know yet.

Joe: Then why are you telling us? I didn't read that yet.

Brooke: Gatsby wants to know something; he told Jordan to tell Nick.

Do you think George Wilson knows about Myrtle and Tom?

Jared: I don't think he knows.

Susan: Why does Tom break Myrtle's nose?

Marie: To prove he has feelings for Daisy.

Alex: Plus they have a kid.

Stephen: Plus that's the way things were back then.

This conversation was lively, and several students participated. I would also argue that it reveals student engagement with the text. These students have interesting ideas and insights, yet they do not seem to listen to one another. Questions go unanswered, virtually ignored, or, when addressed, a single answer is allowed before moving on to another question. Using an overhead transcript of this discussion, we spend one class period discussing it. Which aspects of a lively conversation do they see? Students note that they had many questions about the book, and that a lot of people were involved. "What's missing?" I ask. They laugh self-consciously. "Well, no one answered anyone's questions, accept Susan's, at the end. And even that's not a very good answer," says Marie. "Yeah, it jumps around a lot," adds Alex. We talk about how things could be improved. Making sure that questions have answers before we move on. Writing down our questions before the discussion or as they occur to us, so that we don't have to interrupt right away before we forget. Contrast this earlier conversation with the one that took place on February 24.

Discussion clip, *The Great Gatsby*, Chapters 4 and 5, February 24

Joe: When Tom and Daisy are sitting in the kitchen and Nick looks in on them, what conclusion have they come to?

Melissa: What's really important is what are they talking about?

Alex: They're talking about everything that's happened during the day, everything that's built up. [She gives an example.]

Stephen: He's lost his mistress and he doesn't want to lose his wife; she's lost . . .

Melissa: I think he's trying to console her, be the nice guy, convince her to stay with him.

Marie: Yeah, Tom and Daisy have come to some sort of agreement— they've done the same thing. He can't be very mad because he did it too.

Stephen: It says they move, he just goes from one place to another.

Brooke: Yeah, like on page 82, it says, "He went to France, Caymens, Chicago . . ."

Alex: Did Daisy know it was Myrtle that she hit? What I mean is, when she hit her, did she know that Myrtle was Tom's mistress?

Ellen: I don't think she hits her on purpose, if that's what you're asking. It says Daisy was just driving to try to make herself feel better. I think Myrtle ran after the car wanting to get . . . remember, Tom was driving the car before. I think she wants to get to Tom.

Jared: Yeah, the book says, "She ran out like she knew who it was." I think she definitely thought it was Tom.

Susan: Yeah, and here on page 151 it says Daisy turned away from her then back into her. She tried to avoid hitting her; she was just too scared. I wonder if Tom will find out.

Melissa: If he finds out it will be months or years because Gatsby . . .

Susan: Doesn't he say he'll take the fall? I think the truth will come out.

Dan: It would be best if she stays where she is and he takes the blame.

Chris: Will he still cover for her if she stays with Tom? Won't he be jealous?

Susan: I think he will still cover for her. I mean, it all comes down to this. He loves her.

Looking at this transcript, I celebrate that the pace of this second conversation has slowed considerably. As students sit in the circle, they look at one another and are really listening. An answer, clearly, does not mean the end of the question, and it has become OK to disagree; it's also great to be able to help each other out and corroborate a point. More students are referring to their books and quoting relevant passages.

However, there is still much missing from their discussion. Although they are making some inferences, they aren't following up their discussion of the characters in the book with any discussion of its relevance to their own lives. They are not addressing the author as a consciousness who created the book.

As we read the end of *The Great Gatsby,* we work on developing these skills, by applying the personal and external reality questions from the questioning circle. In one of the final discussions of the text, students supplied more sophisticated questions, but I had also prepared questions to support my students in their zone of proximal development. In general, if students do not yet frame questions that help them discuss an author's generalization, the structures of a text, or the significance of the text to their own lives, I am ready to intervene to help them discuss those issues. The following transcript is taken from a conversation that occurred after students read the last two chapters of the text.

Discussion clip, *The Great Gatsby,* Chapters 6 and 7, March 5

Joe: This book sucks. Who can you like when everyone is such a loser?

Melissa: No one. Daisy and Tom are such rich snobs. They don't care about anyone but themselves. They end up together because they deserve each other.

Brandon: Daisy should have ended up with Gatsby. He loved her so much. Why didn't she go with him?

Melissa: Because she's a rich girl, that's why. He didn't have enough money for her.

Stephen: Or the right name. Even though he made all that money just for her, he wasn't the same as Tom with his polo horses and going to Yale and all of that.

Marie: Well, plus he made all his money and stuff illegally. He was a bootlegger. That's kind of like, OK, this guy likes you so he's going to give you anything you want, but he's going to be a drug dealer to do it. Is that what you want?

Brandon: She's just a bitch that's all. She doesn't care about him.

Ms. Baker: What evidence do you have that Daisy doesn't care about Gatsby?

Brooke: She's sitting at her kitchen table with her husband at the end of Chapter 7, like "No big deal, I just killed someone and my lover is hanging out in the bushes, too bad for him."

Ellen: Yeah, she lets Gatsby take the blame for the whole thing.

Jared: And then she doesn't go to his funeral.

Ms. Baker: And why do you think she should care about Gatsby? Why does returning to her husband make her a bad person?

Jared: Well, if she cared about him, or if she was sorry about what she'd done, it wouldn't be so bad, but she doesn't seem to even care. Nothing changes. She doesn't change.

Brooke: Yeah, plus she knows he's a loser. He has affairs and she doesn't even care. I wouldn't let someone treat me like that.

Stephen: And Gatsby treats her better. He really loves her. He does all of that just to be with her—he makes all kinds of money because he knows she needs money, and he buys that house right across from hers—and he throws those huge parties just hoping she'll show up—man, all for nothing, then she disses him.

Brooke: But I don't know about him either. It seems sort of like a stalker. I mean, all these clippings about her life and buying that house right across from hers. It's sort of creepy. I mean, like, get over it already. She's married, move on.

Ms. Baker: Okay, now I think this might be really important. Does Gatsby love Daisy? Is it a healthy love? Would you want to love or be loved like that?

Stephen: Yeah, he loves her.

Susan: No way, he's obsessed.

Ms. Baker: Instead of revealing Gatsby and Daisy's love in chronological order, the way it occurred in time, the author reveals bits and pieces to us. Part of the story of Gatsby and Daisy is revealed in this next-to-last chapter. What do we learn? And why put it there?

Stephen: Yeah, that's why I say he loved her. It says he loved her. See on page 150, "I can't describe to you how surprised I was to find out I loved her." See, he loved her.

Dan: And he says she was the first "nice" girl he'd ever known.

Brooke: Yeah, but what's he mean by that? Look at all this other stuff. "He had never been in such a beautiful house before." Blah, blah, blah about her house and how many rooms it has, and lots of other guys had already been in love with her. Look at this, "It increased her *value* in his eyes." She's like a piece of meat, or something you buy at the store. She's just a thing to him.

Ms. Baker: Is this how you would want to love or be loved?

Chris: I certainly wouldn't want to love like that. It sucks to be him. I mean, he's totally obsessed, he gives up everything—eventually he even gets killed over her, and she's like "Oh well, too bad, sucks to be you—"

Brooke: Yeah, well, it's not too great to be her either. I mean, she's married to a guy who cheats on her, and the guy who says he's totally in love with her, really, maybe he's in love with the fact that she's wealthy. Those are some great choices.

In this discussion students have moved beyond talking about the characters. They have begun to discuss the significance of what's in the text, and how they feel about it. Through the text, these young men and women are also having an important discussion with one another. What does love mean? How do I want to love and be loved? What constitutes a healthy and good relationship?

Though they do much of the work on their own, and I try to let that work be done by them, I am not afraid of lending them strategies and questions that I think they should be asking. I will follow up by identifying the kinds of questions I asked, showing why they were important, and encouraging and supporting students to internalize and make use of these questions on their own. In the meantime, I will provide the assistance that is needed so they can move from where they are to where I would like them to be.

Teaching Questioning

Jeff likes to say that one goal of a really good teacher is to make herself continually more obsolete. In that spirit, it is not simply enough to question students, or even to help them to more and more competent discussion of those questions. Instead, it is necessary, eventually, to put the responsibility of asking the questions into their power as well.

I like to use literature circles to give students practice with all aspects of discussion skills. Using student-generated questions from literature circles is a great way to teach questioning skills. A typical question lesson might consist of a two-tiered discussion in which students prepare for and meet in literature circles in which all groups are discussing the same piece of literature. At the end of the discussion, students are asked to (1) evaluate the discussion director's questions; (2) star the two most effective questions; and (3) make a list of the reasons they feel those questions are most effective. All groups hand in their best questions, and at the beginning of the second class, a large-group discussion is held using the "best questions" of each group.

Although this large-group discussion will cover much of the same ground as the previous day, it is often richer as students hear new perspectives on questions they have already discussed and had a night to think about. More important for teaching questioning, students have eight to ten good questions to compare. At the end of the discussion I list the questions on the overhead, and students generate a list of characteristics of good discussion questions (see Figure 5.3). The next time we meet for literature circles, I ask students to evaluate their own questions based on this list of characteristics.

Another great strategy to help students generate good questions is to teach Christenbury's and Kelly's questioning circle to students and ask them to generate questions for discussion using the same model that I use. At first students may think the categories seem arbitrary and have trouble writing questions, but as they get a feel for the role of the "dense" question in shaping their choices for other questions, the overall quality of their questions improve. Figure 5.4 shows a set of

FIGURE 5.3
STUDENTS' LIST OF "GOOD QUESTIONS" AND
ANALYSIS OF THE QUALITIES OF GOOD QUESTIONS

Questions	Qualities of Good Discussion Questions
Why do Tom and Daisy seem so unhappy? Why did Nick want to move to Long Island? Why does Myrtle date Tom? Why didn't anyone go to Gatsby's funeral?	These kinds of questions make you think; you don't just say what happened, you have to think about why. Sometimes you have to imagine or use your own life to answer this kind of question. These questions also make you think about the characters like they are real people—you really have to pay attention to them and almost, sort of respect them.
Why does the author include that long description of Dr. T. J. Eckleberg? Why is everything gray and ashes in the valley of ashes? At the end of Chapter 1, what is Gatsby reaching for?	When someone asks a question like this, it makes me pay attention to some detail that I probably just skipped over. It's like it makes you slow down, pay more attention. This is the kind of question that makes everyone open their books and go back and read something over again.
Why is it so important that Nick turns 30? Gatsby seems like he just wants Daisy so he knows he can get what other men want; why does he care so much about stuff like that?	Mostly, questions should be real, like you should ask something that you really want to know. Like that question, about Nick, if someone in the class asks it, I think, "Yeah, good question, why is that a big deal?" But if the teacher asks it, then I just figure she already has an answer and I'm just guessing for the right one. I hate that. Yeah, you can ask a question you might already have an opinion about, but not one everybody knows the answer to. Your discussion question shouldn't be like, "What color is Gatsby's car?"

FIGURE 5.4
STUDENT-GENERATED QUESTIONING CIRCLE
QUESTIONS FOR *THE GREAT GATSBY*

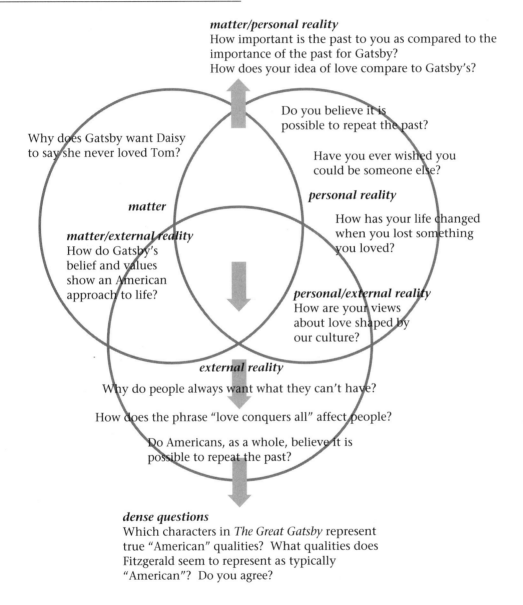

matter/personal reality
How important is the past to you as compared to the
importance of the past for Gatsby?
How does your idea of love compare to Gatsby's?

Do you believe it is
possible to repeat the past?

Why does Gatsby want Daisy
to say she never loved Tom?

Have you ever wished you
could be someone else?

personal reality

How has your life changed
when you lost something
you loved?

matter

matter/external reality
How do Gatsby's
belief and values
show an American
approach to life?

personal/external reality
How are your views
about love shaped by
our culture?

external reality
Why do people always want what they can't have?

How does the phrase "love conquers all" affect people?

Do Americans, as a whole, believe it is
possible to repeat the past?

dense questions
Which characters in *The Great Gatsby* represent
true "American" qualities? What qualities does
Fitzgerald seem to represent as typically
"American"? Do you agree?

student-generated questions using the questioning circles and based on their reading of *The Great Gatsby.*

Remember Joe, the boy who yelled at me, "You're judging me on how I treat my mother"? A year later he asked me to proofread his college application letter. It began this way, "Usually the teacher who most impacts your learning is the teacher you like the best. In my case this was decidedly not true." Joe's letter went on to say that the things he learned in English that year—to think critically about what he read and heard, to think carefully about his place in the world, and to question what and how he wanted to be in it—were things that would stay with him forever.

I'll protest that I did not teach him how to be in the world, but rather how to ask himself, others, and books the right questions about how he wanted to be in the world. The next year, during a break from college, Joe showed up with his Great Books list and asked, "Would you like to read a book with me this summer?" Each year since then we have read a book together, not as a teacher and a student, but as two readers with a text. And we discuss the book not as teacher and student, but as two questioners journeying into the unknowns that are our lives.

Questioning is a powerful teaching strategy. Besides giving a teacher information about students' comprehension and thinking, questioning and discussion provide opportunities for students to explore topics and argue points of view, to interact with one another, to speak as experts in the classroom, and to find out more about their own ideas and beliefs as they are discussed (Christenbury and Kelly 1983, 2). They also assist readers to engage authors and texts in democratic discussion—to ask questions about and perhaps even resist an author's message. In other words, teaching students to ask questions helps them behave as active citizens in their own lives and in the world. However, questioning can only be effective if it is handled in a way that honors students' responses, allows time for students to think and react, and covers areas of natural student interest. Like any other important literacy skill, questioning and discussion should be taught in order that students might continue to outgrow their own present abilities.

6

Building on Different Strengths to Make Reading Visible

In the end, children's knowledge of symbol usage allows them to stock an imaginary world with distant others, to deal with imaginaries in a highly regulated and rational way, to know the structures, events, and processes of the human society lying beyond the community, and to communicate and cooperate with people.

—White and Siegel, *Everyday Cognition*

*I*sn't it ironic that we often fail to practice what we preach? I recently taught a unit on tolerance to my Reading Lab students (see Chapter 8 for an explanation of Reading Lab) and one of my students helped *me* realize that tolerance and respect for differences was a concept that I paid lip service to, but failed to act upon.

We had just finished reading "A Rose for Charlie," a short nonfiction story about a young man who was thrown from a bridge in the neighboring town of Bangor, Maine, because he was homosexual. We had lively discussions about what led to Charlie's death, and one particularly reflective student, Brooke, explained that Charlie's demise was due to the fact that "he wasn't afraid to show people the real Charlie."

One can well imagine the animated and heated debates that took place surrounding that subject. I had organized a unit around the topic of tolerance because it is a real issue for students, is of great importance, and is one that highly engages them. Although the next text in my unit on tolerance, Gary Paulsen's *Nightjohn,* wasn't quite as controversial as "A Rose for Charlie" (a story that was much closer to home) it *did* contain the "shock quality" that helped grab the readers' attention, which then led to more interesting discussions. *Nightjohn* was a good segue to showing how people's lack of tolerance often leads to devastating results. Paulsen's story is about a young slave named Sarny who learns how to read. Her teacher, Nightjohn, a fellow slave, pays a harsh price for teaching Sarny to read and write—his toes are cut off with an ax.

The student who helped me eventually see my own lack of tolerance—in my case a lack of respect for students' learning differences—was a young woman named Brooke. Throughout the tolerance unit, I was impressed by Brooke's insights. Her contributions to our discussions about *Nightjohn* and the Holocaust literature we had read in the past were evidence that she had personally responded to these texts. The readings moved Brooke somehow, and she was always ready to contribute to a class discussion. However, even though she certainly was never at a loss for words, she had not yet realized the strategies necessary to read a text authorially, which was a major focus of my teaching at this point.

As Jeff discusses in Chapter 3, a consideration of the author is an expert strategy essential to democratic reading, one that often escapes both the struggling and more accomplished reader. Rabinowitz and Smith (1998) argue that reading literature is a highly conventional activity, and authors count on their readers to interpret texts in certain ways. A reader can enter into a conversation with an author about issues that matter to them both by thinking about an author's purposes, the reasons he had for constructing his text in a certain way, and the message this construction was meant to convey. This active reconstruction of an author's meaning leads to a conversation with an author about essential life issues through which the reader can construct her own identity and stake out her own beliefs.

But before I could guide Brooke in her authorial reading of a text, her behavior began to change. I assigned a three-page comparison/ contrast paper about *Nightjohn,* which I asked students to contrast with one of our previous readings. I wanted students to get at the authorial generalizations of these texts through the various ways authors constructed their characters and had them change. I thought that a close comparison study of the texts would highlight how different authors constructed different kinds of stories to make different points. Some of my students seemed to do well with this assignment, but it certainly didn't push and support Brooke to examine the textual constructions or to converse with the authors as I had hoped.

While the majority of students busied themselves with the assignment, Brooke held her frowning face up with her fist and doodled on a piece of lined paper. I was circulating around the room, checking on students' progress, guiding and assisting where I was needed, when I noticed her. "Hey, what's going on?" I asked. "You must have some great ideas to write about since you've been contributing so much to our discussions."

Brooke didn't look convinced. "No, not really," she said sullenly.

After some prodding, Brooke finally explained what was wrong. "Look, I haven't gotten a good grade on any of your writing assignments. I think the whole idea is stupid, anyway. You know that I read the stuff—I tell you in every class what I think of the reading, so why do I have to write about it?"

I tried to explain to Brooke why I thought the comparison/contrast papers might help her discover and understand the ways that the authors constructed the texts to make particular points. Brooke didn't appear to be listening. She shook her head and said, "I'm sorry, but this isn't how I learn and understand things."

"Well, it's the way you *should* learn and know things!" I retorted. My first reaction was to defend an assignment that had served me well in my years as a teacher. So why did I have this nagging feeling in my stomach that told me Brooke might have a point? Granted, the writing assignments that I gave my students had served me well—they had even benefited some of my students—but what about the several students like Brooke who just didn't seem to gain from this? A flurry of questions stormed through my mind: Why do I believe that writing a comparison/contrast paper is *the* way instead of *a* way? Why can't I get at my purpose, which is to teach authorial reading to students, through other means? Why can't I use Brooke's strengths and preferred ways of knowing as a means of getting her to think *and* write better?

The more I thought about it, the more I realized Brooke was right. How could I argue with her logic? Students could certainly express themselves in ways other than by writing a comparison/contrast paper. Brooke had her own strengths: she was articulate and made herself clear to others; she was passionate and could defend her ideas; and she questioned and challenged others (as she had just demonstrated). So why couldn't I allow her to use those strengths to her advantage? What more did I want from her?

Well, for one thing, I wanted Brooke to write, and to write well. Writing is an important skill, and I hoped to teach my students to communicate in a variety of ways, including written communication. The problem was that writing was the *only* form of communication that I had been privileging, or at least grading, in my classes. For Brooke, this presented quite a challenge; her ideas were represented to some degree in her written work, but she had difficulty putting into writing exactly what she wanted to say. Brooke's organization wasn't the best, although the structure of her paper was acceptable. Her writing was guarded and dull, and she definitely didn't shine as a writer. Brooke was, without argument, an external processor who contributed and gained the most when she was able to react to and build upon the comments of her peers—oral communication was her niche.

I usually saved Brooke's papers to correct last because I knew that they would fall short of my expectations for written work—and I felt guilty about this. In spite of the fact that Brooke was a critical thinker and an intelligent, reflective, and compassionate person, she earned consistently low grades in my class. This was primarily because all of my assignments involved writing—Brooke's weakness. To compensate for my deficiencies as a teacher, I adjusted my grading scale to a 1 to 10 system. I suppose that I unintentionally wanted to camouflage each 6 and 7 that decent, well-deserving students like Brooke received from me—after all, a *6* sounds a whole lot better than a *60*.

Instead of rationalizing and defending the grades that I issued students, I should have been examining alternative methods for assessing what they had read and learned. And I should have been looking for ways to support and assist them into writing about literature . . . so they could be helped to know what they were thinking, and know how to put that into a powerful form.

In my past practice, I had assigned an occasional project or speech, but finding them monotonous, time-consuming, and difficult to grade, I resorted to the comfort of a writing assignment, a more expedient choice complete with a rubric for scoring that I had created. And now, I considered whether I was assisting students enough through the writing assignments with the steps of knowing how to access material to write about (procedural knowledge of substance) and how to put this material into a form (procedural knowledge of form).

Like an intolerant character from one of the texts we had just read, I was trapped in a "one-response-fits-all" mode and dangerously assumed that all students had an equal opportunity in my class. I had most wanted to teach them to build from their strengths to address their weaknesses. Why had I failed to see that during my unit on teaching tolerance, I did not learn to accept *their* diversity?

Questions led to more questions, and I began to think about how to assist Brooke in improving her reading skills through an avenue other than writing, and how, perhaps, to use her strengths to support her writing skills. Even though writing was more difficult for Brooke, did her lack of skill mean that she could never advance? And if I was unwilling to accept the fact that Brooke's writing skills would always be average, how could I assist her in becoming a better writer?

At about this time, Jeff had been using a method called Symbolic Story Representation (Wilhelm 1997) or Symbolic Representation Interview (SRI) (Enciso 1992) with students in my school. This technique is a kind of "reading manipulative" that allows students to demonstrate in a presentation *what* they are reading and *how* they are reading it through the use of objects or cutouts. Jeff had demonstrated how the technique could be adapted to assist students to use new reading strategies. Could the SRI help Brooke improve her reading, how she shared her reading, and maybe her written communication skills, too?

I was enrolled in Jeff's Young Adult Literature course at the University of Maine at the time that I read *"You Gotta BE the Book,"* and Jeff was working in my school, so I had ample opportunity to learn more about SRIs. In our Young Adult Literature class, Jeff showed us a powerful video of Walter, a young struggling reader who successfully articulates what he has learned from reading a tale called "The Fisherman and His Wife" by using symbolic cutouts and found objects both to tell the story plot (the WHAT—the landscape of action), and to explain how he read and experienced the story (the HOW—the landscape of the reader's consciousness). Jeff's description of Walter's struggle with writing convinced me that I *had* to provide the opportunity to use SRI with students like Brooke. I wanted to teach and sup-

In completing an SRI, the easier of these two challenges is the act of describing the WHAT of the story. The more difficult task for students is to explain HOW they read a text.

port my students in new ways of reading and awareness—to dignify different kinds of knowledge, different ways of representing ideas, and support the use of new strategies—and the SRI seemed like a powerful tool to accomplish all of these goals.

Symbolic Story Representation

The SRI is a technique that assists readers by providing them with an outlet for explaining WHAT a specific text is about and HOW they read it.

The SRI originated as a laboratory technique to open a window into the hidden processes of readers, and to make those processes visible so they could be studied and discussed with readers. Jeff learned this technique from a professor at the University of Wisconsin, Pat Enciso (see Enciso 1992), and he adapted it in various ways to make it a teaching technique that could be used by all the kids in a classroom. He has also experimented with various adaptations of SRI for teaching particular strategies and for approaching particular kinds of texts.

In many ways, the SRI is similar to assigning protocols for reading (see Jeff's use of "Old Horse," in Chapter 3). When writing a protocol, students record what they are seeing, thinking, feeling, questioning, and doing as they read or are read to. The SRI examines the same things, but it can be accomplished through means other than writing, namely through the use of *art*, *artifacts*, and *talk*. This is what made the SRI so appealing for students like Brooke.

When completing an SRI, the student uses an artifact or cutout to symbolize herself as a reader during her reading experience. Some students simply choose to use a cutout (or several cutouts) to represent themselves as readers. They might use a picture of themselves or a combination of pictures and artifacts to help them talk about their thoughts during the reading experience. Others challenge themselves even more and take their symbolic journey to new heights by making their "reader cutout(s)" symbolic, too, in a way that represents *how* they read and responded to the text. I hoped the SRI might help spark creative ideas and focus Brooke's thoughts, which could then assist her in creating an interesting and organized piece of writing

How to Create an SRI: Brooke's Example

It's important to note that SRI is a highly flexible technique that can be adapted to meet students in their ZPD, and can also be adapted to support the use of specific strategies. SRIs can be used to assist students to simply summarize and tell a story. I have seen Jeff use them to assist students simply to become aware that as readers they "see" and "participate" in story worlds, but I have also seen him use them to assist students to read for main idea, to understand and evaluate characters, to recognize and interpret irony, and a host of other particular strategies.

In this chapter, I am demonstrating how I used a particular kind of SRI to help students converse with authors, and this is reflected in my planning sheet (Figure 6.2) later in the chapter. Please be aware that you can adapt the technique to fit your particular purposes with particular students.

Step 1: Select a Scene   *The first step in creating an SRI is to ask students to decide on a scene that they would like to dramatize. This should be a scene to which they had a strong response. It should also be a scene that is pertinent to the "big picture" of the story. Since SRIs take time to create and perform, students should choose one rich scene on which to focus so that they can provide a richly textured representation of what they read and how they read it.*

Brooke chose Robert Cormier's novel, *We All Fall Down*, as her text for her SRI. However, she had some difficulty deciding which scene to select, so I assisted her in the following way. I asked her to pretend that she was Robert Cormier and to create a set of visual tableaux depicting the five most important scenes from the book—scenes that would absolutely require illustrations if artwork were to be added. Once she had identified those scenes, I asked her to role-play Cormier and explain to me why she felt those scenes were important. After the role-playing exercise, Brooke considered these scenes again, and then she placed them in order of importance to the meaning of the story. This activity helped Brooke think about the text in a different way (to move beyond her personal response to consider significance from an author's point of view), and it also assisted her in selecting a scene that was critical to the entire story.

Brooke begins her SRI by giving an overview of *We All Fall Down*. She has decided to dramatize the "trashing scene" in this novel, in which Buddy, a main character, and his friends enter a stranger's house in a drunken stupor. They vandalize the home by urinating, defecating, and vomiting throughout the house until the home owners' daughter, Karen, returns.

Step 2: Consider How You Read

Ask students to reflect on how *they read the text, then have them create a "reader cutout" to symbolize how they situated themselves in the scene. Tell students that this cutout will help their audience understand how they involved themselves in their story while they read. Students should move the reader cutout to show where they are throughout the scene and what they are doing as a reader. For example, the reader cutout might move close to a character the reader cares about. Students can use just one reader cutout or several if they want to demonstrate that they took several different stances or positions as a reader. For example, the reader cutout might shift into the form of a question mark if the reader has a question at a particular moment in her reading. The cutout should reveal things about the reader as a reader of this specific scene.*

It is evident from Brooke's enthusiasm and expressions that, as a struggling reader and writer, she welcomes the opportunity to test her knowledge in an alternative format to writing. She has used tiny straws to create character cutouts, or puppetlike representations. She represents herself as a reader with a small straw attached to a cutout, a colored picture of herself, which she has photocopied on a transparency. Brooke explains, "I always read as if I'm the main character of the book or the character I can most relate to. In this case it was Jane Jerome. I felt like I was Jane, so I used a cutout of what I thought she'd look like and made a transparent picture of myself to put in front of her to show that I was becoming her as I read."

Step 3: Writing Down the Moves

Ask students to list several "moves" (meaning-making strategies) that they made as readers during their scene. They should explain strategies like noticing details and interpreting them, visualizing, connecting to, feeling, thinking about, questioning, or anything else they are aware of doing as they read.

I suggest to students that they reread their scene to help them remember the moves they made and to think about how to demonstrate these in the SRI, and ask them to take notes as they do so. I model how to do this kind of protocol by reading aloud a scene from a book that I'm currently reading. While I'm reading, I stop at various intervals and interject my own thoughts, feelings, and questions to demonstrate what "moves" I make as a reader, moves that would go on my own list of notes if I were preparing my own SRI. Next, I think out loud about how I might demonstrate those moves with my own reader cutout. Modeling during this step is essential because struggling readers especially may not realize the purpose of this activity, which is to help readers realize and emulate what the experts do—visualize and carry on a dialogue with a text as they read.

You will see on the SRI Planning Sheet (Figure 6.2) that students are asked to list their "moves" in preparation for doing their SRI. It's worth noting here that the SRIs themselves provide students with both environmental assistance (from the assignment and from the cutouts they use to tell the story) and with an additional layer of peer assistance, as they teach each other about reading "moves" through their SRI performances and discuss these moves and their meaning.

In demonstrating her first "move," Brooke begins by sharing some of the thoughts she has as she is reading the scene. She tells us that when she reads she is more apt to "side with" or think about the happenings in the story from the perspective of a character who is both female and close to her own age. This realization surprises Brooke; she says she hasn't thought about it before. Now she wonders why this is, what it reveals about her as a reader, and if she might try to relate to a male character or an older one.

Brooke, in describing her second move, says that in this scene she doesn't allow herself "to be Karen when I read because that would be too scary." She discusses how Jane Jerome, the sister to the victim in the trashing scene, is a more sensible character, and how it feels better to read the story from her point of view. Brooke maintains that "being Jane Jerome is tolerable; being Karen would be frightening."

In her third move, Brooke describes how Buddy and a group of his friends enter a stranger's home, destroy their property, and deface the house. As she speaks, she holds up her image on the straw and says, "The first thing that popped into my head as I was reading was to yell at them, 'why are you doing that to people—even people you don't know? What's wrong with you?' " Notice how the reader cutout requirement provides an opportunity for students to think about how they bring meaning to a text, and how it encourages them to do so in new ways. In my observations, students often fail to realize that others could read the exact same text in a completely different way. The cutout requirement makes that notion apparent and visible.

I asked her at this point about why the author would have written such a scene. Brooke thought the author wanted her to be scared and disgusted by this behavior. She then thought that the author may have wanted her to be closer to Karen so she could feel more deeply the hurt caused by such actions. Considering what she thought the overall purpose of the author to be, she felt the scene was a good one, and though it did scare and anger her she felt this was the author's purpose. She emphasized that she did not want to experience the scene any more intensely than she already had.

In her fourth move, she continues to talk about the events as they unfold during the trashing scene and Brooke moves her reader cutout to explain how angry she feels when Karen (the main character's sister) enters the home. Holding up the cutout that represents Brooke as a reader, she says that this scene was "just like those dumb horror movies where the girl goes down the cellar stairs when she knows that there's some kind of monster or creature lurking around at the bottom."

Finally, in her fifth move, Brooke explains that she knew she was "being suckered by the author" because he shared with her things the character didn't know. She was glad to distance herself from Karen so it was not too scary for her. Still, she can't understand why a fourteen-year-old girl isn't worried when the door to her house has been left open. Brooke finds it odd that Karen doesn't hear the trashing going on and run away. She talks about how terrified she would have been if that had happened at her house.

Step 4: *Ask students to consider the author of their story. Students will think about*
Considering *and create an author cutout or symbolic representation that best describes their*
the Author *conception of the author.*

The expectation for using an author cutout is to help the reader to think about the author, to consider how he constructed this scene, and to assist an authorial reading of the text that considers the author's purpose and meaning. The authorial reader considers the reasons why an author composed a text in a particular way and reacts to that.

In her attempt at authorial reading, Brooke discusses how the author talks about the Avenger and how he witnesses the trashing but makes no effort to get help. At this point, she explains her author cutout (actually, symbolic representation in this case), which is the Stephen King novel *Bag of Bones*. She tells us she considers Robert Cormier to be as "freaky as Stephen in the ways that he thinks. Plus I think he wants to scare and shock me, which is just like Stephen. I think he wants me to feel this to tune me in to evil and how it hurts people." She adds, "He's a great writer, and like Stephen, they both always find or make up twists or awful details to their stories, like rapes or murders." I find Brooke's first-name reference to the authors interesting because she is conversing with them in a highly personal way—a way in which most readers are not accustomed.

Once again, Brooke holds up the author symbol (the Stephen King book) and the picture of herself. She holds her arms out wide to separate the two. She is talking about how the author describes what Harry Flowers, the ringleader, does to the girl. The author mentions that Harry holds Karen up against the wall, but he doesn't say for sure that he rapes her. Next, she describes Cormier's depiction of how Harry pushes Karen down the cellar stairs. Brooke tells us that during this time she has a "feeling of total disgust. When the author tells about what Harry Flowers did to Karen. How disgusting. Just the thought makes me sick. I don't like that Robert allowed this to happen to her, no matter what his point is, so I am getting as far away from him as I can." She implied here, as Rabinowitz and Smith suggest (1998), that authors must be responsible to their characters, and that readers should resist authorial visions and meaning that they find immoral.

Step 5: Considering Significance

Because I wanted students to consider the author's message in this SRI, I instructed them to list three general life ideas or motifs that the author seems to repeat and communicate throughout the scene. Students will now think about and create a cutout or symbolic representation that depicts these ideas.

Also ask students to create cutouts or symbolic representations of the setting, the characters in the scene, and any ideas or forces that they wish to dramatize. They may want to use objects to represent some of these things, and to assist students through this process you may want to do a mini-lesson on the differences between a prop and a symbol. Students tend to select realistic props (a football to represent a football), rather than symbols (a maze to represent the intricacies of a football game). I sometimes require students to use a certain number of symbols to push them beyond their tendency to rely on props.

Encourage students to dramatize *rather than to just hold up cutouts and props and talk about them. Explaining that their SRI performance is sort of like a puppet show might help. Drama gives students the opportunity to be even more creative; tell them that creating a drama will help their audience to visualize their story.*

Brooke mentions that several themes and motifs repeat themselves throughout the trashing scene. The first major motif that she notices is that during this particular scene the characters seem to have no regard for others, as is especially evident in their treatment of Karen. She also notices that Harry Flowers and his followers have no consideration for Buddy, one of "their own."

Another recurring theme she identifies is that the characters with personal problems turn to illegal activity in ways that are self-defeating. For instance, Buddy turns to alcohol to redeem himself when all it does is bring him down, and Harry, a character with a seemingly idyllic life, turns to destruction of property and others to hide from his own feelings of neglect and abandonment.

Finally, Brooke observes that people react differently in a group. She makes the astute comment that Buddy probably would have behaved differently if he had been with people other than those in the Harry Flowers gang, and she talks about how Cormier designed the text so that she would feel compassion for Buddy. She also notices that if Karen had been with a group of her peers, her behavior might have been different, too. Brooke tells us that she might not have thought the situation through clearly enough if she had been alone like Karen. If Karen had been with a group of her friends, she might never have gone into the house with the door opened and various items knocked over.

She notices how the characters are associated with images of bodily offal and sees that as a comment on their actions.

Brooke interprets Robert Cormier's message during this scene as "those who are destroyed, destroy." She discusses how Harry, who has seemingly led the perfect life, was probably neglected by his wealthy and powerful father, an attorney, and that likewise, Buddy was all but forgotten by his mother and father, whose lives were consumed by their divorce. Brooke represents these ideas about life or motifs with a fire cutout. She used orange construction paper and made big flames tipped in yellow and outlined in red to create the cutout. She explains that Cormier wants his readers to understand that people are not inherently bad. She talks about fire and says, "When it's used for a good reason, it's useful, but when fire is used the wrong way, it becomes a bad force—evil. Buddy and Harry, after being abused themselves, became bad and evil things, too." When she was asked if she accepted this message of the author, she said that she did.

Step 6: Consider the Author's Message   *Ask students to answer the following questions to assist in their understanding of the scene. Encourage them to create cutouts or symbols for any of these ideas.*

- What do you notice (particular ideas, images, or motifs) within the text that leads you to believe you should pay attention to them? How can you represent this textual coding in your SRI?
- Why do you think the author drew your attention to these ideas? What do you think is her own "take" or generalization about these issues? What in the text makes you think so? How will you show how you noticed and interpreted these authorial moves with moves of your own?
- Please explain how you agree, would adapt, or resist the author's generalization about these issues. How will you show this response through your reader cutout and other cutouts or objects? How has this scene helped inform your thinking about the theme of our unit study?

Next, Brooke demonstrates how she pays attention to the text and remains engaged in authorial reading. Brooke explains that Cormier devotes several chapters to Buddy's troubled home life; in fact, she suggests that he juxtaposes his chapters to illustrate Buddy's involvement with the gang and his family problems. Brooke uses the chapters themselves to represent the textual coding of the author. She flips back and forth showing how one chapter is about Buddy's home life and the next chapter is about his gang involvement. She mentions that perhaps she should have included a symbolic representation of a family in turmoil (to represent Buddy's domestic problems) and a pair of handcuffs to represent what might potentially happen to Buddy if he is caught in illegal activities encouraged by his new gang of friends.

She argues that Cormier specifically constructed this scene to elicit an empathic reading, "so I would feel sorry for Buddy and see how complicated things are—not rush to judgment." Despite Buddy's complicity in the trashing, Brooke believes that Cormier wants his readers to feel sorry for Buddy and understand his situation. She goes on to explain that she knows children who have lived through divorces and she explains that she understands how difficult it is to experience that. Brooke then says, "I do feel sorry for Buddy in a way, but I think that we can't just go out and do bad things because we've had bad experiences."

Step 7: Encouraging the Extras   *Ask students to think about and create extra creative elements that could add to their dramatization of the scene (e.g., music, symbolic representations, found objects, backgrounds, etc.). Students should also explain how these "extras" demonstrate something essential about what they read and how they read it.*

Once students have read either a self-selected text or a required reading assignment, I suggest you have students begin the SRI by using the "Guidelines for Creating an SRI" (Figure 6.1) and the "SRI Planning Sheet" (Figure 6.2). The guidelines provide students with a step-by-step explanation of how to prepare an SRI. The SRI planning sheet then steps in to help organize and focus the students' thoughts on both the general and expert processes of reading. As you will see, the second half of my planning sheet focuses students on authorial reading. When you model an SRI for your students and design a planning sheet, be sure to focus on the particular strategies you want to teach.

After students complete the planning sheet, I recommend requiring a conference with either a peer or the teacher prior to the SRI presentation. This provides students with an opportunity to push their thinking, provides them with additional assistance, and helps them to focus their thoughts and rehearse their dramatization.

I have good luck by allowing students to start their SRI in class by filling out a brainstorming sheet and beginning to find or create cutouts, and then giving them a couple of days on their own to finish up and rehearse. In this way, I use a maximum of two class periods to prepare and perform the SRI. Sometimes students want to watch the best or most creative ones and so I may also plan time for that as a whole class on a following day.

As I noted in step 3 above, when I introduce SRI, I model one that explores my own reading (I do/you watch, from Figure 1.1, Chapter 1). After that, I do one *with* students and ask them to help me use and converse with an author cutout about the textual construction and meaning (I do/you help). Then I have them prepare one of their own with my help in the form of a brainstorming sheet and conferencing (You do/I help). At this point they are often able to perform quite good ones without assistance (You do/I watch). Later on, I might introduce a new strategy to be used in SRI and we would repeat this sequence.

Some students may need assistance to identify important scenes and learn how to interpret them. In Brooke's case, she had intended to focus her SRI on a minor scene in her book, *We All Fall Down*. She was interested in the conversation that existed between a main character and her three friends. Brooke believed that because she found the

FIGURE 6.1
GUIDELINES FOR CREATING AN SRI TO ASSIST AUTHORIAL READING*

Step 1: Select a Scene

The first step in creating an SRI is to decide on a scene that you would like to dramatize. This should be a scene to which you had a strong response. It should also be a scene that is pertinent to the "big picture" of the story. Since SRIs take time to create and perform, you should choose one rich scene on which to focus so that you can explore that one scene in detail. Decide on the important characters, setting, ideas, and forces that will be essential in re-creating and dramatizing this scene.

Step 2: Consider How You Read

Create a cutout or representation of yourself as the reader that will help us to understand how you read and involved yourself in this particular scene. You can use one single cutout or create several to use if you felt like you took different stances or positions as a reader at different points during your reading of a scene. For example, your reader cutout might shift into the form of a question mark if you had a question at a particular time during your reading. The cutout should reveal things about you as a reader of this scene (where you were, how you felt, what kinds of things you did).

You will move your reader cutout to show where you are throughout the scene and what you are doing as a reader. For example, you might move your reader close to a character you care about.

Step 3: Writing Down the Moves

List five moves you made as readers during your scene. You will find space to list these moves on your planning sheet. Moves are things like noticing details and interpreting them, visualizing parts of your scene or characters, or connecting to something that's happening. Anything you feel, think about, or question during your reading is a move. Anything else you are aware of doing as you read is okay, too!

When you perform your SRI you will move your cutouts around to dramatize what happened in the story and _how_ you read it (your moves). It is essential to make extensive use of your reader cutout(s) so that you can demonstrate how you read the scene.

---

*Most of these steps are generally useful for creating an SRI. Steps 4 and 5 and 6 described here are more particular to supporting the goal of reaching an authorial reading. These steps could be revised to support the use of other strategies.

Step 4: Consider the Author

Consider the author of your story. Create an author cutout or symbolic representation that best describes the author. Think about how she constructed your scene. Why was the scene important to the book? Why did the author write it the way she did? How did you react to the way she wrote it? There are spaces for you to answer these questions on your planning sheet.

Step 5: Consider Significance of Textual Details

Create cutouts or symbolic representations for important characters, setting(s), ideas, and forces, or you may find objects to represent things you want to dramatize.

The cutouts can be symbolic (ex. a gun for a soldier, a taco for a selfish person all "wrapped up" in herself, etc.), or realistic props (designed to really look like the person/thing they represent). You may also use a real object to represent characters and ideas (dice for a risky situation or a "gamble," an orange for a person with inner strength, playing cards or game pieces, etc.).

On your planning sheet, list three general life ideas or motifs that the author seems to repeat and communicate throughout the scene. Think about and create a cutout or symbolic representation that depicts each of these ideas.

Step 6: Considering the Author's Message

Finish answering the questions on your planning sheet. These questions will help you better understand your scene. I encourage you to create cutouts or symbols for any new ideas that come up.

Step 7: Include Extras

Think about and create extra creative elements that could add to your dramatization of the scene (e.g., music, symbolic representations, found objects, backgrounds, etc.). You should be able to explain how these "extras" demonstrate something essential about what you read and how you read it.

Step 8: Provide Drama!

Remember, your goal is to *dramatize* your scene. Rather just holding up cutouts and props and telling about them, move them around. Think of it like a play or a puppet show! Be as creative as you like; it will help your audience visualize your scene!

Step 9: Rehearse!

There is an eight- to ten-minute time limit, so be sure to rehearse. The more you practice, the more focused you'll be!

Step 10: Anticipate Questions

You will perform in groups of three to five students, and they will be asking you questions about your scene and how you read it. Try to predict the kinds of questions they will ask you and consider how you will answer.

FIGURE 6.2
SRI PLANNING SHEET FOR SRI TO ASSIST AUTHORIAL READING

Due date: _____

Name _____

Before you begin to prepare your SRI, please answer the following questions to make sure that have thought through how your presentation will meet all criteria. After answering the following questions, please share them with a member of your reading group and then with me. This preconference is required prior to your SRI presentation.

General Processes

1. How does your reader cutout(s) reveal what you did as a reader and how you situated yourself in this scene? How does it describe you as a reader?

2. List five "moves" that you made (things you did, felt, saw, noticed, connected to, thought about, questioned, etc.) as you read this scene.

    A.

    B.

    C.

    D.

    E.

Considering the Author

1. Describe how your author cutout/symbolic representation shows when you considered the author and what you think about the author of this scene or short story. Consider your thinking about how the author constructed this scene and what meaning you think she is trying to convey through that construction.

A. What do you think of the author? How will you show this?

B. What do you think of how the author constructed this scene? How will you show this?

C. What do you think the author means to communicate in this scene? How will you represent this?

2. List three general images, life ideas, or motifs that the author seems to repeat during this scene. How will you represent these with cutouts or symbolic representations?

A.

B.

C.

Discussing/Presenting Your Authorial Reading

1. What do you notice within the text that leads you to believe you should pay attention to these particular ideas?

2. How did you represent this textual coding in your SRI?

3. Why do you think the author drew your attention to these ideas? What do you think is her own "take" or generalization about these issues? How will you show how you noticed and interpreted these authorial moves with moves of your own?

4. Please explain how you agree, would adapt, or resist the author's generalization about these issues? How will you show this response through your reader cutout and other cutouts or objects? How has this scene helped inform your thinking about the theme of our unit study?

5. What extra creative elements did you add to your scene and why (e.g. music, symbolic representations (found objects), backgrounds, etc.)? How do these demonstrate something essential about what you read and how you read it?

exchange interesting, this automatically made the scene important. She needed teacher assistance to understand *how* to choose a scene that was not just interesting to her, but of particular significance to the book as a whole.

It is important to note that modeling and assistance are also necessary during the interview phase that follows the SRI performance if students are to ask the types of questions that extend understanding of our reading, of a story, and of the perspective it presents. A question like, "What made you decide to use fire to represent destruction?" is useful and it encourages the speaker to think more about the *how,* or the process that he went through to read and complete the SRI. A question like "at what points were you aware of the author?" or "why did you represent the author as a priest?" push the reader to consider the author and his treatment of characters and other textual features.

Once students learn how to question and converse with one another, and question and converse with authors, they frequently become engaged in lively conversations with their peers concerning the text and its implications. They question one another and exchange ideas, which challenges students to reflect on their own roles as readers.

Both Hillocks and Vygotsky stressed that we must help students be successful by starting with what they *can* do on their own, in order to lead them from there to accomplish what they *cannot yet* do on their own. All students can be successful if instruction meets their strengths in their zone of actual development and builds from there.

The SRI is a prosthetic device for making reading concrete and, therefore, more visible, more available to the reader and others, and more amenable to social support. This is partly why I encourage the student's audience to ask questions to push his or her reading, thinking, and explanations.

Why Do SRIs Work with Students?

Privileging Student Voices

Brooke's and other students' personal responses to the readings in our unit on differences had been impressive in themselves. But at the same time, Brooke was teaching me that using one method to represent and assess her learning was insufficient. Students like Brooke, at least some of the time, deserve an opportunity to demonstrate their intelligence in a way that suits them.

I decided that by assisting the reading, thinking, and writing of my students, the SRI would serve multiple purposes. Best of all, the SRI would enable me to teach from Brooke's strongest self to help her become a stronger self. It would address weaknesses through her strengths. It would be a democratic move because it would privilege new ways of knowing and learning, and the voices of my students who did not excel at writing would be heard more clearly.

So it was at the end of this unit that I decided to allow students to pursue free reading around our theme and to perform an SRI, and it was this assignment that resulted in Brooke's insightful analysis of *We All Fall Down*. I hoped the SRIs would help them share their reading and encourage concluding discussions around the theme before I made a final writing assignment. While SRIs focus on depicting an episode from a book, I wanted to be sure that my students understood their chosen texts as a whole. To address this, I required students to give a verbal overview of the whole text, and then to focus on the particular scene that they found most powerful or important.

> The SRI is a springboard for sharing how students read particular text segments and therefore of sharing ways of reading.

Some students included scary music as an extra for a Stephen King novel, some of my students have even brought food into class to depict a meal that a hungry character had been longing for. As an extra, Brooke used a champagne bottle to describe Buddy, and she explained that "alcohol is a depressant, and the bottle represents how down and depressed Buddy is during this scene." She talked about how Buddy's parents are getting divorced, and how Buddy just wants to "fit in." Brooke said she viewed Buddy as a "trasher with a conscience," which, she suggests, might be the reason that he turns to alcohol—to absolve himself of guilt. She moved her reader cutout toward the champagne bottle to show that although she doesn't approve of what Buddy is doing (trashing, drinking), she understood how complicated his life was and felt sorry for him. She explained that she wanted to create a special symbol for Buddy because he was the main character and the reason that the book was written. She explains that the bottle also represents Buddy because "all of his emotions are bottled up and he really doesn't have anyone to talk to."

The SRIs supported student discussion by giving them "objects to think with and talk about." If students are able to better understand and make new kinds of meaning with a text by discussing it in this way, then they will be better prepared to write.

Thinking About
Thinking

For the struggling reader, a description of the *what* of a scene might suffice in an SRI—that, in itself, can be quite a demanding task for a student who is not an avid reader. The *what* would simply be an enactment of key events that occurred throughout the story. However, for those students who are capable of describing the *what*, the more exciting and challenging component of this assignment is telling the *how*. By describing *how* they read a text, the students are automatically engaged in metacognition.

In completing an SRI, the easier of these two challenges is the act of describing the WHAT of the story. The more difficult task for students is to explain HOW they read a text.

Metacognition, according to researchers such as Flavell (1979), is the ability to think about thinking. Vygotsky, remember, was very keen that learners be able to name and talk their way through what they were learning. Metacognition is a highly reflective process that requires students to consider and reflect upon their problem-solving strategies and cognitive steps (in the reading experience, in this case). In an effort to have students name the moves they make as readers, I tried to incorporate activities that required students to reflect on their thinking or cognition. I soon found that SRI was a powerful Vygotskian tool for assisting my students to make new moves, approach new kinds of texts, and make new kinds of meaning with texts. It helped me support and nudge students like Brooke to richer and more competent performances.

Assisting Students
with Authorial
Reading

Authorial reading is clearly important for reasons outlined in Chapter 3. However, I had reasons of my own for wanting to assist my students to read authorially. For example, when my students read a book like *Huckleberry Finn*, I wanted them to understand that Mark Twain used offensive terminology to describe people of color because he was trying to represent an undeniable historical period that brought shame to our nation, not because he was racist. On the other hand, as Michael Smith points out (1998), the way that Tom treats Jim in the final chapters is certainly unethical, and if Twain allows Jim to endure this suffering for the sake of humor, then we may choose to resist Twain's treatment of Jim. When I asked my students to make and use an author cutout of Twain during SRIs of these scenes from *Huckleberry Finn*, students were helped to understand the subtext of the story and to converse with Twain about the construction and meaning of his text. The text—and Twain's hand in creating it—was made more visible and available to my students through their use of SRI.

*Students
Enjoy SRIs*

While the SRI assists
the development of
new interpretive
moves and privileges
unique ways of
knowing, it also fits in
with Hillocks' and
Vygotsky's arguments
about the impor-
tance of "playfulness"
and "fun" in the
process of learning.

Increased reading competence and cognitive gains for students make SRIs appealing to teachers, but what makes the SRI appealing to students? The purpose of the SRI assignment is to privilege the unique voice of the student and to provide her with an outlet for sharing different ways of knowing in the classroom. The student's task is to retell a portion of a text she read and how she read it by focusing on a powerful scene and using symbols and props to depict important characters, settings, ideas, and forces at play in the text. According to Gary, one of my former students, the SRI "gave me a chance to show what I know."

The Significance of SRI Symbols

In one of my classes a student used a series of African masks to depict herself as the reader. She had read an old African folktale, and she discussed the ways that she had taken on the persona of certain characters. She claimed that the masks represented her as a reader because although she identified with the characters, she was conscious of the fact that she was herself beneath the mask. In other words, she recognized that she had achieved a kind of double vision. She said, "In one instance, I was a member of the African tribe, but at the same time, I was thinking about the story from my own perspective": the point of view of a sixteen-year-old sophomore from a small town in Maine. Such a "double perspective" is an "expert reading move" (Wilhelm 1997), and one that this student was able to explore and share with others through the SRI.

One area of difficulty that my struggling readers faced while completing the SRI was knowing the difference between a prop and a symbol. As a teacher, I assumed that students could expand their knowledge of symbols (e.g., that the American flag represents our country or that a white dove stands for peace) to include new symbols in their representations. However, when students began their SRIs and brought in artifacts such as a football to represent—you guessed it—a football game, I realized that we had to do more to clarify what constitutes a symbol.

Why are symbols significant? Symbols are more than just a device used to complete the SRI—they are an important component in the lives of all people. From a very early age, children use symbols to understand their world. When I asked Cameron, my three-year-old son, why he had colored the evil faces of the Team Rocket characters in his Pokemon coloring book red, he simply explained, "They're red like fire because they're really mad." Cameron obviously has already come to understand our culture's preconceived notions about what the color red symbolizes, and he used that color to define the personalities of the Team Rocket characters.

White and Siegel (1984) recognize the importance of symbols to human beings. They believe that "in order to transform external relations into internal relations—to build symbolic models of experience— people need to put tokens of their selves and their actions into the model" (272). Throughout this book, we maintain not only that students need to be provided with specific assistance to understand the actual processes in reading, but that they also need to do something with this knowing that evolves from their readerly experiences. The SRI requires students to represent themselves by using symbols or artifacts and to represent their actions or the moves that they make as readers.

White and Siegel's "symbolic model of experience" translates to a rich reading experience. When we read we use symbols to understand a text, which then helps us internalize or relate on a deeply personal level. A word, a phrase, or an entire chapter in a book might remind us of something we have read in the past, a movie we have recently seen, or something we have actually experienced. When completing an SRI, students are required to use symbols to understand the text. By making the use of symbols explicit, the readers are expected to focus on their reading experience in a way that assists them in a more meaningful exchange with the text. They are using concrete objects to understand abstract notions and ideas. Vygotsky emphasized that all learning proceeds from the concrete to the abstract, and the SRI assists in this transformation. Depending on the reader's level of expertise, this might be the first time they have interacted with a text in such a way.

How Does the SRI Measure Up?

I had a hunch that the SRI might serve as the perfect springboard to improved writing skills for Brooke because it would allow her to reflect upon text, how she had read it, and would give her objects to use as she explored and reflected upon her thinking.

This process of symbolization enables readers to take a text that was otherwise "external" or not inherently meaningful, and transform that text to a meaningful, purposeful, way of knowing that helps them make sense of both the text and their world.

It is important to actively assist students at various stages during their construction of the SRI, especially if this is the first time a student has engaged in pursuing a new strategy, such as identifying symbols, or articulating meta-cognitive awareness of reading strategies, or in this case, achieving an authorial reading.

Brooke's written communication skills probably would never have permitted her to convey the highly sophisticated ideas that she was able to share during the performance of her SRI. Moving her reader cutout to display how she was reading helped her "to discover" new insights about the text and her reading. The connections that she was able to make were astute, particularly between the trashers and the victims. Perhaps most eloquent was Brooke's representation of the author's construction of the text. She continually returned to Cormier's text construction to arrive at the conclusion that fire was a symbol that could represent the notion "those who are destroyed, destroy."

Students like Brooke who are intimidated by written assignments are often set back because they try too hard to "get the words down right" and something is lost in the transaction. The writing may not assist them to new understandings and moves as a reader in the way that the SRI obviously does. As I mentioned earlier in this chapter, I wanted to create an assignment to privilege Brooke's preferred modes of communication, but I also hoped to improve her reading and cognitive skills, as well as her writing. After Brooke and her classmates completed their SRIs, I asked them to write an essay based on their authorial reading of the text that they used for the SRI.

As anticipated, Brooke's essay was much more in-depth, focused, and creative than it might have been if she had not gone through the process of completing an SRI. The SRI structured her thinking and assisted her in the construction of a written work that was arguably the best piece of writing she had completed all year. In fact, the SRI served not only as a way to help her achieve an authorial reading and be more aware of her own reading processes, but as a frontloading activity for her writing assignment.

Building a Community of Learners

The SRI, with its focus on the use of symbols to explain a text and one's reading of that text, is more than just an alternative assignment for students. The SRI privileges the voices of students and communal understandings of texts and situations. In my classes, students often used an SRI performance as an impetus to discuss or solve a problem that the text presented to them. A discussion of the text almost always led to a discussion of similar problems by which the students, themselves, were challenged.

Brooke's SRI triggered an intense discussion involving the degree that people should be held accountable for their actions given their past. One student said that her drug-addicted father had abused her when she was a little girl, but that didn't give her the right to "just go out and abuse someone else—or even drugs—if I feel like it." He said he rejected Cormier's plea to understand Buddy. Another student defended Cormier and said that Buddy suffered and so we were being asked to understand but not condone his actions. This was something he was willing to do. It is notable that the author was part of the conversation. I believe this was abetted by putting the author concretely into the SRI as a force to consider and converse with, because the students used the SRI as a way of fueling their conversation.

In my experience, this level of sharing and discussion does not typically take place when students are assigned a more traditional response, such as an essay. By making reading visible and by teaching students to better understand texts, particularly by privileging an authorial reading of a text, notions of the democratic classroom developed naturally. Everyone was using and appropriating other students' representations and stories to talk about issues of great importance to them all.

Students in Brooke's class asked many questions about their presentations and made comments like, "That's a great idea! I should have used that in mine!" or "I never thought of it like that." The SRI provides a unique opportunity for both the students and the teacher to see not only how individuals read a text, but also how they make sense of the world around them. By comparing their thinking and reading to others, students can test and question their ways of knowing against the understandings of their peers and can borrow strategies from each other. Also, once we are able to understand and appreciate that people are complex individuals with different ideas and ways of knowing, then we can begin to work at building an appreciation for diversity.

The notion that symbol usage can benefit people in their understanding of others and how they relate to them in the world is clearly articulated by White and Siegel (1984). These researchers eloquently state:

The use of symbols enables students to reflect on the text, their reading of it, and themselves, and it provides a way to celebrate the diversity of the students and others.

In the end, children's knowledge of symbol usage allows them to stock an imaginary world with distant others, to deal with imaginaries in a highly regulated and rational way, to know the structures, events, and processes of the human society lying beyond the community, and to communicate and cooperate with people. (274)

The SRI is an activity that lays the foundation for building such a community. It can privilege considering the author, and always privileges acknowledging individual ideas, cooperating with others, and bringing one's reading to the table to help the group wrestle with particular issues—all prerequisites to celebrating diversity. For Brooke and her classmates, the SRI provided an opportunity to share their personal thoughts and ideas in a nonthreatening way. Above all, it enculturated them into a literacy club by enabling them to read in new ways, interact with authors, exercise respect and resistance, and giving them a tool for working through readings and ideas expressed there with their peers. And in the end, isn't that the quintessential focus of learning for our students: to know how to connect with and understand one another? What a world it would be if all people could think and behave in such a democratic way. The SRI helps me work in that direction!

7

Assignment Sequencing
Teaching Students Text by Text, Activity by Activity

Give a man a fish, he'll eat for a day. Teach a man to fish, he'll eat for a lifetime.

—Old Folk Saying

I was fourteen, a freshman in high school. My dad, brother, sister, and I lived in a small apartment, and I did not have a desk. Every night after dinner, one of us would clean up and do dishes, and then I would lay out all the homework for that evening across the dinner table. It was the year of Algebra I, and on this particular night I was struggling with a fairly simple problem: $2x + 12 = 22$. I looked that problem over and over, but somehow since second period that morning, I had forgotten where or how to begin. I asked my dad for help. He looked over my shoulder.

"The answer is 5," he told me.

I looked up into his face, wide-eyed. "But how do you know that?" I asked.

He looked at me, baffled. "It just is," he replied.

"Well," I asked, "How did you get it?"

"Get it? I just know it."

"But Dad, there must be some *steps*!" Tears began to well in my eyes.

"Tanya, I don't know how I know it; I just do. The answer is 5. Can't you see that?"

I couldn't. And I didn't know how to begin to see that equation the way he did. As my frustration boiled over, so did my tears. With a wide sweep of both arms, I cleared the kitchen table, books and papers flying, and ran to my room crying.

Thank goodness my math teachers understood teaching better than my engineer father did. At school my algebra teacher could deconstruct that problem for me, reminding me that *x* was a variable; it only meant what the equation said it did. To read the equation, I would need to isolate the variable. In order to do that, I just had to remember that whatever I did to the left side, I also had to do to the right. By moving from easy problems to more complex ones, and by making me learn the correct steps, my algebra teacher took away the mystery of basic algebraic equations until I could (and still can) solve them on my own.

In a simple way, my struggle with algebra illustrates my interpretation of the Vygotskian view of learning. First, I needed help from an expert to learn *how* to solve a basic problem. As I grew in my understanding of algebra, I could benefit from assistance from my peers, and then even from myself. And I was able to bring forward what I had learned in the past and transfer that knowledge to other, more difficult algebra problems.

George Hillocks has produced a body of work dedicated to helping students of reading and writing to take similar steps toward competencies in our field. Some teachers see the word *steps* and shudder at the thought of a return to skill-and-drill instruction. I strongly argue that George's work, and our application of it, is not skill and drill. Instead, it is a democratization of reading instruction in which students are explicitly taught how to read challenging texts and meet the demands of new texts, giving them the language of power and meaning-making moves. Sequencing, teaching students the "steps" or interpretive strategies required to read particular texts, involves sharing the power of expert knowledge for the purpose of doing meaningful work together instead of keeping the power a secret so that it is held only by a few.

But there are some things about teaching English that make this difficult. Like my engineer father, we may be so good at "the solutions" that we've forgotten how we got there, and only know the answers. How do we unlock the mystery behind the opaque processes that make up reading, or the mystery that is hidden in the conventions and readerly expectations of a certain kind of text?

Especially frustrating for novice or struggling readers, I believe, are discussions of implicit or double meanings—symbolism, irony, and theme—and how they are coded. I remember smiling benignly at my first class of students who, thank goodness, did not cry or sweep their texts from their desks (at least not in school!), but who were nonetheless completely frustrated as I pushed them toward more complex readings of texts. So many students threw up their hands in frustration that first year. One student asked, "What do they do, give you a secret decoder ring in college? How do you know that Jay Gatsby's shirts are a symbol?" Another demanded access to my copy of the novel we were studying. "Do you have these answers written in yours?"

As a first-year teacher, I took all of these questions as a good sign; I was just happy to know more than they did. It was only after a year or two of teaching, when I had had a chance to catch my breath, that their questions became disconcerting. When I felt safe enough to listen to their questions empathetically, when I could hear the frustration in their voices, my answers became less satisfying to me. "It just *is,* read this passage with me. Can't you see that?" or "You'll get better with practice" just didn't ring true when they didn't know what they were practicing, and I didn't know how to assist them to do it.

I thought I was trying to teach students how to read. Yet unlike algebra processes, the steps I took to becoming a competent and mature reader had never been pointed out, or I had forgotten them as they had become more natural to me. Like my father with the algebra problem, I knew the answer but was less sure how I got it. I needed to "take off the top of my head" as Nancie Atwell (1987) says, and show myself, as well as my students, the processes of reading.

Jonathan Culler (1975) has made this argument:

> We do not judge students simply on what they know about a given work;
> we presume to evaluate their skill and progress as readers, and that pre-
> sumption ought to indicate our confidence in the existence of public and
> generalizable operations of reading. (quoted in Hillocks and Smith 1988,
> 44)

If there are "public and generalizable operations of reading" (particular interpretive moves or steps), then shouldn't we be teaching students what these operations are? Otherwise, we must admit that we are teaching texts, not teaching reading. We are teaching declarative knowledge, not assisting students to take on expert procedures of knowing and acting.

Our job as English or literature teachers, according to Culler's argument, is less about teaching books than it is about teaching processes with which to approach books. But what are the things we know and do that make texts come alive for us? In "Sensible Sequencing: Developing Knowledge About Literature Text by Text," George Hillocks and Michael Smith (1988) argue that expert readers must make use of in-depth knowledge of concepts, genres, and discourse conventions when they read, and to know how to set in motion the interpretive processes each of these require of readers. Therefore, these are essential things language arts teachers should work to help students learn if they are going to mature as readers who can learn from text.

In order to help students "own" these operations or processes of reading, we must organize instruction much as a coach organizes practices, by: (1) creating situations in which students can practice the skills they need to develop; (2) giving them time and adequate support to do so; and then (3) allowing them chances "that count" to show what they know. Instructional sequences are a way to teach students "something that [will] matter across texts" (Smith 1998, 74).

There are many advantages to developing such sequences for teaching in the English classroom. Such a sequence can become a unit that is built around any central required text. Knowledge and strategies can be developed through activities with one text and then brought forward and applied to the next. For instance, in contrast to typical American literature instruction, in which Walt Whitman is paired with Emily Dickinson (although the strategies required to read their work are entirely different), Whitman could be paired with Allan Ginsberg as part of a popular culture unit on shock and breaking the rules to communicate. Students would learn strategies for reading free verse poetry by reading Whitman that could be immediately applied to a reading of Ginsberg's free verse. Likewise, the concepts of popular culture and defamiliarization could be traced and developed through readings of both authors. Both process and concept can be developed text by text. What is learned with Whitman can be brought forward to, built upon, and amplified through a reading of Ginsberg.

Instructional Sequences

An instructional sequence is like a ladder set up to help students gain knowledge, in which the set of readings is sequenced along with carefully planned instructional support so that students will build knowledge text by text as they go through the sequence. In order to design an instructional sequence, teachers must first know where they are going. It helps to start by stating what students will know and be able to do by the end of the sequence. This can be stated as a heuristic—or set of problem-solving strategies—for noticing, understanding, and interpreting through the use of the required procedures. The sequence should then take students through a series of learning activities that move, as Jeff is fond of saying, "from order to adventure and independence" and from the most accessible and easy to the most challenging and sophisticated text. By the end of a sequence, readers should reach new understandings of and gain control over problem-solving heuristics that they can articulate and use on their own. In fact, the unit should end with a chance for students to *demonstrate* that they own the heuristic or big understanding and use it on their own.

Jeff developed the following criteria for creating an instructional sequence when I took a graduate class with him. I still find these criteria (Figure 7.1) useful and helpful to me when designing new reading sequences.

Talking About Theme Most middle and high school English teachers are required to teach "reading for main ideas" or reading for "theme." As a matter of fact, "main idea" and "theme" generally appear at every level of middle and high school English curricula and textbook series scope-and-sequence charts. Given that this is so, one might expect that by the time students arrive in my eleventh-grade English class they would "know" how to read for theme and be sick to death of "learning" it. Although the latter is often true, my experience has shown me that the former is not.

Although most of my students can define the literary term *theme* with varying degrees of success (declarative knowledge of substance), and many of my students can make general statements about the themes of "school" books when asked to do so, few are able to defend those general statements in clearly articulated arguments based on textual evidence, and fewer still recognize or talk about themes in their

FIGURE 7.1
READING SEQUENCE—PROPOSED CRITERIA

A **ladder** is a set of texts on the same theme or topic, proceeding from least complex to most sophisticated—or if you will, most accessible to most challenging.

A **sequence** is like a ladder except that it is a set of readings that are sequenced along with specific instructional support so that students will build knowledge text by text as they go through the sequence.

1. Know where you are going before you start designing the sequence. State what kids will know and be able to do by the end of the sequence. Conceptual knowledge goals can be stated in a "Big Understanding Statement." Procedural or genre knowledge goals can be stated as a heuristic—or set of problem-solving strategies—for noticing, understanding, interpreting through the use of the required procedures or genre conventions.

2. The sequence should proceed from most accessible to most sophisticated text. It should start where kids are in terms of skill and knowledge, provide preconditions for growth, and then support them in moving beyond their current abilities, helping them to outgrow their current selves as they are moved through their ZPD (zone of proximal development).

3. It is helpful to begin with a frontloading activity or reading that connects kids' real-life experiences, concerns, and questions to the issues that will be pursued through the sequence. Always consider how to connect kids' need for personal relevance with the need to develop socially significant strategies and knowledge.

4. The sequence should explicitly work to build student knowledge of procedural strategies, genre knowledge, or conceptual knowledge. (Some sequences do all of these things.) This knowledge should be built incrementally text by text. You should cite up front what is being sequenced and what will be required of the reader.

5. The sequence could end with a specific "bridge" or a "pairing," i.e., a more accessible YA text that pairs up with a more difficult canonical text in such a way that it prepares the student to build the procedural strategies, conceptual or genre knowledge to more fully understand and respond to the more canonical text.

6. The sequence should work in some way to assist readers in more competent performances, making new strategies and knowledge visible and public.

7. Readers should reach new understandings or problem-solving heuristics that they can articulate by the end of the sequence. In fact, the unit should end with a demonstration that students "own" the heuristic or big understanding.

independent reading. (They do not possess, in other words, procedural knowledge of substance. See Campbell, et al. 1998 for a review of data from the last several NAEPs.) If our purpose is to prepare independent readers and thinkers, then, in the procedure of recognizing, understanding, and discussing main ideas or themes, it appears to me that we are failing. And if students do not have procedures for understanding textual significance, then they cannot converse with authors, they cannot think with or apply textual ideas, and in my opinion, they have fallen far short of the goals we should have for them.

Reflecting on my own algebra experience, this makes sense to me. Knowing the correct answer to that algebra problem brought me no closer to knowing how to solve, or even to read, the problem. Knowing the definition of the literary term *theme*, or even hearing an English teacher's explanation of *the theme* of a certain work of literature, brings students no closer to being able to read a text themselves for that information. They have not yet learned "generalizable knowledge" that they can bring with them from text to text.

George Hillocks (1980) states it this way: "when [literary] structure is approached simplistically, as it tends to be with the 'list of elements,' the instruction does little to enhance the students' comprehension of literature." Yet, "to treat them in depth is beyond the interest and sophistication of most secondary school students" (305–306). The teacher's work, then, must be to "identify levels of comprehension skills relevant to reading literature, determine the levels at which students comprehend literature, and plan for instruction accordingly" (306).

But before we teach students how to read a text to discern the theme, I think we need to make clear to ourselves and our students why talking about theme is important. As with all learning, we need to take Applebee's (1996) advice and "focus on knowledge-in-action rather than knowledge-out-of-context." Theme isn't important just because it is in every scope-and-sequence chart. Rather, understanding an author's generalization—hearing the argument that is made by the text—is important because it is, as Peter Rabinowitz (Rabinowitz and Smith 1998) says, "what makes talking back possible" (14). In other words, approaching a text from an authorial reading—asking "What does this text mean to the audience for which it was intended and how do I feel about that?"—allows a reader to enter into an important discussion with the author. But, as Rabinowitz points out, if a reader doesn't first hear what a text says, "there is nothing to disagree *with,* and debate and dispute are replaced with talking at cross purposes" (15). George Hillocks suggests that we should discuss with our students the "significance" of a text rather than its "theme." He argues that "until students see the significance of what they read . . . they cannot begin to enjoy a text that focuses on more than action."

In his research concerning what is basic to the comprehension of literature, Hillocks has developed a seven-question informal reading inventory that statistical analysis has shown to be hierarchical. (See Chapter 5 for a careful review of the questioning hierarchy.) In other words, if a student is unable to answer a question lower on the hierarchy, then he will be unable to answer any further questions in the sequence since the earlier question is a stepping stone to the later one. Looking at this hierarchy (Figure 7.2), you will note that question level 6, "author's generalization," corresponds almost directly to what English teachers call "theme."

This might very well explain why students often struggle with questions concerning theme. Many of our students' trouble with "theme" may come about because we begin our instruction at a level above their ability to comprehend. In other words, we may be trying to teach students beyond their zone of proximal development—reaching them, rather, in their zone of "frustrational development." Therefore, in order to help students make sense of an "author's generalization," we need first to develop their abilities to deal with the literal and inferential questions lower on Hillocks' hierarchy than level 6.

The following instructional sequence is designed to help students develop and internalize those skills that are necessary in order to deal in a sophisticated fashion with the abstract concept of "theme." This will allow them to understand a text's "significance" so they can converse with authors and each other about issues of great human importance.

One key piece of the work I have done with Jeff and Julie is coming to understand that students do not learn what they do not value. I have very few students, especially those who are emergent readers, who embrace sophisticated structural analysis of literature, no matter how exciting that may be to me. However, most students *are* interested

FIGURE 7.2
HILLOCKS' QUESTIONING HIERARCHY

Examples are based on Chapters 1 and 2 of John Steinbeck's *Of Mice and Men*

Literal Level of Comprehension

1. Basic Stated Information

   The information this question asks the reader to find is important to the text, is prominent, and is repeated.

   Ex. Where are George and Lennie going at the beginning of the story?

2. Key Detail

   A detail that is important to the plot, usually appearing at a key point in the story and having a causal relationship to the things that happen in the story.

   Ex. What does George tell Lennie he should do if he gets into trouble?

3. Stated Relationships

   The reader must find the relationship that is said to exist between two pieces of information. This relationship is usually causal and must be stated directly, usually only once.

   Ex. Why is Carlson interested in Slim's new puppies?

Inferential Level of Comprehension

4. Simple Implied Relationships

   These questions ask for information similar to that elicited by level 3 questions except that they are NOT directly stated in the text. The inferences made at this level are drawn from a few pieces of information closely grouped in the reading passage.

   Ex. Why does George expect Curley to pick a fight with George?

5. Complex Implied Relationships

   These are inferred from many different pieces of information. The task is complex because the reader must identify the details, figure out the pattern that exists among them, and then draw the appropriate inference.

   Ex. In Chapter 2 Lennie says, "I don' like this place, George. This ain't no good place. I wanna get outta here." Give at least three reasons that Lennie might feel this to be a "bad place."

6. Author's Generalization

   These questions are different from the questions at level 5 because they ask the reader about ideas implied about the world outside the work itself.

   Ex. How might Steinbeck explain a person's motivation for taking care of another person or staying in a difficult relationship? Give evidence to support your idea.

7. Structural Generalizations

   Questions in this category require the reader to explain how parts of the work operate together to achieve certain effects.

   Ex. Because George and Lennie arrive in the morning while most of the men are working, the first person they really talk to is Candy. Give at least two explanations for why Steinbeck might have introduced these characters in this way.

in discussing the "big questions" of life. School, in my opinion, should push students to think about the things that matter to them and to stake out some personal philosophies about themselves and the world before they are sent to live in it. Thus, I designed an instructional sequence conceptually around the idea of dreams and opportunities.

At a conference several years ago, I heard a woman say that in most communities, 90 percent of the top 50 percent of students will leave the area, but 90 percent of the bottom 50 percent of students will stay in the area. We've already argued that we must care about *all* of our students, particularly those on the margins. But if what this speaker stated is even partly true, then as members of any community, we have an additional reason to be personally concerned about the · dreams and aspirations of those students who are in the bottom half of their class—they will be our neighbors, their children may someday also be our students. Yet I am concerned that many of my students seem unable to articulate and work toward a goal for themselves or a hope for their world or their community. Because I worry about their long-term vision (or lack thereof), part of our democratic work in this unit will be for everyone to think about what they hope to achieve in their lives, what they might hope to achieve for others through their lives, and how they might achieve those things.

The classroom activities and discussions are designed to develop specific reading skills while engaging adolescents in thought, writing, and talk about a topic that is meaningful to them.

Instructional Sequence: Developing Procedures for Recognizing and Understanding an Author's Generalization

Step 1:
Introductory
Activity

Sequences always begin with an introductory activity. (See Chapter 4 for more "frontloading" activities.) These activities are generally "non-literary" in nature, and might involve activities such as surveys, opinionnaires, or role-playing. Such activities should activate or build knowledge about a generative concept or process.

Introductory activities help students state their own opinions and knowledge on a particular subject, introduce key concepts of the works to be studied, ask questions, and set goals. This induces purposeful reading, which thereby increases comprehension (Kahn, Walter, and Johannessen 1984, 9).

The sequence I designed to help students read for an author's generalizations in the context of a unit on dreams and opportunities begins with an opinionnaire. Students agree or disagree with the statements concerning "dreams" (Figure 7.3). Next, as a whole class, we discuss each of the statements. I ask students to support their opinions with reasons and examples, and I encourage them to disagree and de-

FIGURE 7.3
STUDENT OPINIONNAIRE

Dreams, Opportunities, and Success Opinionnaire

This survey asks you to consider your own ideas about your dreams and opportunities, and about achieving success. In the space provided mark whether you agree or disagree with each statement.

	agree or disagree
1. I can be anything I want to be.	_____
2. Success always comes to those who wait.	_____
3. Our dreams are always good for us.	_____
4. "Dreams lift up fools."	_____
5. Carpe diem! (seize the day)	_____
6. In America, everyone has an equal opportunity for success.	_____
7. Success depends on good luck.	_____
8. "Men are masters of their fates."	_____
9. If at first you don't succeed, try, try again.	_____
10. "If at first you don't succeed, try, try again. Then quit. No use being a fool about it."	_____

bate each other's positions. I ask students to keep the opinionnaires for discussion of different characters' and authors' opinions on the issue of "dreams" later in the unit. In this way, the frontloading activity serves as a template for future response and understanding of the character and authorial perspectives various texts will introduce.

Step 2: Simple Text: Teacher-Directed Activity

Procedures that are new and difficult for students can best be introduced with accessible texts. Accordingly, I like to read picture books aloud to high school students. Once they get over their shock, most come to enjoy this activity. In the case of discussing themes, picture books are an excellent place to start. Many children's stories clearly state their themes, and the characters and situations are less complex than they are in most stories or novels written for older readers. Furthermore, they provide not only textual but also visual cues by which the reader understands the story. Beginning the instructional sequence with a text that incorporates visual cues helps students see the procedure by which we read textual cues as well.

Learning proceeds from the *concrete* to the *abstract,* from the known to the unknown, from the familiar to the "distant from home," from simple to complex, visual to nonvisual, external to internal. We must sequence instruction and make reading processes visible to students by taking them from where they are to where we want them to be.

Such work also helps students to move, as Hillocks and Vygotsky argue they must, from the known to the unknown.

Usually, I begin with the picture book *Uncle Jed's Barbershop,* by Margaree King Mitchell. In this text, Sarah Jean, an adult African American woman, recounts her Uncle Jed's quest to open his own barbershop. The story is set in the rural southern United States and begins during the Great Depression. The narrator's uncle experiences several setbacks. First, he has to give all his savings to the doctors in the white hospital so that they will treat the narrator during an illness. Next, he loses all his savings in a bank closing. However, Uncle Jed never loses sight of his dream. Finally, at the age of eighty, he opens his barbershop. The book ends with Sarah's observation, "He taught me to dream, too."

In order to begin our work in understanding and stating themes, I start with Hillocks' questioning hierarchy. I first read *Uncle Jed's Barbershop* aloud without interruption, and then I ask the class a question that requires them to identify basic stated information, such as, "What happened to Uncle Jed?" This question is easy to answer and thereby allows everyone to feel comfortable participating in the discussion. I continue to direct the discussion with questions that elicit key details (e.g., "Where was the narrator treated during her illness?") and stated relationships (e.g., "Why did Uncle Jed lose all the money that he had saved?"). This read-aloud and question/answer discussion should elicit the literal information needed to understand the text. Although I may skip questions or activities focusing on the literal level of comprehension later in the sequence, when I know them to be in my students' zone of actual development, at this point these questions—as well as the simplicity of the text—allow all students to participate and gain confidence to speak during class discussion. If there are students who cannot answer these questions for this text, I recognize that they may be in need of serious remediation (Hillocks 1980, 307). At this point, I read the book aloud again, but this time I ask students to stop me at any crucial points that develop Uncle Jed's character. I might model this by interrupting the reading myself to make a comment, such as, "Hmmm . . . this is interesting to me. Uncle Jed just gave all his money to the doctor so that Sarah Jean could be treated. Even though he won't be able to have his barbershop now, he doesn't look very sad. As a matter of fact, he looks quite happy."

At the end of this reading, I ask students to work on a level 5 question. Knowing how to challenge students and when is a matter of practice and knowing the texts as well as your students, but with this simple text and more than one reading, I feel comfortable asking most classes to try something a little more difficult. That is, I ask them to make some inferences that require them to work with many pieces of information, or to deal with a "complex implied relationship." In this case, I ask students to write three words to describe Uncle Jed. Our goal is to answer, "What kind of man is Uncle Jed?" Next they work in groups of three to five students to compare lists and come to agreement about which word *best* describes him.

Once each group has negotiated an agreement, they work together to list all the evidence from the text that supports their choice. Here I am asking students to make an inference based on many pieces of evidence and to actually pull that evidence from the text in order to show *how* they know *what* they know. Finally, each group presents their argument: "Uncle Jed is _____." At the end of this discussion we might debrief in a conversation about which groups had the best evidence to support their claims and how the other groups might have chosen a better adjective or more effectively supported the claim that they made.

Finally, with so much information, both stated and implied, in the hands of all students in the class, we are ready to work with the more abstract concept of the author's generalization—to talk about the ideas implied by the text about the world beyond the text. Note that I don't ask students to make statements about theme. As Hillocks (1980) argues, such statements are often very general: "The theme of this book is dreams." This kind of topic statement is not useful in helping us understand textual significance or an author's generalization. Instead, I ask students to return to our opinionnaire and choose the statement that they think Mitchell would most agree with. We then use the same group procedure as before in which students discuss their choices as a group, come to consensus about the best answer, use evidence from the text to support their answer, and present their argument to the class. I often also have students engage in a debate, awarding points for each piece of evidence or warrant offered to support a particular theme. This makes sure that the text and author are part of the discussion.

At this point students have carefully studied one text to come to a determination about the author's generalization. I want students to make an argument for their understanding of what *Uncle Jed's Barbershop* "means." More important for this sequence, I want them to know *how* they came to know that. Therefore, through class discussion, we begin to compile a class list of the types of questions we answered before coming to our determination of the author's generalization (theme). I ask students to think about and categorize the sorts of questions we asked and answered about the book. Through their participation and my coaching, we develop a list that looks something like the list in Figure 7.4. I keep this list posted in the classroom for students' easy reference as we continue to work on developing our "theme-finding" strategies.

Step 3: More Complex Text: Teacher, Group, Independent   This second set of texts involves students in reading poetry, often the emergent reader's nightmare. I begin with fairly easy poems and offer students some choices because I want them to see that while poems make some different demands on readers than stories, they are neither impossible nor horrible to read, and that although they may need different reading strategies for poems, and even for different types of poems, much of our heuristic for understanding an author's generalization applies across genres. We begin with a class reading and discussion

FIGURE 7.4
STUDENT DISCUSSION-GENERATED HEURISTIC

Questions to ask of a text in order to talk about theme:

1. Theme and plot:	What happens? (briefly summarize the main events) What is it about? (What seem to be the most important events? How are those events tied together? What do they have in common?)
2. Theme and character:	Who is the main character? What does that character say and do? What does the character's behavior suggest about people in general?
3. Theme (author's generalization):	What does this text mean? What does it seem to be saying about life or about people?

of Langston Hughes' "Dream Deferred." For this reading, I give all students a clean copy of the poem with wide margins. They may take notes, write questions, and in any way mark their copy. I have found that students' comfort with poetry greatly increases when they can physically interact with it.

On our first reading, I read the poem aloud and ask students to try to explain how this poem is different from a story. I want students to note that there are no characters and no plot or story line; as they say, "nothing is happening." Therefore, students will need to develop some other questions for their heuristic. I read the poem a second time, performing a "think-aloud" (see Chapter 3) of what I am doing as a reader to understand the poem. I ask students how reading this poem is different from reading a story, and we brainstorm the different things I noticed and the different moves I seemed to make. If students don't mention this, I point out that because poetry is language in its most condensed form, all the words are important, and I must pay special attention to images and the larger meanings they suggest.

Then I read the poem a third time, or invite a student to read, and ask students to highlight or underline any words they cannot define. Our discussion may then begin with a definition of the word *deferred,* through which we need to all understand that the poem is about a dream that is "postponed," "delayed," or "withheld" (the literal level of comprehension). Next I ask students to work individually to sketch the images that Hughes associates with a dream deferred (key details). I want emergent readers to sketch or draw these images because these readers often shut out poetry, believing that because there is no story line or characters the poem is ethereal and beyond their understanding. I hope that the sketches will bring the ethereal to a concrete (literal) level.

Students share their sketches with a partner and consider the following questions:

- What do these images have in common?
- How is each different?
- What is suggested by the similarities and differences?

I want students to note that all the connotations are somewhat negative (they may argue about "syrupy sweet"), but that they have very different suggestions about the kinds of negativity. I might ask them, for instance, to rate the images from least to most terrible. In this discussion students are stating implied relationships.

To move students toward discussion of the author's generalizations, I employ a drama activity. In this case, I ask groups of students to represent each of the images in the poem as a figurative representation of human behavior in a "snapshot" or "tableaux" drama, a frozen scene depicting physical and/or emotional relationships through characters' gestures, expressions, and/or actions, often accompanied with an explanation of the scene. (See Wilhelm and Edmiston 1998 for a full description of this and many other drama strategies.) In other words, students *physically show* the appearance and feelings of a human who may be "a dried-up raisin" or a "festering sore," or who "explodes." Using the technique of "forum theater," each group presents their tableaux, and other groups discuss, challenge, and augment the depiction. Variations of the tableaux are tried. For example, the figures in the tableaux may be brought to life to talk with or be interviewed by us, or a caption or commentary may be added to the picture, or one picture may melt into another and then freeze again in a kind of "slide show."

Once discussion has concluded and we have "seen" each image in a human form, I ask students to reread the poem and consider what generalizations Langston Hughes might be making about life and human experience. Students might see this poem as a warning to the dreamer, or perhaps to anyone who stands in the dreamer's way. Since the dream could be any dream, the poem is general in its implications. I might direct students to consider Langston Hughes' race. How does that knowledge develop or challenge their reading? Finally, I ask each tableaux group to consider the poem as a whole and to prepare a choral reading of the poem that uses their voices and body language to depict the generalization that they see as most appropriate. For example, should the poem be read with sadness, in anger, in defeat, or as a warning? After we have heard all of the choral readings, the class gathers for a whole-group debriefing.

At the end of this discussion, I want students to see that they have added some new types of questions to their heuristic for questioning texts in order to understand and state themes. Can they name what they have done? How would they write it, in their own words? Through discussion, we add to our class list, which is still posted for students' reference. Our new list of questions for a text looks something like Figure 7.5.

Of course, I want students to practice their work with poetry, and the assignments in Figures 7.6 and 7.7 provide examples of assignments that ask students to practice—with peers and independently—at questioning texts that do not have explicit characters or plots. Notice the application of Lev Vygotsky's ideas about teaching and learning. As students become more capable, I make sure that the assistance is gradually changed, from expert (teacher) assistance, to peer and environmental (the structure of the activity itself) assistance, to self-assistance. Also remember that our "big project" in this sequence is for students to consider their dreams and aspirations. By writing their own poem students "talk" through writing about dreams and aspirations.

> Teaching episodes must be carefully sequenced to cohere and be coherent to students.

Step 4: A Complex Text: Group and Individual Student Work

Working with Alice Walker's short story "A Sudden Trip Home in the Spring," I expect students may struggle a bit. This story "ups the ante" because it has more complex characters, encompasses a major theme and some minor ones, and deals with a situation that is far removed

FIGURE 7.5
STUDENTS' REVISED HEURISTIC

Questions to ask of a text in order to talk about theme:	
1. Theme and plot:	What happens? (Briefly summarize the main events.) What is it about? (What seem to be the most important events? How are those events tied together? What do they have in common?)
2. Theme and character:	Who is the main character? What does that character say and do? What does the character's behavior suggest about people in general?
3. Theme (author's generalization):	What does the author "mean"? What does the author seem to think, or want us to think about, by telling us this story?
4. Theme and language:	What are the connotations of the words that the author uses? Is there a pattern in the language? Do the images have similarities and differences—what do those similarities and differences mean?

from my students' lives in several ways. Sarah, the main character in "A Sudden Trip Home in the Spring," is the only African American student in her college dorm. In the story, she is called home for her father's funeral. Not only are most of my Maine students personally removed from issues of race by virtue of living in an almost ethnically homogeneous community, but they are also historically removed from a world in which desegregation of public institutions is new and frightening.

At this stage in the sequence, I remove some of the scaffolding seen in earlier assignments. To begin, students read the story independently (I do not read it to them) and they briefly summarize the

FIGURE 7.6
GROUP POETRY READING ASSIGNMENT

Traveler

He swore to God he'd get out
By sixteen, seventeen at the latest
And when twenty hit,
And him still there,
It hit hard,
And from then on he carried
This heavy anchor inside
That said
You ain't goin' nowhere, son,
So just get your ass on home.

—Cynthia Rylant

Directions:

1. In your group have one person read the poem aloud; highlight any words you don't know.

2. As a group, define any words that anyone doesn't know.

3. Sketch the major image(s) of the poem, share with a partner, share with the whole group. Discuss the similarities and differences in your pictures.

4. What connotations do you see in the words/images of this poem?

5. What does the author "mean" in this poem?

6. Once your group has decided on an answer to #5, prepare a reading of your poem that expresses that meaning.

7. Prepare and present your choral reading to the whole group.

---

main events of the story (basic stated information) by themselves. I ask them to bring to class a written copy of their summary as well as any questions they have as we begin to tease out the themes of this work.

To begin discussion, I ask the whole class a few questions to move them from looking at basic information toward making some inferences about the text (Where is Sarah when the story opens? What is

FIGURE 7.7
INDIVIDUAL POETRY WRITING ASSIGNMENT

1. List all the images that the poets you have read have associated with dreams.

2. Organize this list in a way that seems appropriate to you (dreams to come, dreams defeated; positive, negative; etc.).

3. Choose one section of your list that you are interested in writing about. Write three new images that you would add to the list describing this sort of dream.

4. Using a combination of your images and other poets' images, create a poem that describes this sort of dream.

5. Give your poem a title that describes the type or state of this dream.

she studying at this school? Who are her friends?). Then we begin using more drama strategies to extend this process. Jeff has helped me use drama in my classroom in many ways. In what he calls "correspondence drama," students take the role of a character and "correspond" by writing a letter, postcard, telegram, and so forth to another character or to someone outside the story.

After we read "A Sudden Trip Home in the Spring," I ask students to take the role of Sarah and answer one of the following questions in the form of a letter from Sarah to her brother:

1. How does Sarah feel about her place with the other girls at school?
2. How does she feel about her father?

Both of these questions require students to consider complex implied relationships. Rather than reading and grading all of these letters myself, I ask students to inform one another's reading by using their letters to create and present a choral montage, a group reading of the most poignant or salient points of each student's letter, organized in a meaningful and/or lyrical way. Here are the directions for using a choral montage in your classroom:

1. Students work in groups.
2. Each group uses the letters that answered one of the questions.
3. Each student receives a letter written by someone else and under-lines the phrase or sentence that she believes is the most powerful, interesting, or important.
4. Each group member reads aloud the sentence she has chosen.
5. The group then organizes these sentences in a way that forms a story, a poem, or a chant and practices reading their sentences aloud in that order. Phrases may need to be changed, added, or even deleted to ensure that one line leads to the next in a coherent way. In this way, the revision process is public and visible.
6. When the groups are prepared, each presents their choral reading.

The resulting montages naturally explore answers for each of the two questions. The oral performances of the montages allows students to hear Sarah's voice and feelings in a number of their classmates' voices.

I want my next question to help students focus on language and metaphorical images, much as we did when we looked at the themes of the poems in step 3. I ask students to work in groups to consider Sarah's exchange with her friend Pam, in which she speaks of "one faulty door in a house with many rooms," and then sketch the image, considering what it looks like in human terms. Each group will supply one sketch. Who or what in Sarah's life does that metaphor describe? I ask students to answer and defend their answers with other evidence from the text (complex implied relationship).

The final group question deals with the character of Sarah. Focus-ing on the conclusion, I ask students to consider how Sarah has changed by the end of the story:

1. What does Sarah's decision to carve a figure of her grandfather in stone mean?
2. How would you characterize Sarah's change of attitude toward her family?

Both questions also ask students to explain complex implied relation-ships. The questions also provide environmental assistance to students in developing their "theme" heuristic by focusing their attention on the fact that changes in character are often clues to the story's theme. This is an example of something about reading literature that I want them to name and internalize and bring forward to all future readings. Their heuristic for understanding an author's generalization should now include, "How has the character changed? What does such a change suggest about people in general?"

Ready to discuss the author's generalizations, I next post the following list of abstract nouns on the board: *love, courage, peace, freedom, dignity, defeat, pride, survival, understanding, forgiveness.* Students choose those they feel apply to Walker's story and list those words and a brief explanation for choosing them in a reading journal. Then they share their journal entry with a partner to explain their choices. Working in pairs, students next look at the words they both chose and begin to decide which are part of the major (dominant, repeated) theme. Students collaboratively craft a thesis, a one-sentence statement that reveals the theme of this short story, and then they complete what Kahn, Walter, and Johannessen (1984) named an "evidence extract" (15):

1. I ask students to write a claim concerning a piece of literature (in this case, they use their thesis).
2. Next, they list a certain number of pieces of specific evidence that support their claim.
3. Students can then peer-edit each other's works to make sure that each piece of evidence is specific and does support the claim, and help one another to revise their lists where necessary.

In Vygotskian terms, this activity provides peer assistance. However, should students be operating beyond their zone of proximal development, expert (teacher) assistance can be provided. For instance, I might provide the evidence from the text and ask students to explain how that evidence supports a specific claim (i.e., I can move back on the assisted performance continuum from "You do-I help" to "I do-You help"—see Chapter 1).

Before we move on to step 5, in which students will work with a longer—but probably not more complex—text, with less teacher direction, here is a good place to add to our heuristic. Students are now familiar with the idea that themes are concepts and must be discussed with abstract nouns. They should also recognize that the *significance* of a text can be seen as the author's claim concerning a concept. Through class discussion, I want to tease that out as a separate step in the heuristic. They should add to their heuristic something like this:

Themes involve concepts about life, the human condition, and other broad, philosophical ideas. Try to pick out the concepts that the writer is discussing—the meaning of and reasons for words and actions. We state themes using concept words (such as *love, courage, peace, freedom, dignity, defeat, pride, survival, understanding, forgiveness, anger, sadness, hope*).

The richest and most powerful teaching assists students on various levels (expert, peer, environmental, self) and in various ways (models, structures, talking through and naming, questions, feedback, real-world contingencies, and so forth).

When students articulate and use a heuristic enough (how much is enough depends on the difficulty of the task and the abilities and knowledge of the students), they internalize it as a set of problem-solving strategies they will carry forward with them into the future. A good heuristic not only helps students see what they should do in order to complete a certain reading task, but it also helps them see and name common errors that many novice readers make. If errors occur, especially among several students in the group, you might want to add a "what to watch out for" list to your heuristic. Figure 7.8 shows a list of problems my students often encounter as they try to understand and state themes in their reading.

FIGURE 7.8
PROBLEMS STUDENTS ENCOUNTER
IN UNDERSTANDING THEME

What Should We Watch Out For?

1. Confusing subject for theme. The subject, remember, is what happens on the surface of the story, and only in the story. The theme is more about the purpose of the story, the reason the author had for writing it. Theme should state generalizations that go beyond the world of the story.

2. Leaving out important details. The theme must not disagree with or fail to consider any important details of character or plot.

3. Looking for the moral of the story. Although some texts do have a moral as a theme, many, especially more modern and more complex texts, have themes that are more subtle than morals about how we should live or behave.

Step 5: Short to Long, Easy to More Difficult: From Group and Independent Reading

To this point, we have read several short stories together and focused on theme. Along the way, we have continued to refine and use our heuristic. Now that we are nearing the end of this assignment sequence, students read a full-length novel without a lot of teacher direction. The novel, John Steinbeck's *Of Mice and Men*, is short, relatively easy to read, and highly engaging. It deals with two men's pursuit of their dream to own a small farm.

As we begin step 5 of the sequence, I want to diagnose the students' progress, so I give the seven-question quiz shown earlier in Figure 7.1. The students' answers help me work individually or in groups with students who are still struggling at any level below 6 on Hillocks' hierarchy.

> A sequence must continually increase in complexity to engage students and support them to more competent performances.

Students who seem to be doing well complete the literature circle assignment in Figure 7.9 with little teacher intervention. Note, though, that the literature circle roles themselves provide environmental assistance. The structure of the task helps students remain focused on the steps they have learned for paying attention to a text's significance. When they have completed their roles students meet in literature circle groups to discuss their assignments, using group discussion to assist one another in developing their readings. I often have students record their literature circle meetings so that I can check in and, when necessary, offer expert (teacher) assistance.

Step 6: More Difficult, Full-Length Text: Independent Reading

At this point, I ask students to work independently to apply their heuristic to a novel of their choice from the following list:

The Color Purple by Alice Walker
Their Eyes Were Watching God by Zora Neale Hurston
Black Boy by Richard Wright
Monster by Walter Dean Myers
Roll of Thunder, Hear My Cry by Mildred S. Taylor

With my guidance, students choose the book that most matches their interests and their abilities as demonstrated throughout this unit. Students read their texts independently and are responsible for keeping learning logs that show consideration of every aspect of their heuristic.

I provide workshop time during this assignment so students may consult with me and their peers and so I can monitor progress and

FIGURE 7.9
LITERATURE CIRCLE ROLES ASSIGNMENT

Student Directions	Finish reading *Of Mice and Men*. As you read, think about what message Steinbeck might want to convey to us. Think about what purpose the plot, the characters, the setting, and the language might serve in making that message concrete. Each member of your group will prepare to be the expert in one area of the heuristic and lead your group's discussion of it. As a final project each group will coauthor a paper discussing the central theme of *Of Mice and Men*.

Literature Circle Roles

Summarizer	Summarize the subject of the book. Who are the main characters? What are their relationships to one another? What are the main events of the story?
Character Analyzer	Keep an eye on the two main characters, George and Lennie. What crucial points in the story develop these characters? What generalizations can you make about the characters? What might each character's behavior suggest about people in general?
Language Watcher	What particular words or phrases do you notice as you read? What do you notice about the language of the characters? Is it different from the language of the narrator? Write down and bring to discussion particularly noticeable or important passages.
Connector	Relate important ideas in this book to yourself and other works we have studied. What do the events in this story make you think of? Who do the characters remind you of? How do these similarities relate to our discussions of dreams and opportunities?

Group Discussion Guidelines

*Pay close attention to any "concept words" that arise in your conversation. Decide which ones are part of the major (dominant, repeated) theme. Try to use some of those words to state the major theme of *Of Mice and Men*. Be sure to look for clues to Steinbeck's theme in the climax and the ending of the novel.

*In your discussion consider which generalizations about characters seem to you to be part of the major theme.

*State the central idea of this story. **What does this story mean to the audience it was intended for?**

*Check your work. Have you stated themes that incorporate all the major ideas of the novel? If you stated the theme of this novel as a moral, is that appropriate here?

*How do you feel about what the story means for the audience it was intended for? Do you accept, adapt, or reject this message from the author?

intervene if students are struggling. They may use several note-taking techniques we have explored together, including double-entry draft notes, in which they copy down passages from the novel in one column and responses to or notes about the passage in the other. They may include literary letters to me or one another in which they explore their own thinking and ask questions about the text.

Finally, students write a paper that explains the central theme of their novel, backing up their reasoning with evidence from the text (this sort of literary analysis is a requirement in many high school level courses). I often tell students that the final step is a big leap if

FIGURE 7.10
STEPS OF ASSIGNMENT SEQUENCE PRESENTED IN CHAPTER 7

Step	Type of Text	Type of Activity	Purpose
1	None	Student-interest	Pique student interest
2	Children's story	Teacher-directed	Model desired responses Direct learning
3	Poems	Teacher-directed	Direct learning activities Model Build confidence
		Group work	Support each other's learning Practice learned skills
		Independent work	Practice learned skills
4	Short story	Group and independent work	Practice learned skills Support each other's learning Work with new texts
5	Easy novel	Group and independent work	Work with longer text Support each other's learning Apply learned skill to more difficult task
6	Novel	Independent work	Demonstrate ability to apply new skills independently

there are no steps built, but a baby step if all the steps leading up to it are in place. Their papers should be easy to write if their thinking and writing as they read is focused on applying the questions in their heuristic. The final draft of this paper, combined with the student's learning log, should demonstrate the student's ability to independently read in order to understand an author's generalizations, or the themes, of a full-length text. I ask them to conclude their paper with a personal evaluation of the text's theme and in what ways they would embrace, adapt, or resist that theme in their own lives.

Frying
Larger Fish
Throughout this unit, I have continually asked students to consider not only "What does this text mean?" but "What do I think about that?" Students have worked to reconsider and redefine their own dreams, or to compare their dreams and their sense of the value of dreams to others'. As we conclude our unit, I ask students to do two things:

1. Write a "dream statement," which should include a goal or dream for the future as well as a plan for achieving it.
2. Write a letter to eighth graders that discusses the idea of dreams or aspirations and offers them advice that might help them as they enter high school.

By the end of the unit, Leon, a notorious class clown, was willing to admit that he did have a dream for his future: to become a teacher. In words that were quite moving for me to read, the next year his letter of application to the state university system concluded:

> I've dreamed of becoming a teacher for years now, and after having Ms. Baker my junior year, I have become totally excited to begin college and achieve this aspiration. The thinking and reading I did during junior English convinced me that I can make this dream can come true, so I know I can succeed.

When the learning we do in school begins to affect how students choose to live and act, then I know one of my goals has been achieved.

Throughout this sequence, students engaged in a number of learning activities. Some may be uncommon in most classrooms, and others should feel hauntingly familiar to anyone who has taught or learned in a traditional school setting. Some teachers may feel that the questions in this sequence look conspicuously like the questions at the end of each selection in their American literature anthology. "If this is so," they might ask, "why go to all this trouble when the selections and questions have been so neatly arranged for you in that anthology?" The answer, I think, is crucial to how we plan instruction.

Questions at the end of each selection in an anthology rarely, if ever, make connections among its individual texts. While these questions provide our students with the *opportunity* to make generalizations about the kinds of questions readers should ask, they do not state these generalizations explicitly, and none but our most thoughtful students will ever internalize these questions as clues about how to become better readers. In fact, in schools where answering questions at the end of the textbook selection is a primary classroom activity, *reading becomes a task to complete in service of answering those questions.*

On the other hand, the sequence in this chapter (and instructional sequences in general) is inquiry driven. It asks students to pursue, over time, their evolving understandings around a central issue, and to internalize, through practice, the kinds of questions used in a particular process of reading. Therefore, *asking and answering the questions becomes a task to complete in service of reading, which is in service of personally relevant and socially significant inquiry.* At their best, we believe, sequences ask students to *complete their reading in service of a larger democratic project.* This chapter offers one version of a democratic project: to explore and share perspectives on dreams and opportunity. Chapter 8 offers another example of such a reading project, as older students engage with preschool authors to create books together.

Sequencing is a democratic pursuit because students are helped to develop knowledge of the reading game and its rules in a supportive, step-by-step fashion so they can all play, eventually, on their own. Sequencing lets them know that reading is not a mystery privy to an elite few or a privilege of an inner sanctum, but a pursuit they all can participate in and enjoy, something that Jeff's student Jack calls out to be able to do in his poem at the beginning of Chapter 2.

I learned how to "do" algebra by watching a teacher demonstrate the process through which equations could be solved, by practicing that process on increasingly more difficult problems, and by having a teacher or friend intervene and reteach the steps to me whenever I forgot, became confused, or lost my way. Receiving the answer to the problem I was trying to solve did not help me understand the problem or how to solve it. If we expect students to become better readers independent of our guidance, we must take a hint from our colleagues in math and science and begin to reorganize our teaching by:

1. Creating instructional sequences that show our students *how* we read certain kinds of texts
2. Helping them practice those processes on increasingly difficult texts
3. Intervening with reteaching or redirecting when they forget, become confused, or lose their way.

We must help them develop some *steps* and problem-solving processes to use on their own. The sequence I've described here has helped nearly all of my students to effectively read for, articulate, and justify author's generalizations they've identified long after this unit is over. This is a significant achievement that our national assessments show few of our students reach. My own students reach this achievement, I believe, because I take the time to assist them over time to internalizing ways of reading through sequences such as this.

8

Reading Together

Power forces us to change. Only love can move us to change.
Power affects behavior; love affects the heart.

—Brennan Manning

In small groups in which everyone feels that a great deal
depends upon his actions, and learns to act upon his own
responsibility instead of losing himself in the anonymity of the
mass, social patterns grow up in which individuality can almost
certainly develop.

—Karl Mannheim

Reading Buddies: High School Students and Preschoolers Learning from Each Other

Teaching in new ways not only changes students, it also changes us as teachers. By carefully attending to students and their needs, we mature and grow as teachers.

I taught both English and reading at Old Town High School. I had around twenty-five students in my English classes, and a smaller class load in the Reading Lab, where I taught reading. Each reading class contained approximately twelve students, most of whom were identified as needing assistance in reading (although some more expert readers enrolled in the course as an elective). The Reading Lab was formerly structured so that students worked on a self-paced individualized program that utilized worksheets to assist in comprehension. Once ten comprehension questions had been answered correctly on individual reading cards, the student could then progress to the next card. The first thing that I did when I was hired was to dispose of this program and implement activities to facilitate group learning and more democratic and purposeful endeavors. I wanted to assist students to be able to see their own expertise and build from there to improve their strategies and widen their interests. Influenced in this regard by Jeff's *You Gotta BE the Book*, I wanted them to work with others on important projects that involved reading, to live through and visualize their reading, to reflect on the constructedness of texts, and to use what they learned from reading to develop social awareness and undertake new kinds of social action.

But I fell short of my good intentions and continued to teach in ways that did not match my evolving theories of learning and reading. As a result students like Chad challenged my instruction. A sarcastic sophomore and a struggling reader, he complained about my assignments on a fairly regular basis. "I'm sick of writing these stupid summaries over the *Reader's Digest* articles!" I couldn't blame him because, quite frankly, I was tired of reading daily accountability reports that lacked interest and luster. Reading aloud to Chad's reading group was a better alternative as students appeared to actually take in some of the information being read to them, but judging from follow-up discussions, about 40 to 50 percent of them were still not reading on their own with a level of engagement that I would have preferred. And even if they were comprehending the texts, what did this understanding teach my students about themselves? How was their reading helping them in the bigger scheme of things? And, perhaps more important, what could I do to make these reading experiences more personally relevant and socially significant? I needed a real-world project that would contextualize our reading activity and make it more purposeful.

Finally it clicked, my colleague Martha Pojasek and I had been trying to develop a plan for an upcoming teacher research project, but we hadn't had any success so far. We knew we wanted to work together, but we were teaching on the opposite ends of the age spectrum. I taught grades 9 through 12 English and reading classes, while Martha owned and operated her own preschool. We wanted to have our students collaborate on a project, but we couldn't decide what that project would be.

Reading Buddies Projects had been cropping up everywhere, and the benefits of such a joint venture were well documented. If we did such a project, though, how would we know for sure when students were ready to be guided to the next level of literacy performance? Was it possible to create a project that would honor the social and emotional differences of each student? In what ways could we provide assistance and support to all students as they worked within their zones of proximal development, cognitively, socially, and emotionally? And finally, how would we guide students in their partnerships in ways that would help them become more productive, tolerant, and decent human beings?

Martha and I wanted to guide our students in the type of reading buddies projects we had read about, but in addition to tackling the lack of interest in reading (which was mostly prevalent at the secondary level), we wanted to address the lack of interest in writing. Furthermore, it was important for us to expand the preschoolers' knowledge to help them reach new understandings about print. Together we developed an implementation plan that we hoped would encourage students to use their social learning environment to become excited and enthusiastic about a literacy endeavor, and one that would help students celebrate themselves and each other. Further, I hoped the project would help my students to appreciate authors and their purposes as they helped preschool authors to construct a story that conveyed a message of importance to them. Just maybe I would nudge my reluctant readers to a more nuanced appreciation of authors and authorial reading.

Why a Lecture Just Won't Do

Five-year-old Josh leans closer to the camera—an intentional action used for effect—as he tells about his favorite "sca-a-a-wy" part in the book. His otherwise shrill voice is toned down several octaves as he whispers his way through a description of the haunted house. "And all the lights were off, and there was a broken window in the house, and there was a big noise, and—BOOM!" Josh holds his belly and laughs in an exaggerated fashion as he imagines how much he has just frightened his reading buddy, Shelly. In the next breath, Josh is up off the floor and right on to another tale about Ewoks and different creatures from *Star Wars*.

Just like Josh, all young children seem to be programmed to tell tales—tales of fantasy, action, horror—you name it. But somewhere along the way as children grow into young adults, they deny themselves (or are themselves denied) permission to be involved in storytelling. I am deliberately conflating the term "storytelling" here with the term "literature" because, depending on the age of the student in question, the terms could mean the same thing. Little Joshua's literary repertoire might consist of Mercer Mayer books that are read to him by family members, while Shelly, a high school student, views literature as being comprised of the classics or books by Gary Paulsen or Toni Morrison. No matter how one defines "literature," though, by the time I see my reading students at the secondary level, typically their drive and enthusiasm for literary endeavors such as storytelling, writing, and reading is at an all-time low.

George Hillocks has convinced us that one-sided modes of instruction account for much of the apathy and lack of enthusiasm in our students' literary endeavors. Willinsky (1991) says, "Teachers tend to isolate the literary work from the general project of language—[which is] trying to represent and often remake the world" (4). This was true of my former teacher-centered, information-driven, historical approach to teaching: a classic example of how educators tend to segregate what they teach from student lives and real inquiry, which establishes nothing short of artificial, meaningless lessons on a particular subject.

Even good middle school readers experience changes in their habits and attitudes toward literary activities by the time they reach high school—and sometimes even sooner. No longer are they spending hour upon hour making their way through a scrumptious series like the Nancy Drew books. Instead, they choose to test their world through social trial and error rather than through the literature that once shaped and informed their lives. This is not without good cause, either. If students aren't being explicitly taught "how" to read the more complex texts they face beyond early elementary school, then it stands to reason that they will seek alternative ways to learn about their world.

While the socialization process is a crucial and necessary component to any child's development, so too, I'd argue, is one's exposure to texts and strategies for reading. If students aren't exposed to a variety of texts, they will never learn strategies such as authorial reading, which teaches the student that literature is created by real people to explore issues of profound importance to being and living. The author constructs her text in a deliberate way in order communicate a certain meaning. This meaning or interpretation of the text can then be embraced, adapted, or resisted, and the reader can "read against the grain" to use the text to derive an alternate understanding. In the end, exposure to texts and strategies to reading underscore the notion that stories and arguments and other texts are essential and world-changing.

Through literature we can develop the ability to assess situations and people who are from another culture, and certainly out of our realm of direct contact. Learning about the life of a gang member, for example, is a lesson that we hope our children never experience firsthand. However, if we teach in an area where this is a reality, reading about it may help bring us together. Reading offers vicarious exposure to different types of people and situations without the threat that might otherwise exist. Story writing, telling, and reading are unique and powerful ways of knowing about life, if only for the simple fact that stories help us make sense of our world and the people around us, and help us re-envision and consider how to remake the world.

So why the declining interest in literacy at the middle and high school level? Perhaps storytelling is seen as "fun," which has traditionally not been analogous with secondary education. Maybe story writing, telling, and reading are viewed more as a pastime or hobby, like collecting baseball cards, so some do not regard it as "real work" that furthers one's high school education. In my experience, students equate "real work" with what they believe connects to the real world and, ultimately, to their future. A more convincing argument for the decline might be that educators are unintentionally not providing the direct instruction that secondary students so desperately need in order to be successful readers and writers with more complex texts. Certainly, a plethora of research exists to support this notion (cf. Hillocks 1986; Nystrand et al. 1997). At any rate, "the [traditional] teaching of literature could be responsible, if only in part, for the current literacy crisis" in our country (Willinsky 1991, 4).

And literacy crisis there is. Over the past two decades, the National Assessments of Educational Progress (NAEP) have made clear in their reading report cards that despite a basic level of literacy that exists among seventeen-year-olds, students have persistently failed to read or write with any degree of depth or analysis.

Evidence of this occurs in my own school, where teachers have been faced with consistently average to low reading and writing scores on the Maine Educational Assessment. Willinsky urges that "if there is more than a passing interest in what we have made of literacy in the English curriculum, then perhaps educators and the public at large might be ready to consider whether something more could be made of language in schools" (4).

So what can be done to remedy the current literacy crisis in our country and in our own schools? Clearly an approach different from the ones teachers have taken in the past is needed. Research indicates that taking into account the social situations in which students learn best is a factor that is often overlooked. White and Siegel recognize that "cognitive development may be tied closely to children's widening experience with socially structured learning situations of their society" (White and Siegel 1984, 7). There is indeed a connection between the social conditions to which we subject our students and their intellectual development. If this social aspect is so important to the education of our students, then why do we, as educators, neglect our students' need to learn in social conditions that motivate them and help them advance?

Beyond the scope of reading to improve cognition is the need to read in order to learn more about oneself and others. We need to read to inquire together into essential issues, and to take action on these issues. We need to read to function effectively in a democratic society by using texts as objects with which to argue and think. Our data demonstrates that the students in the project I will now describe became more literate, more self-knowledgeable and self-confident, and more supportive of one another throughout the project.

The Reading Buddies Project

Eighteen-year-old Christine is probably not the normal choice for a selected case study. She is not a struggling reader, and my reading program did not rescue her from the dregs of failure, thus transforming her literary world. Quite the contrary, Christine is a polite young woman with a good work ethic and a decent reader, but something in her literacy life was missing. It seemed to me that Christine had lost her passion for reading. True, on her own time she read a couple of John Grisham or Isaac Asimov books a month, but this was more a perfunctory routine for Christine. For Christine, reading was more a school-sponsored activity rather than a self-sponsored one. It was as though she had an internal supervisor in her mind saying, "Alert! Alert! The end of the month is approaching! You need to finish one more book to fulfill your quota!"

My reading classes took place every other day, as was normal for all subjects taught according to our block scheduling. Like an obedient student, Christine would attend her reading class on Fridays, the day of book talks, prepared to discuss her latest endeavor. She was motivated by a drive to complete the assignments, not by the act of reading itself. Her comprehension skills were good, her vocabulary above average, but for all that, Christine's enthusiasm for literacy was not what I hoped for. I wanted to see her eyes light up when she talked about books. I wanted to see her run to class and implore other students to read something that had really moved her. I wanted her to get pumped up about reading!

While I focused most of my time and energy on students like Brad, Karen, and James—the ones who loudly proclaimed that they hated reading and who struggled accordingly—it was students like Christine who really got under my skin. After all, she possessed all the skills to be a great writer and reader, but she lacked the passion. She lacked what is arguably the most important quality of a literate person—a love of words, a love of the power of language to move us, and a love of what that can do for us and others. In fact, despite her great strengths, she revealed that she did not plan to attend college.

What resource is there for the student who is not moved by literature or by learning? A true love of words, whether that comes in the form of telling a story, writing one, or reading one, could be fostered when students are engaged in work with a real-world purpose. It is my hunch that Christine lost her passion for writing and reading because she wrote one too many book report, filled out one too many worksheet, and took one too many quiz about the material she was reading at any given time. The Reading Buddies Project that Martha and I developed was the "real-world work" under proper social conditions that inspired Christine and sparked her renewed passion for words—and for sharing words with others. This experience also helped her see new life possibilities for herself.

Project Goals

The primary purpose of this project was for high school and preschool students to form a partnership to improve reading and writing skills and to learn to work together for democratic purposes. Each pair of students was instructed to create a coauthored and coillustrated story, and in the process, we were able to expose students to various texts and textual conventions. The primary mode of communication would be by audio- and videotape because transportation was difficult to arrange and because we wanted preschoolers to tell an original story that high school students could translate and put into book form.

My high school students read a favorite children's story to their preschool partner on videotape so that participants could "meet" their buddy. Next, preschoolers recorded their own *original* stories on audiotape so that high school students could transcribe them. The transcriptions were not expected to be exact, in fact, high school students were encouraged to think about the essential elements of a story (e.g., a beginning, middle, and an end, a conflict or challenge, protagonists and antagonists) and to make necessary changes. Utilizing audio- and videotapes helped us solve our transportation crisis and gave high school students an opportunity to really focus on the stories as told by their buddies.

It just so happened that we had the exact number of students so that each child was able to be paired with a buddy. Twelve students from various reading classes volunteered to participate in the Reading Buddies Project, and there were twelve preschoolers. Students who did not participate elected to complete an inquiry project to fulfill the requirements of my class. During our eighty-minute blocks, I assisted both reading buddies participants and regular members of my reading classes. While I asked for volunteers in order to get students who were more willing to take this project seriously, I highly recommend pursuing this project with only *one* class of students.

Journal Excerpts The following excerpts are from my journal. I wrote them during the
That Chronicle time that the Reading Buddies Project was implemented in my class.
the Reading Figure 8.1 shows an outline of the project overall.
Buddies Project

Figure 8.1
Outline of Reading Buddies Project

Preschool Teachers

1. Secure permission slips for preschoolers to participate in project.

2. Ask students to bring in favorite book.

3. Enlist parents in writing the profile of students, or work with students to compose individual letters.

4. Communicate any important or sensitive information to high school teacher in order to help students be successful.

5. Discuss profiles/letters with high school teacher. Pair students, but take plenty of time to consider individual preferences, personalities, and so on.

6. Announce buddies! Give students their letters from high schoolers, then discuss perceptions.

7. READ! READ! READ! Read lots of children's books, and have students practice favorite children's book. Students will give feedback to one another.

8. Students read (or tell) favorite children's book to buddy on video.

9. Exchange videos and more buddy letters with high school teacher and share with students.

10. Continue to view video. Begin making audiotapes of students telling original stories. Work independently with each student. Use leading questions to help students formulate stories.

11. Discuss commonalities with students. What are things in the stories that are the same? What is different about this story? and so on.

12. Continue to read buddy letters, watch videos, and prepare for Reading Buddies Day. This will help students establish familiarity with their buddies, and it will continually expose them to the elements of a story.

13. Plan the celebration of Reading Buddies Day! Decorate the room, prepare a snack list, etc.

High School Teachers

1. Write invitation letter to students explaining Reading Buddies Project.

2. Ask students to bring in favorite children's book.

3. Have students compose their own profile/letter to be shared with buddies (include pictures, designs, etc.).

4. Class project—design a cover for letters to reading buddies (*Hint: Place all letters in slipcovers—preschoolers will read them over and over!*)

Figure 8.1
(Continued)

5. Discuss profiles/letters with preschool teacher. Pair students, but take plenty of time to consider individual preferences, personalities, and so on.

6. Announce buddies! Give students their letters from preschoolers, then discuss perceptions.

7. READ! READ! READ! Read lots of children's books, and have students practice favorite children's book. Students will give feedback to one another.

8. Students read favorite children's book to buddy on video.

9. Exchange videos and more buddy letters with preschool teacher and share with students.

10. Teach students to take double-sided notes (actual transcription on one side: thoughts, questions, ideas, and drawings on the other).

11. Audiotapes of buddies telling original tales arrive. Share with appropriate buddy.

12. Use dual headsets to transcribe with students.

13. Begin composing stories.

14. Students complete rough draft and peer editing.

15. Discuss illustrations, how to separate pages, how to capture the interest of your readers, etc.

16. Students prepare final draft of book and share with classmates before Reading Buddies Day.

Day One   Today I presented my third-period class with an invitational letter requesting their participation in the Reading Buddies Project (Figure 8.2). I want this program to be viewed as a privilege for these students; not just one more "quick-fix" to gain literary skills, so I wrote a letter that I thought would set the tone. I hope the kids see this as an opportunity to make a difference in their own lives, the lives of the preschool students, and even in the lives of their own children someday. I asked the kids to bring in their favorite children's book to read to their buddies. I don't know why I'm surprised, but so many of them mentioned that they couldn't even remember their parents reading to them as children. Some of my fondest memories are of curling up on my mother's lap and reading *Blueberries for Sal.* What a shame to think that these kids missed out on that!

FIGURE 8.2
READING BUDDIES CHAPTER (INTRODUCTORY LETTER)

Old Town High School

240 Stillwater Avenue • Old Town, ME 04468 • 207-827-3910

Improving Storytelling / Writing Skills Across the Ages

Fasten your seatbelts! You have just agreed to participate in an exciting project which I hope will improve your overall reading skills. Researchers have shown that there is a direct link between improving a high school student's story-telling and story-writing skills by working with primary-school children. So get ready to have fun, and hopefully learn a lot!

We are working from a specific time-frame, so please be sure to accomplish the tasks in the order that they are given. Please note that we will complete this project on April 10th, at which time we will take a field trip to a Bangor day-care center. The following tasks will need to be accomplished before this date:

1) Write a letter to your "Reading Buddy" telling about yourself. I will give you the name of your partner in the next couple of days. Information that you might want to include would be a self-description including your hobbies. You might want to talk about your preferences in reading. Attach a picture of yourself to your letter. The letter can be as creative as you would like to make it. You will be receiving a similar letter from your reading partner soon.

2) Select a children's story to read to your reading partner on videotape. This may involve taking a visit to the library or raiding your little sister's book shelf in order find a good book. Once you find a book, practice reading it to me or to a partner, and let me know when you're ready to make a video tape of you reading the story aloud. When you're finished reading the story on videotape, tell your reading partner (on the tape) why you chose to tell this particular story.

3) You will be sent a tape of your reading partner telling a story. Your next job is to transcribe the tape, put it in book form, and illustrate it.

4) Meet with one other student working on this project and discuss what makes a story work. Next, write an original story and reproduce it on pages. Be sure to leave ample space for illustrations. Prepare for our field trip where you will tell your story to your reading partner, and together you will illustrate and discuss it.

I talked to Martha this afternoon. She introduced the project to her preschoolers by explaining that they have the opportunity to work with high school students who are going to read to them and help them create books. She said that she asked students to think about their all-time favorite books and to bring them to school tomorrow. Martha tells me that even though most of her students won't be able to read the words on the page, they will be able to describe the illustrations and tell the story based on their own recollections. She explained the project to parents today, and each willingly signed a release giving permission for their child to work with a reading buddy at the high school. Tonight Martha is going to write a profile on each preschooler explaining their hobbies, interests, and so on. She'll drop it off to me in the morning.

Day Two   Martha dropped off the profiles of each preschooler today. She included some sensitive information for me to know about one of her students. It seems that one boy was recently adopted and has had to change his name. Apparently his biological parent has threatened to take him back, although he doesn't have custody. Martha and I discussed who we might pair this little boy with since he is pretty fragile right now. I think Tracy would be a good choice—she's such a nurturing kid. She has brothers and sisters and a heart of gold. I'll explain to her that Bobby is having some hard times and that she needs to be extra sensitive to him. I will also need to talk to Tracy about privacy issues, considering that Martha explained how forthright Bobby is about his family situation. It occurs to me that it might make sense for Tracy to write a more uplifting story with Bobby, especially if he begins to focus too much on his family problems.

During class I had my students compose their own profiles. The only guidelines I gave them were that they had to tell about themselves in the letter, include their interests, and talk about what types of things they like to read. Brad, of course, asked what to write for that because he doesn't like to read anything, but once I told him that he could write down comic strips if he chose to, he was fine. (See Christine's letter, Figure 8.3.)

With the exception of a couple of students, this is a tough bunch. Every lesson that I've done with this group throughout the year has been like pulling teeth! They really haven't been excited about any-

FIGURE 8.3
CHRISTINE'S LETTER TO JUSTIN

Hello Justin!

My name is Christine. I am a reading student at Old Town High School. I have brown hair and brown eyes. I LOVE to read.

I have a younger brother named Justin, and a younger sister named Vanessa. They both like to read too. We have a pet parrot named Peso. He is dark green with a red tail. I put a picture of him on this card. I have another parrot named Sonali, she is light green and has an orange beak. She is LOUD! She likes to eat spaghetti. Here is a picture of her too.

I like to read stories about the future. Have you ever read a story where people are put in a spaceship, or use shuttles instead of cars? I love those stories, they kind of remind me of Star Trek. Do you watch that show? Star Trek books are future books too. I have never read a Star Trek book, but I would like to.

What books do you like to read? I look forward to reading with you.

Your Friend,
Christine

thing. Was I ever surprised when they decided as a group and without my direction that they should put all of their letters together in a book. Derek volunteered to design a cover, which he entitled "Color Me Creative." It was really cute! Each student helped color the cover that he made on poster board, which included a large drawing of a box of crayons. On each of the crayons were the high school and preschool students' names. Nearly everyone has decided to bring in pictures of themselves and their pets and to include little drawings or graphics for their introductory letters.

Day Three   Martha and I met this morning to compare profiles. We decided who should be paired with whom based on what we knew about the students and on the profiles they wrote. We paired Justin and Christine because of their interest in science fiction. Amanda and Toby are going to be buddies because they both really love dogs. Bobby and Tracy will be buddies because of Bobby's family situation. Tracy will work really well with him, I'm sure. I think it's a good thing that we really thought about how to pair the kids; we paired the extroverts with the students who tend to be shy, hoping that they would have more of an opportunity to connect. Amanda's really nervous about working with such little kids because she's an only child. She keeps telling me that she doesn't "have a clue" about little kids. She and Toby, her buddy, both love animals, so I think that will be a great springboard for their collaborative efforts.

Day Four   I told my students who their buddies are today. I gave them the individual profiles that Martha had written about their reading buddy. We read lots of stories aloud. Then we practiced reading their favorite children's stories aloud. This was a lot harder than I thought it would be! Dawn really struggled with *A Tale of Peter Rabbit.* She had difficulty with the words, and when that happened she would forget to hold the book so that the kids would be able to see it on camera. She decided to read the words first and to hold up the pictures after she finished each page.

What a great class we had! We spent the afternoon laughing, reminiscing, and reading. Three of the girls recited *The Cat in the Hat.* It was pretty hilarious. In this day alone there has been more excitement over books and reading than in all of my classes combined throughout the whole school year. I can already see that this group is becoming more supportive of one another and more unified. A week ago Brad would have dumped all over Dawn for making mistakes when she read her story on video. Instead, he supported and encouraged her by admitting that some of the words in her story would have "messed me up, too." If I had known that this project would make gentlemen out of kids like Brad, I would have done this with all of my students!

Martha emailed me earlier. She's already started videotaping her students. Only two of her kids can really read. The others just "read" from memory, so they won't need much practice time. She said that she is taping each of her preschoolers individually. She has them hold up their books and either read the words or just tell about each illustration. She's bringing the videotape over tonight. Can't wait!

Day Five   I just videotaped my students reading their favorite children's books. This will be a good way for the students to get to know each other, and since our schools are thirty minutes apart, we won't have to worry about the logistics of transporting our kids from one place to another until Reading Buddies Day at the end.

Practice didn't make perfect in Dawn's case, but all my students (even Brad) were engaged and wanted to do a good job at this. I notice that the struggling readers are playing experts (novice experts) and learning by providing peer assistance. When Dawn struggled, Brad and Amanda attempted to help her "sound out" the difficult words. This peer assistance would have been an embarrassment before, but now I see that students are really able to read books in their ZPDs without feeling self-conscious.

The videotaping took the entire eighty minutes of class, so the kids volunteered to come after school to watch the preschool tape and "meet" their buddies for the first time. Now that's a first! I can't remember a time when any of them have willingly offered to come in after school to get caught up on their work.

We had fun—we made popcorn, and the kids just cracked up over how excited the preschoolers were. Shelly's buddy, Joshua, was really animated, and the high school students laughed a lot when he told his "sca-a-a-wy" story. Each time a new little "buddy" came on, someone would whisper, "Pssst—whose buddy is this? Amanda is he your buddy?" This is just the type of reaction I've been waiting for! It's almost like it's their own little brother or sister who's on video—they all look so proud when their buddy comes on! I've gotta run to Martha's after school so she'll have our videotape to show her kids in the A.M.

Week Two   I just got off the phone with Martha. Her kids watched our videotape today. She said they watched it at least six times in a row. They love it! It's funny, she said the reaction of the preschoolers wasn't all that different from the high school students—they were all trying to figure out whose buddy was whose, too!

Martha has her work cut out for her this week! She's been working hard to get the preschoolers thinking about stories that they want to "write." She said she read them several of their favorite class books, and then she started taking students out of the group individually to tape their stories. During this time the other preschoolers were engaged in an activity with the teacher's aide. Martha said that Justin was really funny when she worked with him. She reminded him that the story he would tell would be sent to Christine and made into a book. Martha brought up his tape this afternoon, and on it you can hear her say, "OK, Justin, what kind of story would you like to tell to Christine?" He tells quite a little tale about wizards, a mean witch, a stone, and a "one-arm-ed, two legg-ed mouse." (See Figure 8.4 for Christine's depiction of this "mouse.") It was a riot! In the next few days Martha will be finished with the rest of the audiotapes. We decided to use audiotapes instead of videotapes for this part of the project so that it will be easier for the high school students to transcribe the preschoolers' stories.

My students have been reading tons of children's books to get ideas for the books that they'll soon be writing. Some of the kids have even been emailing their buddies. Martha and her aide have been helping the preschoolers read their email. The high school students are learning about illustrating and the importance of writing for your audience (in this case, three- to five-year-olds, which, in some respects, is more challenging than writing to someone from their own age group).

Week Three   The hard work begins today for my kids. Some students have volunteered to come after school again so that I can help them transcribe their buddy's story. They can't wait to have a turn to listen to their tape. We've been using a tape recorder with double headsets, so that I can transcribe right along with the students. I taught the students how to take double-sided notes. On one side they record exactly

FIGURE 8.4
CHRISTINE'S DRAWING OF JUSTIN'S "MOUSE"

Later that night, Zeth woke from a fitful sleep and saw that the jewel had been stolen. He quickly threw on his robe and hurried off to retrieve the stone. He met with poisonous spiders that tried to eat him alive, but he threw them off and continued on his way.

Just before entering the witch's dungeon, he met up with Annabelle's partner, Moss. He was a gigantic mouse with six legs, two heads, and two tails. He roared at Zeth, but Zeth just paralyzed him with a deadly stare and went into the castle.

what their preschool buddy is saying on the tape, and tonight they'll take those notes home and use the other column to record their thoughts, ideas, and illustrations before they prepare their rough draft. (See Figure 8.5.) All year long I've tried to get these guys excited about writing and reading. I have worked hard at choosing interesting prompts and exciting reading material. I have even gone so far as to choose risqué material to capture their attention. Still, though, I have seen happier and more enthusiastic faces at funerals than when I assign a prompt or read aloud. Finally, the tables are turning!

Week Four Oops! We didn't finish the transcriptions today, so I called Martha to let her know that we'd need a couple more days. Each transcription takes about forty minutes! Thank goodness so many were willing to come in during study halls and after school, or we'd be finishing this project in July!! With Vygotsky's "zone of proximal development" in mind, I transcribe right along with the students whenever I can, and then we compare notes. By discussing our thoughts on how to proceed with the story, I am able to think about the next best step for each student. It also allows me to show specific and clear examples of story elements that they might want to use. For example, Christine's zone of proximal development is at a different stage than Brad's. Through our discussion I was able to see that she is ready to learn about irony and surprise endings to incorporate in her writing. Brad simply needs guidance in composing a beginning, middle, and end.

Right now Martha and her kids should be reading the profiles of the high school students and watching that videotape (over and over again, so she tells me). She said that her preschoolers love repetition, so they really don't feel like there is a delay in the project. The only concern that Martha has is that her VCR will wear out! Ha!

Most of my students are finished with their transcriptions and double-sided notes, which include their "book" ideas. Now they just have to start their rough drafts. The preschoolers' ideas sometimes do not flow in a logical storylike order, so it has been difficult for my students to know how to proceed with their stories. We've been discussing various ways to structure the stories. We talked about finding a beginning, middle, and an end amidst the preschoolers' often jumbled words. Then we discussed the patterns that were emerging in different pieces. Christine mentioned that in Justin's story he keeps

FIGURE 8.5
EXAMPLE OF DOUBLE-SIDED NOTES

Story of Josh's "four legged brother"
Casey does funny tricks in the
snow.
He looks like nothing
Casey has four legs.
He can almost fly.
Teacher: Is casey a bird? No.
          Is casey a dog? Yes.
I will tell you what kind he is.
  —Draws Casey.
If Josh was home with him:
he'd do funny tricks in the
  snow like eating and jumping.
When Casey's inside the house
Sometimes he gets my toys.
when I'm not playing with
  them.
  He carries them around but.
Mom + Daddy gives them.
He swallows my toys.
Last night when Mamma and.
Dad put me to bed, he.
swallowed a towel with
  balloons. The whole thing.

— this would be a good title.
Not sure if he wants this
theme to carry through.

—

          Draw a flying dog
  maybe with startled looking
  birds.

— Show Josh in the snow
    running. Then the
    two eating dinner.
— Picture of Casey bringing
    his toys over.
—, Have Casey chewing
      toys and getting scolded
— Chewing a towel and
    getting scolded.
— Maybe this could be
    a story of poor
    Casey who doesn't know
    how to behave and
    think they don't love him
    but they really do.

talking about Ewoks and wizards, so she decided to backtrack and include those characters in her piece because they kept resurfacing. Joel mentioned that his buddy keeps talking about strange tricks that a Martian does, so he's decided to include one of the more descriptive tricks in his book. I reminded them to think about how they would illustrate whatever it is that they were thinking of including in the book. That also helped them weed out what information they wanted to include and what they didn't. Dawn was afraid to leave anything out because she has a little brother who has a great memory. She said, "If he tells you something and you get one little bit of his story mixed up, he has a fit!" It's nice to know that they're thinking about their audience this much!

My students are beginning to understand what I want them to know about stories and working together. Christine's dialogical approach to writing and her efforts at refining her story demonstrate her understanding of the importance of revision. Brad struggled to find an ending to his story, so it is apparent to me that he is beginning to get a sense of story structure. For Joel, it was important to make the points and themes of his "Martian" book clear, and he did so by adding lots more detail. The greatest lesson learned by every student in this project is the importance of working together and assisting one another—a lesson that hopefully will transfer to their adult life and in their roles as citizens of their respective towns and of this world that we all share.

Week Five   My students continue to work on their stories. Their rough drafts are done, and the stories have already been put into book form. We had a class discussion about how to divide the words into pages. The pages are all numbered, and they just need to start illustrations. Joel has already started. He didn't want to draw, so he decided to cut pictures out of magazines—he thought his story would look better that way. I encouraged him to draw and told him that his four-year-old buddy probably wouldn't be too critical of even stick-figuring drawing, but he insisted on magazine cutouts. He ended up finding this cartoon-type picture of a little boy, and he cut out three legs and glued them to the little boy's head. Brandon wrote about a Martian that does strange tricks, so Joel used that picture to illustrate that particular page. He thinks Brandon will get quite a kick out of it, and I'm sure he will too. We'll share stories as soon as all are complete.

Week Six, Day One   How frustrating! We're still behind schedule and Martha's poor kiddies are still reading those letters and watching that video for the past two weeks now! I called her this morning to tell her that we're almost finished. She says that they've actually been working on preparing for "Reading Buddies Day," which will be on May 11th. The preschoolers have been making color-coded balloons out of colored paper, and Martha has been writing their name on one balloon and their buddy's name on the other. They'll hang the balloons up as decorations on the 11th. They've also been planning what snacks to have and discussing how the afternoon will be organized. They're working on a huge class "thank-you" poster to display on that day as well. With any luck, we should be done tomorrow.

Week Six, Day Two   Finally my students have their books finished! They were so particular about their books that it took longer than I expected. I think that's a good thing, though, because it helped them assist one another and become a lot more immersed in the project. Since the high school students mainly transcribed the original stories of the preschoolers and then illustrated, Martha and I thought it would make sense to reverse the process. We wanted the buddies to be able to do an activity together, so I assigned a final project for them to complete over the weekend. They're going to create one more book for their buddy, but this one will be on their own and without illustrations. The high school students will write the story this time, and the preschoolers will have an opportunity to illustrate. Our plan is to share the first books at the beginning of Reading Buddies Day in a large group, and then break into smaller groups and read the pages of the second book created by the high school students. Then we'll have the high school students and the preschoolers coillustrate.

At the mention of the creation of a second book, the high school students became very excited (funny, a few weeks ago they'd have been moaning and groaning). It seems that the Vygotskian tables have turned; as my students have become more expert readers and writers, they are now assisting one another. Without any suggestion from me, the students started talking about sequels to the first books that they wrote. Some in the class didn't know what a sequel was. Joel explained that a sequel was like the second part of a book, and one of the kids brought up the sequels to the movie *A Nightmare on Elm Street.* They discussed different ways that a sequel might be composed, and Shelly talked about how she might write a sequel to her wizard book.

Do I even need to comment about the social ramifications here? These kids are building relationships based on their newly gained "expertise" as readers and writers, and here I sit taking notes! Too good to be true! They're all looking forward to the 11th when they'll meet their reading buddies for the very first time. They'll coillustrate their second books on that same day.

Reading Buddies Day   It's finally here! I wonder how excited the preschoolers are if my high school kids are practically bouncing off the walls? The van will be delivered at 11:00, and we'll head over to the preschool then. Amy has to call home because she forgot her permission slip. I'll write more when we get back.

WE'RE BACK! What a day we had! You could not believe the excitement the minute we walked into that preschool. I had the video camera all ready to go, and Martha was ready with her Minolta. We hadn't even discussed how to begin the day, and it was a good thing, too, because the kids had that all figured out. The room sounded like a day at Disney, and the reading buddies immediately found each other in the crowd. Martha and I looked at each other and shrugged, then stayed out of the way as much as possible.

On the ride home Christine told Dawn that it turns out that she was right about kids and their memory. She said that Justin told her that she got the Ewok named Wicked all wrong, that he wasn't supposed to look the way that she had drawn him. We all got a good laugh over that one! The drive home was fun and filled with stories and jokes about the preschoolers, but everyone got pretty quiet as we pulled up to the front steps of Old Town High School. "Geez, it's a bummer that it's so near to the end of the school year," Joel said as he climbed out of the van. "Do you think it would be all right if I emailed Brandon for a while longer?" A few of the other high school students said that they wanted to do the same. More pleased than you know at the connections they had made with the preschoolers, I said, "I think

Reading Buddies Working Together: Joel and Brandon

Brandon would be pretty disappointed if a guy who makes Martians as well as you didn't keep in touch."

The Benefits of Buddies

The Reading Buddies Program was completed on May 11th. This meant that I would only see the seniors in the class for five or six more visits in the reading lab until graduation. Christine was one of those students. Assessing a senior's enthusiasm for schoolwork in the months of May and June is like hunting in the Maine wilderness for zebras—not a likely prospect. Yet here the opposite was true. In her last five classes in the Reading Lab, Christine helped coordinate a final breakfast meeting for our reading class at a local restaurant. During our meeting, she talked about her writing, children's stories, and literature with more passion than I thought possible. Where she had once talked about getting a job and getting married, this project had allowed her to see new interests, strengths, and possibilities for herself. She was now exploring the possibilities of writing for publication, attending college, and maybe even teaching.

Christine had always been a good student, but she seemed to have been an indentured one. In her case, her good grades in reading and English did not mean that she was applying what she had learned to her own life. Once she had participated in the Reading Buddies Project, she began to think about reading and writing in different ways. The Reading Buddies Project was a social learning project that truly made a difference for this young woman.

Nine out of the ten students in this project, many of whom were seniors, continue to visit and keep in touch with me. Dawn joined the Marines and writes frequently. Joel went to college in Vermont, and Dan is married and living in Florida with his wife and her two children. The other students live in the Old Town area and drop by the high school on a regular basis to talk "books."

Christine called me about a year after the project. She had spent an entire year writing children's stories, and she asked if I would edit her work before she sent it off to a publisher. She had already sent a prospectus and a sample of her work, and a publishing company had expressed interest in her material. Christine had created two fantastic tales. One was an adorable story encouraging kids to take care of the environment, creatively written from the point of view of a piece of garbage. The other story was about a little boy whose day goes all wrong.

Christine is still waiting to hear from the publishing company. She recently sent me an email to ask for advice about whether or not to hire an agent for her publications. After our conversation, I'm sure that if this first company isn't interested in her work, then she'll keep looking until she finds someone who is.

It would be presumptuous of any educator to believe that one classroom project was so influential that it shaped the future of her students. In Christine's case, she had all of the necessary literary skills to be an excellent writer; she just lacked enthusiasm for writing and reading. When I asked if she thought that the Reading Buddies Project had any role in encouraging her to be a writer, Christine replied,

"Well, put it this way: I doubt that I would have been confident enough to send my work to a publisher if I hadn't had some practice writing and working with kids. When I saw how into my story Justin was, I knew that I wanted to write more. It makes a difference if someone is really interested in what you write."

Evidence of Success

Although I have presented a great deal of information about Christine and Justin in the context of this chapter, their case study was not the only way that I evaluated the Reading Buddies Program. I examined the outcomes of this program under the lens of "social learning theory." This theory is a traditional and well-established model that assists in the examination of a particular program. Social learning theory provides guidelines for evaluating any program and is especially useful for programmatic evaluations in schools. Based on this theory, I was able to identify that the Reading Buddies Project provided knowledge to students about reading, writing, and cooperative learning (the entire project was constructed to address these areas), which then led to a change in the motivation and intentions of the students (demonstrated in their willingness to participate in literary activities). Once students were willing to participate in the activities, this led to a change in practice (students began to read and write more on their own, and they were willing to come in after school to work on the project). The ultimate outcome was that my students were more enthusiastic and engaged readers (as witnessed by Brad's positive attitude toward reading, Joel's wish to continue the project, and Christine's hope to publish future works). Students demonstrated a "change in knowledge, change in attitude, increase in feelings of self-efficacy, higher motivation, mastery of skills, and heightened sense of responsibility" (Weiss 1997, 45) that are emphasized in social-cognitive theories.

Initially our goal was to improve storytelling and story writing across the ages, but many more notable events developed. We noticed that as a result of the storytelling, reading, and story writing, all students involved had a greater sense of self-confidence and built valuable communication skills. In the words of one struggling reader, "I learned that I can communicate with young kids."

The preschoolers, though of varying writing and reading abilities, realized the importance of their audience. The children had preconceived ideas about how their stories would look and sound. They were particular with their buddies when they examined the illustrated stories. "You made a mistake; it should have been a *grizzly* bear," emphasized one preschool boy. One child was even able to recall his original taped story in great detail. He corrected and excused his buddy by saying, "Really, he, Ewok, gets captured, but I forgot to told you that."

The preschoolers were very protective of their buddies during the coauthoring process. They did not welcome intrusions by Martha or me. When I attempted to question Toby about his illustration, he responded curtly, "Uh, can we just draw now?" All students were highly engaged with each other and were driven to complete their books to their satisfaction. When the day was finished, the preschoolers were saddened by the buddies' departure. Following that final day, the preschoolers read the published pieces daily and often watched the video of their buddies' storytelling—apparently repetition really *does* work for them!

Invariably the high school students would voice their amazement at how exceedingly difficult it was to get a clear picture of the preschoolers' stories. You see, though they did not phrase it this way, they wanted to get at an "authorial reading" of the text. They wanted, as one student expressed it, to "make a book that captures what the little guy means."

All of the students were surprised by the fact that the transcriptions caused them to reflect on their own strengths and weaknesses in reading and writing. The entire process fostered authorial conversations. For example, Joel explained to Amanda that Dr. Seuss expected her to read Sam-I-Am's character as a naïve and innocent little creature who "only wants to share something that he enjoys with others." Amanda had been reading Sam-I-Am's character as an annoying character whose sole purpose it was to tantalize and torment. An interesting debate ensued, and Joel finally persuaded Amanda to see his (and Dr. Seuss') point of view.

While the underlying assumption of this project was that students would learn how to improve their ability to write, to tell stories, and to read, some students also learned an even more valuable lesson. One student who was reluctant to work with a buddy at first but brave enough to try said, "I learned that working with little kids is not for me." Both Martha and I were struck by the maturity of this young student.

Back to the Beginning

As a teacher, I have come a long way since my "let's summarize the *Reader's Digest*" days. There had never been a lesson that I have taught, or a project with which I have been involved, that has so significantly furthered the literacy skills of my students as our version of reading buddies. This social learning experience enabled my students to be more in touch with their feelings by providing a vehicle for purposeful self-reflection and examination. I have witnessed a drive, an intensity, and a passion in all of the students involved that seemed nonexistent before. Undoubtedly, this project generated the kind of knowledge and compassion in students that will certainly transfer to others in their lives. If ever there was a learning experience that truly enculturated secondary students into a democratic society, then this was it.

And this is only the beginning! The possibilities and benefits are endless! When other students heard naysayers like Brad boast about his involvement in the Reading Buddies Project, they demanded to be

FIGURE 8.6
SOCIAL LEARNING THEORY MODEL FOR BUDDIES

Reading Buddies Project provides knowledge of literary (reading and writing) and social skills.

Students show evidence of improved reading, writing, and socialization skills.

Knowledge of literary and social skills leads to a change in motivation and intentions of students (willingness to engage in literary activities).

The change in student attitudes toward reading and writing leads to a change in practice—students go beyond willingness to participation in literary and social activities.

part of their own social learning projects involving literacy. After attending a bookmaking workshop, I taught my students how to paint and create their own special "books" in which they could write poems, quotes, or personal thoughts, or that they could give as gifts. We designed our own books, wrote children's stories on the pages, and read and presented them as gifts to the students at the Stillwater Montessori School. I created and wrote a book about a recent trip to the beach right along with my students. It was called *Near the Ocean Blue,* and I read it and presented it to my son, Cameron, who attends Stillwater Montessori.

Each endeavor of this sort has had a ripple effect on the people surrounding the project. As one project leads to another, one person's interest sparks an interest in yet another person. One student in my class developed her own social learning project by designing a website for teen writers. Using the Internet, students send their stories to her, and she selects which ones to feature on her website. She receives submissions because other students have spread the word. Even my three-year-old son has created several projects of his own. After watching "Mommy" write her book, Cameron began to spend hours "writing" his own masterpieces. In turn, Cameron has demonstrated to his cousin how to create a book, and his cousin has practiced making his own. As Cameron continues to create his books, I share in the fun and work alongside him. The greatest hope for any teacher has now become a reality for me. The students that I once taught have now become the teachers of others. Funny, isn't it, how we've come full circle?

When my colleague Martha Pojasek and I were invited to present at the spring conference for the National Council of Teachers of English (NCTE) in Albuquerque, New Mexico, we felt like tennis-great Serena Williams must have when she beat Martina Hingis in the Grand Slam of tennis in 1999. We had "won" the privilege of sharing our success stories with teachers from around the country. What had begun as a small teacher research project in Jeff's Teacher Research class at the University of Maine had blossomed into a literacy project that had changed the lives of some of our students, and certainly our own approaches to teaching, forever.

Re-envisioning Reading and the English Classroom

"[T]eachers develop or adapt curricular structures on the basis of their own views of the students whom they teach and their ideas about the nature of learning . . . what happens in class is likely to be based on the teachers' own interpretations of the text or curricular guidelines."

—George Hillocks, *Ways of Thinking/Ways of Teaching*

"We must not be afraid of dreaming the seemingly impossible if we want the seemingly impossible to become a reality."

—Vaclav Havel, *The Art of the Impossible*

*I*t's inevitable. Early in every school year, sometime after the first few weeks have passed by, I go into the teacher's lounge and I hear it. "The kids are getting dumber every year!"

If I could predict when I would hear this pithy pronouncement I would wear my T-shirt that announces "I know it CAN'T be true BE-CAUSE I heard it in the lounge."

I resist this sentiment about students for several reasons. First of all, I don't think there's any evidence that it's true. Secondly, it doesn't match my experience. Thirdly, it blames the kids and ignores all other factors in learning, most notably the teacher. Most importantly, this sentiment is pessimistic and, therefore, I have come to believe, under-mines student potential and the possibility of democratic learning.

In George Hillocks' reviews of teaching, he's found that most teachers are what he calls "objectivists." (Other reviews of English teaching reach the same conclusion.) In other words, such teachers believe that teaching can be reduced to telling (see teacher/curriculum-centered teaching in Chapter 1). George's own research in the teaching of English compels me that teaching cannot be reduced in such a way. In George's masterful study *Ways of Thinking/Ways of Teaching*, he found that these objectivist teachers tend to be negative and pessimistic about student potential.

Though George uses rich case studies to show how the complex ways teachers think about students and other things like learning, curricula, purposes, etc. affect how they teach, I will summarize briefly here. George found that many teachers are what he calls "pessimist objectivists" and that these teachers simplify and fragment instruction in such a way that their students are denied the very opportunities, tools, and supportive, holistic, real contexts for learning that they need to be motivated, see the sense and use of what is being learned, to apply their learning, and to succeed. These teachers exert maximum control over curricula, students, and learning activities that tend to be lectures, recitation questions, worksheets, and tests. They reduce complex issues and strategies and emphasize "coverage." They assess at the end of units, and tend to blame students for not learning, since teaching is telling and they have made the information available to students. They don't look to students for feedback or to student participation and learning as a source of evaluation that may help them teach better. Probably as a result of this and their stance about teaching, they do not reflect on how they may change their practice.

Constructivist teachers, on the other hand, are optimistic about their students' ability to learn (it's interesting that George found no pessimistic constructivist teachers in his study). They take responsibility for student learning and believe that students can learn almost anything if given the appropriate help. Such teachers tend to be much more aware of their purposes and much more reflective about whether they have met these purposes. They "research" their classroom, and constantly revise their teaching depending on students' interests and needs, and feedback actively solicited from the students.

Their teaching may be structured at times to help students learn new strategies and content, but as student expertise in any area grows, the instructional context becomes more open ended. This teaching nearly always involves meaningful purposes and contexts (often negotiated with students), an inquiry orientation, group work, and specific local-level purposes that serve a shared global goal. Such teachers will transform the learning environment in order to transform student participation. They address strategies and issues at a high level of complexity. They believe that learning and knowledge exist in the actions of participants (not the teacher). They take more time to do fewer things and to do these things thoroughly, providing lots of practice and support. They emphasize learning, and learning as performance. They assess and evaluate student learning continually so that they can change how they are teaching to make it more effective (Hillocks 1999).

Democracy Under Siege

It's compelling that George's research has repeatedly found that such inquiry-oriented teaching (in the sense of helping kids to read and write as a form of inquiry in the context of pursuing big inquiry questions, AND in the sense of the reflective teacher researching her own teaching and students' learning) brings much greater learning gains for students than other treatments.

I would argue that not only is such optimistic and constructivist teaching demonstrably much more effective, it is also more democratic. Pessimism leads to authoritarianism and control. Optimism about your students leads you to be more optimistic about democracy, and to lend more control and tools to the students. Students learn what they have the opportunity to learn. They cannot become active and ethical agents of democracy unless they have had the opportunity to learn how to do so.

When I think about this, I'm always reminded of my first year of teaching when I taught a huge senior boy named Harry. Harry was Greek, wore a black leather jacket, and towered above me. He was in the 12–5 track, the lowest of the low. He was a goof-off with a ready smile and an even readier excuse for whatever mischief he was inevitably involved in. I really liked him.

One day I was notified that Harry had socked the assistant principal and I was to take work down to "The Closet," a small windowless and airless cell where students served the dreaded ISS—in-school suspension.

When I visited Harry there, I asked him why he had sucker punched the assistant principal.

His answer: "I HAD TO!"

"You had to?" I answered, incredulously.

"Yeah," Harry repeated, "I HAD to. He made me mad, so I HAD to punch him!"

In our ensuing conversation, it became clear that Harry really believed that he had very little control over his actions. One thing happened, and you had to react in a particular way. It was equally clear to me that Harry had learned this lesson, at least in part, from school. There was one way of doing things. There were no options nor opportunities for exploring various possibilities. One had little control over one's own activity, and therefore little responsibility for it.

Such an attitude, encouraged by particular ways of thinking and of teaching, puts democracy under siege. Unfortunately, many teachers feel that there is only one way to teach and exhibit the same attitude.

Constructivist teaching, on the other hand, is like surfing on the crest of the future's breaking wave. It requires us to place our vulnerable butts over a great yawning gulp. Since students have more voice and control, the classroom takes on a life of its own that is less in *our* control. Perhaps that's why many teachers resist constructivist teaching. (But then maybe we'd like to bring back a King and become a colony again?)

We've argued in this book that democracy always gets lip service as the higher purpose of American education, but that this purpose is rarely served by the way teachers teach and schools operate. To Julie, Tanya, and me, democracy is not a mode of governing, but a method of associated learning and living, of being respectful and responsible to each other for higher and mutually beneficial purposes, of developing ways to respectfully and responsibly converse and argue with each other, and of sharing knowledge, language, and power.

We've argued that lecturing is not democratic, and that neither are "natural" learning environments that do not actively share nor negotiate mutual purposes and ways of knowing. We've also maintained that both these "one-sided" approaches fail to recognize the great complexity of both the *content* and the *processes* that are required for expert reading. We know from our own experience and teacher research that our students CAN become readers if they are provided with consistent and explicit support to use strategies that they do not yet use on their own, and if these strategies are developed and then used with big purposes and relevant tasks in ready view. Our students are capable of reading new texts and completing complicated tasks if they are helped to develop the necessary tools and to integrate these into their learning repertoire.

This requires a kind of binocular vision on the part of both student and teacher—the ability to focus simultaneously on a local-level strategy and a final global-level goal that the strategy will serve. The strategy may be foregrounded, and then backgrounded, but both the strategy and the immediate purposes it can serve will be kept in sight at all times.

We've argued in this book that it is essential for us to help students "decode" and internalize the hidden processes of reading and making meaning with texts. Likewise, we want to help them decode the hidden mores of human interaction, and we think this can be done through our work together with texts. Just as we articulate the often unconscious social processes of reading and bring them to light so we can help students understand, adopt, manipulate, and evaluate them, it is also our job to bring to light the possible perspectives, opinions, and alternative actions regarding vital issues. These perspectives need to be articulated and respected in a public space so they can be worked through and sorted out. All democratic processes of making meaning include paying respect to other perspectives, and then making judgments and taking action.

We see democracy as an experiment in adventurous living. Democratic living parallels the journey of learning—from order to adventure. In order to get to the adventure and independence, you need to develop the tools, the knowledge, the respect, responsibility, and authority to do your own independent work. Such learning requires both teacher and student activity. To learn, a student needs a teacher and a structure that leads to the development of independent abilities. To teach requires pedagogical content knowledge, including knowledge of content and problem-solving processes that are given over to the student. As strategies are developed, students need to know how the srategies will be used in the near as well as more distant future. And once the skills are developed, the teacher must help provide opportunities for meaningfully enacting and independently using the new skills. This planned obsolesence of the teacher is an essential part of good teaching.

Creating a Subculture

In the bestseller *Tuesdays with Morrie*, Morris Swartz tells us that we have to create our own democratic subcultures to resist larger cultural trends.

We agree and think that we need to create such subcultures in our classrooms, in our profession, and in our society. We hope that we've shown how we have taken steps toward creating such a subculture in our own classrooms through inquiry-oriented instruction. Such instruction often leads to social projects like when Jeff's students create video documentaries about local studies or public service announcements about water use, when Tanya's students conclude a unit on dreams by creating story quilts about dreams for the future (given to newborns and their parents), or when Julie's class takes on coauthorship roles with their preschool reading buddies.

We hope you may have some sense of how we have created a subcultural teaching community through our work together in the Maine Writing Project, through our book clubs (that invite in distant teachers such as George through their books), through our work together in our Professional Development Network (that allows us to work together to teach middle and high school students as well as preservice and in-service teachers), and through our professional conjoint activities such as teacher research projects, making professional presentations, and pursuing writing projects together (such as this book). The work we've done together, as Vygotsky would maintain, could not have been done by any of us alone. We've shared visions, purposes, books, and strategies that have helped each of us to outgrow our current selves.

Dealing with Standards

We each want to create a classroom where existing and emerging standards are met, not by moving through long checklists of skills and learning results, but by using integrated, intelligently sequenced approaches. Standards, particularly at the state level, threaten to undermine good teaching as the focus is put on long lists of skills and factual knowledge that can only be really and deeply learned in authentic situations, through relevant tasks, and though incremental and repeated engagements. The sheer number of standards to be met in our own state encourages teachers to just tell students what they are supposed to know, though this clearly works against good teaching and learning practices and against the purposes of democracy.

This is not to say that we are against all standards or against all tests. We can imagine tests that are a product of teacher expertise and social conversation about what's worth learning, and that help kids to learn as they develop actual performances. It just so happens that we think we are currently working with bad tests that do not help educate kids and whose secret mission is to maintain a repressive class structure (see Lemann 1999). Since we believe this, we also believe that we must argue against bad tests and work toward better ways of assessing students. This is one of our own professional "contact zones."

We want rich units of instruction and communal activity where a wide variety of standards are met through the kids' activity, and new skills are internalized and named after the work is completed. After this we can say, "we met all of these standards as a consequence of this work together."

Engaging the Politics of Literacy

Finally, we want classrooms where the politics of literacy are foregrounded, where kids come to understand the politics of texts, and where teachers work for political ends.

We want classrooms where we work hard to make conceptions of literacy, reading, speaking, and other issues part of the class.

We should be aggressive in pursuing ends that we deem important to democratic living. One of the lessons of Susan Hynds award winning book *On the Brink* (1998) is that teachers who wish to remain politically neutral avoid conversations that are vitally important to students and to learning. We believe that politicized teaching is more respectful of students rather than less so because it recognizes that they are important, have the ability to understand, embrace, and resist, and that they are up to meeting vital challenges. Such teaching grants students responsibility as it lends them expertise.

Such teaching is not indoctrination, it is orientation into larger cultural conversations in which they are invited to take part. *We care about our students as teachers not simply by sympathizing or empathizing with them but by caring about what and how they understand, read, and think and live.*

On the global level, we want our goals to be clear to our students, and open to discussion and negotiation. We want to let them know where we are going and why, to negotiate, discuss, and deal with the politics of this decision.

We also want to deal with the politics of local-level activity. For example, we want to be constantly asking: Is this a good discussion? How do we know? What are the costs and benefits of how we are doing it? What role are you playing in it? Are you happy with this role? What could we do differently?

We want kids to build and apply their own politics and critical standards to everything we do.

Certainly, we want our students to have cultural capital, to have access to the kinds of knowledge and information that are useful and powerful. But this is not the only thing we want for them, and we don't want them to have this access without thinking about it.

We want them to ask: Why does X count more than Y? Why does the *New York Times* have more cachet than the *Bangor Daily News*? Should this be the case? With all stories and topics?

We want students to pit canonical works against noncanonical works from the same period or about the same topics and explore why one is canonical and the other is not, what is gained and lost by that, and to understand that they can embrace the noncanonical and resist the canonical if they so choose.

Why did the textbook writers put the one-page Indian chant next to twenty pages of *The Federalist Papers* and why did we spend much more time on the Federalist Papers? And what effect does that have on how we think about the Indian chant? How does the anthology itself work to make the Native American chant superfluous and how do we feel about that?

Finally, we want ourselves as teachers to be respectful political beings within our classrooms, schools, school systems, and profession. We want to envision and work for change, which we know will only come over time and through slow but consistent work and conversation. One of the most powerful ways we know of for teachers to work for change is to be aware of *what* we are doing and *why*. If we do something in the classroom, we must think it is a good way to do things and should be willing to document and argue that this is so. We need to become teacher researchers documenting our own practice, and either proving through our classroom results that our work does work, or use the disconfirming evidence to improve what we are doing.

As teacher researchers, we should share the work we do with students with supportive colleagues, to parents, and to the community; we should tell our stories and present our work. The gist of this book is us telling you "This is what we did with our students, why we did it that way, and this is what happened and what we learned as a consequence." This kind of teacher research is vital to a profession, since a profession, by its definition, is supposed to create its own knowledge, critique its own emerging understandings, build and apply its own gatekeeping strategies and critical standards. If we do not then someone from the outside, someone with less caring and knowledge of kids and of literature and of pedagogy, will do so for us. And this happened in our field.

The stakes are high. And the race, as all of us know, is a challenging one to run. The course of each year is not one we will get through without some pitfalls and twisted ankles. But we know that we can run the race and finish it strongly. Thankfully we have our own coaches, most notably George Hillocks and Lev Vygotsky, to train and guide us on our way.

Works Cited

Allen, J. 1995. *It's Never Too Late: Leading Adolescents to Lifelong Literacy*. Portsmouth, NH: Heinemann.

Allington, R. 1999. *Literacy Education for the Future: A Day with Richard Allington*. October 14, 1999. Augusta, ME: Augusta Civic Center.

Applebee, A. 1993. *Literature in the Secondary School: Studies of Curriculum and Instruction in the United States*. NCTE Research Report No. 25. Urbana, IL: National Council of Teachers of English.

Applebee, A. 1996. *Curriculum as Conversation: Transforming Traditions of Teaching and Learning*. Chicago, IL: The University of Chicago Press.

Applebee, A. 1998. *The Teaching of Literature in Programs with Reputations for Excellence in English*. Report Series 1.1. Albany, NY: Center for the Learning and Teaching of Literature, 1998. Microfiche.

Applebee, A. 1999. Building a Foundation for Effective Teaching and Learning of English: A Personal Perspective on Thirty Years of Research. *Research in the Teaching of English* 33: 352–66.

Atwell, N. 1987. *In the Middle: Writing, Reading and Learning with Adolescents*. Portsmouth, NH: Heinemann.

Beach, R. 1993. *A Teacher's Introduction to Reader Response Theories*. Urbana, IL: NCTE.

Berk, L., and Winsler, A. 1995. *Scaffolding Children's Learning: Vygotsky and Early Childhood Education*. Washington DC: NAEYC.

Bizzell, P. 1994. Contact Zones and English Studies. *College English* 56(2): 162–69.

Bleich, D. 1975. *Readings and Feelings: An Introduction to Subjective Criticism*. Urbana, IL: NCTE.

Bleich, D. 1978. *Subjective Criticism*. Baltimore, MD: Johns Hopkins University Press.

Bleich, D. 1998. *Know and Tell*. Portsmouth, NH: Heinemann.

Bloom, B. 1964. *Stability and Change in Human Characteristics*. New York: Wiley.

Bloom, B. 1976. *Human Characteristics and School Learning*. New York: McGraw-Hill.

Bloom, B. (Ed.) 1985. *Developing Talent in Young People*. New York: Ballantine.

Booth, W. 1988. *The Company We Keep: An Ethics of Fiction*. Berkeley: University of California Press.

Brown, J., Collins, A., and DuGuid, P. 1989. Situated Cognition and the Culture of Learning. *Educational Researcher* 18: 32–42.

Bruner, J. 1986. *Actual Minds, Possible Worlds*. Cambridge, MA: Harvard University Press.

Burke, K. 1968. Psychology and Form. In *Counter-Statement* (2nd ed, pp. 29–44). Berkeley and Los Angeles: University of California Press (original work published in 1924).

Campbell, J., Voelkl, K., and Donahue, P. 1998. *NAEP Trends in Academic Progress. Achievement of U.S. Students in Science, 1969 to 1996; Mathematics, 1973 to 1996; Reading, 1971 to 1996; Writing, 1984 to 1996*. Washington D.C.: ED Publications.

Christenbury, L. 1994. *Making the Journey: Being and Becoming a Teacher of English Language Arts*. Portsmouth, NH: Boynton-Cook/Heinemann.

Christenbury, L., and Kelly, P. 1983. *Questioning: A Path to Critical Thinking*. Urbana, IL: NCTE.

Collins, A., Brown, J., and Newman, S. 1992. Cognitive Apprenticeship: Teaching the Crafts of Reading, Writing, and Mathematics. In *Knowing, Learning and Instruction: Essays in Honor of Robert Glaser* (L. B. Resnick, Ed.), pp. 453–94. Hillsdale, NJ: Lawrence Erlbaum.

Culler, J. 1975. *Structuralist Poetics: Structuralism, Linguistics, and the Study of Literature*. Ithaca, NY: Cornell 250 Press.

Cziksentimihalyi, M., and Larson, R. 1984. *Being Adolescent: Conflict and Growth in the Teenage Years*. New York: Basic Books.

Cziksentimihalyi, M., Rathunde, K., and Whalen, S. 1993. *Talented Teenagers: The Roots of Success and Failure*. Cambridge, England: Cambridge University Press.

Delpit, L. 1988. The Silenced Dialogue: Power and Pedagogy in Educating Other People's Children. *Harvard Education Review* 58: 280–98.

Dewey, J. 1927. *The Public and Its Problems*. New York: Henry Holt and Company.

Dewey, J. 1944. *Democracy in Education*. New York: Free Press. (original work published in 1916).

Dorn, L., French, C., and Jones, T. 1998. *Apprenticeship in Literacy: Transitions Across Reading and Writing*. York, ME: Stenhouse.

Durkin, D. 1979. What Classroom Observations Reveal About Reading Comprehension Instruction. *Reading Research Quarterly* 14(4): 481–533.

Enciso, P. 1992. Creating the Story World. In *Reader Stance and Literary Understanding: Exploring the Theories, Research and Practice* (J. Many and C. Cox, Eds.), pp. 75–102. Norwood, NJ: Ablex.

Esslin, M. 1987. *The Field of Drama: How the Signs of Drama Create Meaning on Stage and Screen*. London: Methuen.

Fish, S. 1980. *Is There a Text in This Class? The Authority of Interpretive Communities*. Cambridge, MA: Harvard University Press.

Flavell, J. 1979. Metacognition and Cognitive Monitoring: A New Area of Cognitive-Developmental Inquiry. *American Psychologist* 34(10): 906–11.

Freire, P. 1970. *Pedagogy of the Oppressed*. New York: Continuum.

Gevinson, S., and Smagorinsky, P. 1989. *Fostering the Reader's Response*. Palo Alto, CA: Seymour Publications.

Glassman, 1994. All Things Being Equal: Two Roads of Piaget and Vygotsky. *Developmental Review* 14(2): 186–214.

Goldblatt, E. 1995. *'Round My Way: Authority and Double Consciousness in Three Urban High School Writers*. Pittsburgh, PA: University of Pittsburgh Press.

Goodlad, J. 1984. *A Place Called School: Prospects for the Future*. New York: McGraw-Hill.

Greene, M. 1978. *Landscapes of Learning*. New York: Teachers College Press.

Grossman, P. 1990. *The Making of a Teacher: Teacher Knowledge and Teacher Education*. New York: Teachers College Press.

Hamel, F., and Smith, M. 1997. "You Can't Play the Game If You Don't Know the Rules": Interpretive Conventions and the Teaching of Literature to Lower-Track Students. *Reading & Writing Quarterly* 14: 355–78.

Heath, S., and McLaughlin, M. 1993. *Identity and Inner City Youth: Beyond Ethnicity and Gender.* New York: Teachers College Press.

Hillocks, G. 1980. Towards a Hierarchy of Skills in the Comprehension of Literature. *English Journal* 69 (March): 54–59.

Hillocks, G. 1986. The Writer's Knowledge: Theory, Research and Implications for Practice. In *The Teaching of Writing. 85th Yearbook of the National Society for the Study of Education* (D. Bartholomae and A. Petrosky, Eds.), pp. 71–94. Chicago: University of Chicago Press.

Hillocks, G. 1995. *Teaching Writing as Reflective Practice.* New York: Teachers College Press.

Hillocks, G. 1999. *Ways of Thinking/Ways of Teaching.* New York: Teachers College Press.

Hillocks, G., with Ludlow, L. 1984. A Taxonomy of Skills in Reading and Interpreting Fiction. *American Educational Research Journal* 21 (Spring): 7–24.

Hillocks, G., and Smith, M. 1988. Sensible Sequencing: Developing Knowledge About Literature Text by Text. *English Journal* 77(6): 44–49.

Hoetker, J., and Ahlbrand, W. 1969. The Persistence of Recitation. *American Educational Research Journal* 6: 145–67.

Hynds, S. 1998. *On the Brink: Negotiating Life and Literacy with Adolescents.* New York: Teachers College Press.

Kahn, E., Walter, C., and Johannessen, L. 1984. *Writing About Literature.* Urbana, IL: NCTE.

Lave, J., and B. Rogoff. 1984. *Everyday Cognition.* Cambridge, MA: Harvard University Press.

Lemann, N. 1999. *The Big Test: The Secret History of the American Meritocracy.* New York: Farrar, Straus and Giroux.

McCallum, R. 1988. Don't Throw the Basals Out with the Bathwater. *The Reading Teacher* December: 204–207.

Meek, M. 1983. *Achieving Literacy: Longitudinal Studies of Adolescents Learning to Read.* London: Kegan Paul.

Moore, P. 1997. Models of teacher education: Where Reading Recovery teacher training fits. *Network News* (Fall), 1–4.

Moore, D., Bean, T. Birdyshaw, D., and Ryckik, J. 1999. Adolescent Literacy: A Position Statement. *Journal of Adolescent and Adult Literacy* September: 98–106.

Myers, K. 1993. Twenty Better Questions. *Elements of Literature: Teaching Notes.* Austin: Holt, Rinehart and Winston.

National Assessment of Educational Progress. 1981. *Reading, Thinking, and Writing: Results from the 1979–80 National Assessment of Reading and Literature.* Denver: National Educational Commission of the States.

Nystrand, M., with Gamoran, A., Kachur, R., and Prendergast, C. 1997. *Opening Dialogue: Understanding the Dynamics of Langauage and Learning in the English Classroom.* New York: Teachers College Press.

Ogle, D. 1983. K-W-L Plus: A Strategy for Comprehension and Summarization. *Journal of Reading* 30: 626–31.

Paley, V. 1992. *"You can't say 'You can't play.'"* Cambridge, MA: Harvard University Press.

Papert, S. 1996. *The Connected Family.* Atlanta, GA: Longstreet Press.

Postman, N. 1995. *The End of Education: Redefining the Value of School.* New York: Knopf.

Postman, N. 1999. *Building a Bridge to the 18th Century: How the Past Can Improve Our Future.* New York: Knopf.

Pradl, G. 1996. *Literature for Democracy: Reading as a Social Act.* Portsmouth, NH: Boynton-Cook/Heinemann.

Rabinowitz, P., and Smith, M. 1998. *Authorizing Readers: Resistance and Respect in the Teaching of Literature.* New York: Teachers College Press.

Raphael, T. 1982. Question Answering Strategies for Children. *Reading Teacher* 36(2): 186–90.

Rogoff, B. 1990. *Apprenticeship in Thinking.* New York: Oxford University Press.

Rogoff, B., and Lave, J. 1984. *Everyday Cognition: Its Development in Social Context.* Cambridge University: Harvard University Press.

Rogoff, Matusov, B., and White, S. 1996. Models of Teaching and Learning: Participation in a Community of Learners. In *The Handbook of Cognition and Human Development,* (D. Olson and N. Torrance, Eds.), pp. 388–414. Oxford, UK: Blackwell.

Rosenblatt, L. 1938. *Literature as Exploration.* New York: Appleton-Century-Crofts.

Santa, C., et al. 1985. Content Reading in Secondary Schools: Learning Across the Curriculum. Kalispell, MT: School District No. 5.

Schenk, D. 1992. *Data Smog: Surviving the Info Glut.* San Francisco, CA: Harper.

Scholes, R. 1985. *Textual Power.* New Haven, CT: Yale University Press.

Shulman, L. 1986. Those Who Understand: Knowledge Growth in Teaching. *Educational Researcher* 15(2): 4–14.

Shulman, L. 1987. Knowledge and Teaching: Foundations of the New Reform. *Harvard Educational Review* 57(1): 1–22.

Smagorinsky, P., and Smith, M. 1992. The Nature of Knowledge in Composition and Literary Understanding: A Question of Specificity. *Review of Educational Research* 62: 279–306.

Smith, F. 1978. *Joining the Literacy Club: Further Essays into Education.* Portsmouth, NH: Heinemann.

Smith, M. 1989. Teaching the Interpretation of Irony in Poetry. *Research in the Teaching of English* 23(3): 254–72.

Smith, M. 1991. *Understanding Unreliable Narrators.* Urbana, IL: NCTE.

Taylor, B. T., Harris, L. A., Pearson, P. D., and Garcia, G. E. 1995. *Reading Difficulties, Instruction, and Assessment* (2nd ed.). New York: McGraw-Hill.

Tharp, R., and Gallimore, R. 1988. *Rousing Minds to Life: Teaching, Learning and Schooling in Social Context.* Cambridge, UK: Cambridge University Press.

Vygotsky, L. 1934/1986. *Thought and Language,* trans. A Kozulin. Cambridge, MA: Harvard University Press.

Vygotsky, L. 1956. *Selected Psychological Investigations.* Moscow: Izdstel'sto Pedagogical Academy. Nauk: SSR.

Vygotsky, L. 1978. In *Mind in Society: The Development of Higher Psychological Processes* (M. Cole, V. John-Steiner, S. Scribner, and E. Souberman, Eds.). Cambridge, MA: Harvard University Press.

Weiss, C. 1997. Theory Based Evaluation: Past, Present, and Future. *New Directions for Evaluation* 76: 41–55.

Wells, G., and Chang-Wells. 1992. *Constructing Knowledge Together.* Portsmouth, NH: Heinemann.

White, S., and Siegel, A. 1984. In *Everyday Cognition: Its Development in Social Context* (B. Rogoff, and J. Lave, Eds.), Cambridge, MA: Harvard University Press.

Wilhelm, J. 1996. *Standards in Practice, 6–8.* Urbana, IL: Teachers College Press.

Wilhelm, J. 1997. *"You Gotta BE the Book": Teaching Engaged and Reflective Reading with Adolescents.* New York: Teachers College Press.

Wilhelm, J., and Edmiston, B. 1998. *Imagining to Learn: Inquiry, Ethics and Integration Through Drama.* Portsmouth, NH: Heinemann.

Wilhelm, J., and Friedemann, P. 1998. *Hyperlearning: Where Projects, Inquiry and Technology Meet.* York, ME: Stenhouse.

Willinsky, J. 1991. *The Triumph of Literature/The Fate of Literacy: English in the Secondary School Curriculum.* New York: Teachers College Press.

Literary Works

Albom, M. 1997. *Tuesdays with Morrie.* New York: Doubleday.

Carnes, J. 1996. A Rose for Charlie. In *Us and Them: A History of Intolerance in America.* New York: Oxford University Press.

Berube, M. 1996. *Life as We Know It.* New York: Pantheon.

Bradbury, R. 1967. *Fahrenheit 451.* New York: Simon and Schuster.

Burningham, J. 1978. *Would You Rather?* New York: Crowell.

Cormier, R. 1974. *The Chocolate War.* New York: Dell.

Cormier, R. 1991. *We All Fall Down.* New York: Dell.

Fitzgerald, F. S. 1925. *The Great Gatsby.* New York: Collier.

Golding, W. 1962. *Lord of the Flies.* New York: Coward-McCann.

Greenlaw, L. 1999. *The Hungry Ocean: A Swordboat Captain's Journey.* New York: Hyperion.

Hughes, L. 1988. What Happens to a Dream Deferred. In *America in Poetry* (Charles Sullivan, Ed.). New York: Henry Abrams.

Hurston, Z. N. 1991. *Their Eyes Were Watching God.* Urbana: University of Illinois Press.

King, S. 1998. *Bag of Bones.* New York: Scribner.

Krakauer, J. 1996. *Into the Wild.* New York: Villard.

Kurlansky, M. 1997. *Cod: A Biography of the Fish That Changed the World.* New York: Penguin Books.

McCarthy, C. 1965. *The Orchard Keeper.* New York: Random House.

Melville, H. 1959. Bartleby the Scrivener. In *Four Short Stories.* New York: Bantam.

Mitchell, M. 1993. *Uncle Jed's Barbershop.* New York: Simon & Schuster Books for Young Readers.

Myers, W. D. 1999. *Monster.* New York: Harper Collins.

Norris, L. 1982. Shaving. In *Question and Form in Literature.* J. Miller, R. Gonzalez, and N. Millett, Eds., pp. 81–85. Glenview, IL: Scott Foresman.

Old Horse, 1970. In *How to Read a Book* (Eileen E. Sargent, Ed.). Newark, DE: International Reading Association.

Paulsen, G. 1993. *Nightjohn.* New York: Delacorte Press.

Rylant, C. 1994. *Something Permanent.* New York: Harcourt Brace.

Silverstein, S. 1964. *The Giving Tree.* New York: Harper Collins.

Staples, S. 1989. *Shabanu: Daughter of the Wind.* New York: Knopf.

Stearns, John A. "In the Blink of an Eye." Reader's Digest. April, 1989, pp. 99–101. Originally published in *Sciences.*

Steinbeck, J. 1965. *Of Mice and Men.* New York: Modern Library.

Swift, G. 1996. *Last Orders.* New York: A. A. Knopf.

Taylor, M. 1976. *Roll of Thunder, Hear My Cry.* New York: Dial.

Trumbo, D. 1939. *Johnny Got His Gun.* New York: J. B. Lippincott.

Walker, A. "A Sudden Trip Home in the Spring." *You Can't Keep a Good Woman Down.* Harcourt: 1981.

Walker, A. 1982. *The Color Purple.* New York: Harcourt Brace Jovanovich.

Wright, R. 1991. Black Boy. In *Later Works.* New York: Library of America.

Index